Quietude

QUIETUDE

A Musical Anthropology of "Korea's Hiroshima"

Joshua D. Pilzer

OXFORD
UNIVERSITY PRESS

Oxford University Press is a department of the University of Oxford. It furthers
the University's objective of excellence in research, scholarship, and education
by publishing worldwide. Oxford is a registered trade mark of Oxford University
Press in the UK and certain other countries.

Published in the United States of America by Oxford University Press
198 Madison Avenue, New York, NY 10016, United States of America.

© Oxford University Press 2023

Library of Congress Cataloging-in-Publication Data
Names: Pilzer, Joshua D., author.
Title: Quietude : a musical anthropology of "Korea's Hiroshima" / Joshua D. Pilzer.
Description: New York, NY : Oxford University Press, 2023. |
Includes bibliographical references and index.
Identifiers: LCCN 2022027293 (print) | LCCN 2022027294 (ebook) |
ISBN 9780197615096 (paperback) | ISBN 9780197615089 (hardback) |
ISBN 9780197615119 (epub) | ISBN 9780197615126 | ISBN 9780197668368
Subjects: LCSH: Japanese—Korea (South)—Hapch'ŏn-gun—History—20th Century. |
Music—Social aspects—Korea (South)—Hapch'ŏn-gun. | Atomic bomb victims—
Japan—Hiroshima-shi. | Atomic bomb victims—Korea (South) | World War, 1939-1945—
Refugees—Korea (South)—Hapch'ŏn-gun. | Children of atomic bomb victims—Korea (South)
Classification: LCC DS904.6.J3 P55 2022 (print) |
LCC DS904.6.J3 (ebook) | DDC 951.9/004956—dc23/eng/20220803
LC record available at https://lccn.loc.gov/2022027293
LC ebook record available at https://lccn.loc.gov/2022027294

DOI: 10.1093/oso/9780197615089.001.0001

CONTENTS

Preface   *vii*
A Note on Transliteration   *xix*
About the Companion Website   *xxi*

1. Introduction   *1*

2. "Korea's Hiroshima"   *21*

3. Between Worlds: The Hapcheon Atomic Bomb Victims Welfare Center   *51*

4. Yi Suyong   *69*

5. Bae Ilmyeong   *93*

6. The Arts of Institutional Life   *115*

7. Han Jeongsun   *143*

8. Epilogue   *174*

Appendix: Resources for Support and Activism on Behalf of Atomic Bomb and Radiation Victims   *177*
References   *181*
Index   *187*

PREFACE

This book demonstrates a way of musically appreciating the world, but it is not primarily about music or people who make music. It is a musical encounter with a rather remarkable group of people and the everyday arts of survival that they practice to make life possible and worthwhile.

In 2003, in the midst of my dissertation research in South Korea on the song and verbal art of survivors of the Japanese military "comfort women" system of sexual slavery during the Asia-Pacific War (1931–45), I met a man named Kim Hyeongryul. He was born in 1970, the same year as I, and was thirty-two years old. He had been born with a congenital immunoglobulin deficiency that made him extremely susceptible to pulmonary infections and had stunted his immune system. He was sick practically his entire life, and for a long time he didn't know why.

When Hyeongryul was a young man, his mother told him about living in Hiroshima in the 1940s. She was one of the estimated 70,000 Koreans in Hiroshima at the time of the atomic bombing of that city on August 6, 1945. She had moved there with her father, who like many others had been recruited for munitions factory work in the Hiroshima military industrial production complex. Another approximately 30,000 Koreans were living in Nagasaki.[1]

Tens of thousands of the Koreans living in Hiroshima died in the bombing. But Hyeongryul's mother was one of the roughly half who survived, and she like all the others was exposed to large doses of radiation.

As Hyeongryul sought for explanations for his condition he read about other children of bomb victims and discovered many similar cases. He became convinced that he and others like him were victims of the genetic

---

1. Hiroshima and Nagasaki Korean populations are estimates from current studies by the Korean Atomic Bomb Victims Association (Hanguk wonpok pihaeja hyeophoe 2020).

legacy of the bombs. He also viewed himself, his mother, and other Koreans like them as testaments to the horrible intersection of the Japanese imperial exploitation of Korea and the racism that allowed the United States to justify its genocidal use of nuclear bomb technology on Asian civilians.

In the early 2000s, South Korean society, in the wake of the social movements for democratization, reunification, and workers' rights of the 1980s and 90s and the end of South Korean military dictatorship that these movements brought about, was actively re-examining its colonial, wartime, and authoritarian pasts. Many victims of Korea's twentieth-century sufferings had started to come forward. Hyeongryul found allies in the "comfort women" movement, and among those working on behalf of victims of forced labor and military conscription during Japanese colonialism and the Asia-Pacific War. He decided to dedicate his life to pursuing justice and social welfare for victims like himself (see Kim Hyeongryul 2015 and Figure 0.1). Despite his health struggles, he founded the Korean Second Generation Atom Bomb Sufferer's Association (Hanguk wonpok 2-se hwanuhoe) in 2002, and served as its director.

Hyeongryul and I met at a retreat for victims and activists of Japanese colonialism, where I had traveled with several survivors of the "comfort women" system. He and I were on our way to forming that special kind of relation that older Koreans call *gapjang*, friends born in the same year.

A year later he and his father visited the exhibition of "comfort women" survivors' songs and portrait photographs that I was holding with the Japanese activist and photographer Yajima Tsukasa in a Seoul art gallery. Over dinner that night he invited Yajima and myself to visit Hapcheon, often called "Korea's Hiroshima" in the press. Hapcheon is the rural district from where most victims of the Hiroshima atomic bomb were recruited, where most of the Hiroshima Koreans went after the war, and where many of their descendants live. Hyeongryul told us about this fascinating place, and suggested we look into doing a similar sort of exhibition about Korean bomb victims. Yajima and I expressed polite interest and said we would look into planning a trip to Hapcheon. I had been entirely unaware that there were so many Korean victims of the atomic bombing of Japan, despite being an American and having studied Korean music and society for eight years.

That was the last time I saw Hyeongryul. He died the next May, at the age of thirty-five, five days after returning from a Japanese symposium on the plight of Korean atom bomb victims and their children.

In the weeks after his death my expression of interest in the Hapcheon project became an unspoken promise. After five more years of work on the "comfort women" survivors project, which became a book (Pilzer 2012), I finally visited Hapcheon in 2010, hoping to lay the groundwork for an

Figure P.1 Kim Hyeongryul on the cover of a 2015 collection of his writings, *I Gave My Life for Anti-Nuclear Human Rights* [*Naneun banhaek ingwone moksumeul georeotda*].

ethnography of song and voice among Korean bomb victims and their children.

I embarked on this project without thinking too much about it, mostly in the spirit of keeping that promise, aside from a vague thought that it made sense following on my "comfort women" survivors' song project. I also wasn't thinking about the fact that I was an American about to land in the middle of a historical legacy for which my country was largely responsible, and that I was about to live among people who were still suffering and dying because of that history. I would soon, however, have ample opportunity to realize this, and would be moved to action in the face of these people and that legacy.

Mainly I was thinking of Hyeongryul, about my promise, and about his wish that people in Korea and abroad knew about the plight of Korean bomb victims and radiation sufferers. I was thinking also about Hyeongryul's voice, in testimony and in conversation, which sounded so strong precisely because he worked so hard to breathe and to speak.

There are various snippets of that voice in the internet archive. MBC News aired a thirteen-minute documentary about Hyeongryul on August 16, 2017, twelve years after his death, and one day after the seventy-second anniversary of the end of the Japanese colonial era.[2] He can be heard giving a brisk and articulate formal speech: "Speaking of the Japanese imperialist war of aggression, I think it is incumbent upon us to recognize the reality that this history of *insanity* penetrates [breath] the bodies and minds of Korean second-generation radiation sufferers [breath] to this day."

1

Like much media in the annual commemoration of the end of Japanese colonialism, the news segment emphasized Korean victimization at the hands of Japan, leaving aside Hyeongryul's pointed critiques of American militarism and his own government's indifference towards victims. But through the mists of nationalist victimology, we hear his remarkable eloquence and also his struggle to speak. We can hear the twists and turns of his belabored voice. His voice breaks on the word "insanity" (*gwanggi*). Just after that he takes two breaths, barely a second apart. For many who heard it, Hyeongryul's struggling voice became a symbol of the movement on behalf of Korean atom bomb victims and their children. The echoes of that voice still resound.

There is much to be felt and understood in this voice, if we listen carefully. That is what I have tried to do in Hapcheon since 2010: to attend very carefully to others in the pursuit of the understanding of them, their experiences, their suffering and hopes, and—especially—the arts of survival that they have cultivated to make life work and make life worth living. This book documents that process of listening and attending to others.

Listening can mean many things—one can listen for something, or to someone, or listen in on a conversation, and so on.[3] It is often used to refer to intentional hearing. But for me listening is much more: it is the beginning of an ethical encounter with others which is also an inquiry into their lives. It involves asking, and being listened to, and being "copresent," sociologist Erving Goffman's pithy word for how people can be present for and available

---

2. http://imnews.imbc.com/weeklyfull/weekly01/4387758_17924.html?menuid= weekly01.

3. In his 2016 essay Tom Rice enumerates many of these—listening as a kind of searching (listening for), as a kind of attentiveness (listening to) and as a kind of tuning in and even surveillance (listening in) are a few.

to one another (Goffman 1963: 22). It is inherently relational. It involves much more than gleaning the meaning of what people say; it requires one to listen to their voices, to their manner of speech or singing, to quiet, to the spaces in between, to silences.[4] Listening, too, is not a holy grail but only a starting point, inaugurating a kind of attentiveness that involves the other senses, which are not really isolable anyway. In the course of trying to attend to others very carefully, I watched gestures, expressions, practices of walking, exercise, craftwork, and other kinds of movement.

The road to this listening and attentiveness, however, is beset by obstacles. The North American cultures I come from are some of the worst at listening and attending to others in the world. Silence, when it is permitted at all, is reserved not for listening but for planning one's next assertion. North American academic culture teaches you the sleight of hand by which questions are turned into statements, their question marks removed. We are left to seek answers—which is of course the whole point of scholarship—on the sly. The mythology of academia paints the figure of the lone, penetrating intellect (Killick 1995) that pierces obscurity—natural phenomena, unfamiliar and foreign cultures and practices—rather than stopping, listening, and changing in the interest of understanding. I inherit this insensitivity, this phallic and colonialist version of knowledge as conquest and mastery. I do my best to reject this model of academic inquiry in this book.

For a long time, the Western anthropological means of overcoming the penetrating intellect idea has been to surrender oneself to a new context and become transformed in the creation of anthropological knowledge. The routinization of this has long been held up to scrutiny for presuming that anthropologists are outsiders and anthropological subjects are others—typically racialized others—and for other important reasons.[5] But I believe that in many ways we are all outsiders to others and even to ourselves, and that such transformation is always necessary, even and especially in the pursuit of self-understanding.

This is certainly true in the case of this book. The gulfs of experience and power which separate me from my interlocutors were immense at the outset, and they loom larger in my mind as time goes by. Unlike the people I write about, I am not Korean or Korean Japanese, not a survivor of war, and do not live with illness or disability. I have had the advantages

---

4. This phrase recalls Hedges and Fishkin's *Listening to Silences: New Essays in Feminist Criticism* (1994), an homage to Tillie Olsen's groundbreaking *Silences* (1978), about the silencing and absence of women in English-language literary canons.

5. See James Clifford's foundational essay "On Ethnographic Authority" (1983), one of the works that inaugurates this tradition of critique.

of a privileged Western life and membership in the elite world of academia. The Korean bomb and radiation victims in this book grew up in the hardscrabble society of postwar South Korea. Many are cancer survivors, many live with disabilities and chronic illness, and those of the first generation witnessed one of the most horrific and incomprehensible events in human history.

And yet while these disjunctures and the ignorance they produce are inevitably stones in my passway and limitations of this inquiry, they are also the starting points. They are injunctions for me to listen without assuming understanding or even the possibility of understanding. Many people in this book told me of things completely beyond my imagination. There are few points of identification where I could simply say "I understand." There rarely are for anyone, but in the race to identity and the race to knowledge we often pretend they exist. That is true for most people who claim understanding of victims' experiences, whether they claim that understanding is based on a shared national heritage or something else.

So I listen because I don't know. Doing this, as Korean bomb and radiation victims share space with me, and as we make ourselves variously present to one another, we make connections that form the foundations of potential understanding. First-generation survivors and I speak Japanese and Korean in common, and we have common interests. All of these points of intersection are little bridges that bring us closer together. They hold out the hope that in this meeting I can refine and transform my limited ability to listen and perceive, grasp something of these remarkable people's life experiences and their arts of survival, and convey some measure of that to the reader.

My typical American ignorance of the global legacy of US nuclear weapons was also a crucial starting point for the work because it bound me to the project. I have been alive for all but twenty-five of the years since the US used Japan as a convenient laboratory for the world's first nuclear weapons, and yet it took me until my mid-thirties to really sense the extent to which I inherit that legacy. I feel that Americans should not be content to ignore the broad spectrum of present-day suffering that is the result of American militarism in general, and the use and testing of nuclear weapons in particular—in Asia, the Pacific, and North America, and in Iraq, Afghanistan, and elsewhere through the use of depleted uranium. It is my hope that in a small way this book, the first English-language book about the Hiroshima Koreans and their children, will raise awareness of one of these communities and the challenges they face. I include an appendix which describes ways one can become involved in the interests of bomb and radiation victims the world over.

In the rural Korean Southeast my Americanness was taken rather differently than one who is familiar with the well-earned anti-Americanism common in South Korean progressive society might expect. Hapcheon is in the heart of the conservative Southeast, the birthplace of dictator Chun Doo-Hwan, a place where most people, rightly or wrongly, are grateful to Americans for their role in the Korean War and the long cold war between the two Koreas. And yet America is also the country of the bomb, and over the years bomb victims and radiation sufferers offered me many rather polite and strident criticisms of the American use of the bombs and the US government's attitude towards them in the present. But victims have a range of opinions about the use of the bombs and what they would like from the US by way of recognition, apology, reparation, and other things. Most people feel that taking an interest in their case is the proper starting point, and they were very willing to contribute to my study. I think the study was also interesting to some because I expressed an interest in getting to know them as people, and learning from them, and gleaning something of their arts of speech, testimony, and song, rather than using them as oral historical resources to understand the past. Several members of the older generation who came to feature prominently in the book were pleased to have someone to speak with in Japanese, sometimes even more so because I was not from Japan, although we spoke in Korean as well.

The particularities of my subject position had much to do with the people that were drawn to participate in the project, and that is but one reason why this book does not speak for all of the Hapcheon community. It consists mainly of ethnographic writing concerning around ten people, which is more than my previous book, which was about three women. That is largely because of the size of the community, and the shift the project took away from music, which made it easier for me to include people. And yet the experiences and expressive lives of a smaller number of people—Shim Jintae, Yi Suyong, Bae Ilmyeong, and Han Jeongsun—form the core of the book. This is first because it is a book based in our ongoing relationships, and second because there was so much diversity to be found in those few cases that broadening my focus would have cost me that richness.

The different contours and qualities of my relationships with the people in this book make for an unevenness of depth and breadth among the chapters. Most of that is accounted for by the myriad ways that bomb and radiation victims cultivate quietude and silence in their expressive lives. I respect these silences because they represent or express absence, loss, peace, and other things. I also respect them because efforts to withhold and forget are themselves arts of survival. I do not try to explain them away or dig beneath the surface. In research and in writing this book I found out about many holes in the world about which I was ignorant. Victims wish to have these things acknowledged, not probed and dispelled. In any case, that cannot be done. Absences and withholdings are presences in their own right, made and kept by human beings. This book is a study only of the selves and arts that people showed me. It is a product of my "rigorous commitment to the surface(s)"[6] into which bomb victims and radiation sufferers have put so much of themselves. Absences and that which is withheld are important features of these surfaces.

For all of these reasons this book can be nothing more than a beginning, which is why it has no real ending. Its oversights and faults are many and I alone am responsible for them. It does short shrift to many of the theoretical sources that inspire it, in the interest of staying focused on its subjects. It probably makes interpretive leaps it shouldn't, although hopefully most such unwarranted interpretations ended up on the cutting room floor. I am also responsible for all of the translations, unless otherwise noted in the acknowledgments.

In sharp contradistinction to these things, I am not solely responsible for the good parts of this book: they were made possible by a great many people. I am indebted to the many Korean first and second-generation bomb victims, social welfare workers, activists, and others who made it possible. Kim Hyeongryul made the first bridge for me, inviting me to Hapcheon, "Korea's Hiroshima." I hope this book will honor his memory and his legacy and make some small contribution to the cause he held dear. Activist Kang Jesuk, who is active in both the "comfort women" movement and the movement on behalf of Korean bomb victims, provided another crucial link and introductions which brought me to Hapcheon.

Once I arrived in Hapcheon, the years of assistance, patience, friendship, and wisdom of Han Jeongsun, the President of the Hapcheon Peacehouse, and Shim Jintae, the director of the Hapcheon Branch of the Korean Atomic Bomb Victims Association, have been absolutely invaluable. These two remarkable people, who feature so centrally in the book, have changed my life, and I am forever grateful. In addition to sharing with me their own artistry in the pursuit of life, justice and peace, they introduced me to countless others in Hapcheon who would become crucial to the project. They drew my attention to the particularities of "Korea's Hiroshima" and pointed out where assumptions from my former work led me astray. They encouraged me to set aside the term "survivor," which is profoundly loaded for those who experienced the bombs and their aftermath, and use the terms "bomb victim" and "radiation sufferer" in this book, which are preferred terms in the social movement on behalf of survivors.[7] They found me places to live

6. Martin Stokes, personal communication.
7. In my work with Korean "comfort women" survivors, I had become quite adamantly opposed to the characterization of survivors of sexual violence as "victims." Although I acknowledged that victimization is important for many reasons, I felt that the discourse of victims and victimization in the South Korean understanding of the "comfort women" had grown oppressive, enabling different kinds of paternalism, appropriation, and ignorance about survivors and

in Hapcheon, and they see to my health and well-being when I am there. If I could eat Han Jeongsun's *doenjangguk* (soybean paste soup) every day I am certain I would live forever.

I owe a similar debt of gratitude to Yi Suyong and Bae Ilmyeong, who each have their own chapter in this book, for sharing their wisdom, strength, kindness, and much more with me. Yun Sugi and Gu Gyeong-won were unstintingly generous with their time; they took me and my family out to lunch many times over the years, bounced my children on their knees, and were excellent swimming partners. An Buja, An Wolseon, Kim Iljo, Jeong Ilbun, Jeong Hoyeon, and many other first-generation survivors of the bomb who live at the Hapcheon Atomic Bomb Victims Welfare Center have contributed to this work.

I am most grateful also to the staff of the welfare center for all of their support, particularly Facilities Director Kang Suhan, who became a good friend of mine over my time in Hapcheon. I am equally indebted to the Hapcheon Peacehouse and the Korean Atomic Bomb Second Generation Sufferers Association, for providing me with places to live over the years and for facilitating the work in general. I owe a special debt to the many survivors of Japanese military sexual slavery—Pak Duri, Mun Pilgi, Bae Chunhui, Yi Okseon, Yi Yongsu, and Pak Onglyeon in particular—who first showed me that it was possible to keep living in the face of such suffering, and who shared with me their rich performances and practices of selfhood and survival.

I also thank the many academic colleagues, students, and friends who have contributed their thought and sacrificed their eyes to this book. I am grateful to my colleagues Farzaneh Hemmasi and Jeff Packman, Jim Kippen, Annette Sanger, and Lyndsey Copeland and to my advisees Yun Emily Wang, Nate Renner, Jonathan Wu, Nicholas Goode, Sangah Lee, and Bradley DeMatteo for their readings of the work. The students of my Winter 2018 and Winter 2022 graduate seminars on Ethnomusicology without Music helped me refine my thinking about how to do an ethnomusicology of quiet, especially Andrew Janzen.

I am grateful to the Canadian Social Sciences and Humanities Research Council (SSHRC) for the Insight Grants that funded this work in its

their experiences. Sharing this sentiment, the "comfort women" movement in South Korea has gradually moved away from the moniker "victim" (*piheja*) and toward "survivor" (*saengjonja*). When I began this project on Korean experiences of the atomic bomb I was intent on continuing in that vein. But in the context of the atomic bomb, the term seems to highlight one's own survival by contrast with those who did not survive, and so for many the term is an upsetting one. In addition to this, Korea's atomic bomb victims and their children are people whose victimization and suffering have yet to be properly recognized in Korea, Japan, the United States, or elsewhere; and for this reason the movement, which is largely composed of and run by victims themselves, has chosen labels like "victim" and "sufferer" in pursuit of such recognition.

development and final stages. My SSHRC research assistants Na-Young Ryu, Sangah Lee, Nate Renner, Yun Emily Wang, and Bradley DeMatteo provided much invaluable support. Na-Young and her husband Hyoung Seok Hwang provided essential transcriptions of interviews. Brad was a meticulous line editor and a thoughtful commentator. Yun Emily helped with the calligraphy in classical Chinese that is part of Chapter 6, on "The Art of Institutional Life." Nate provided several quite useful transcriptions of Japanese-language interviews and newspaper articles. Sangah checked my translations of song lyrics and other interviews, provided incisive and thought-provoking critique, and translated a core interview.

Special thanks is due to the force behind all of this, Oxford University Press Editor Norm Hirschy, who provided moral support and meticulous editing, and put together a very productive review process for the book. I am profoundly grateful to him, to editor Tim Rutherford-Johnson, and to the two anonymous reviewers for their criticisms, corrections, and encouragement, all of which has greatly improved the book. I am honored and ever-grateful that reknowned *pansori* master, author, and photographer Bae Il-dong lent me his amazing photo of Dobong Mountain to be the cover of this book.

I am grateful to the many scholars whose ideas inform this book, and although I have tried to give them credit throughout, since I do not dwell at length on any of the work's theoretical inspirations I will mention some people here. I am grateful to Alia O'Brien, whose discussion of quietude in her fine PhD thesis (2020) inspired my use of the concept. I thank Aaron Fox and Steven Feld for inspiring me to cross the thresholds of music to other things, and for helping me to think about the voice. I am grateful as well to Amanda Weidman and Nicholas Harkness for their pioneering work in the anthropology of the voice (Weidman 2014; Harkness 2014), which has helped me think about the many voices in this book. Anthropologists of social suffering have helped me think through the performances and discourses of suffering which play through and around the Korean bomb victims scene (Kleinman et al., 1997), as have scholars of disability (Kim Eunjung 2017) and its performance (Sandhal and Auslander 2005). Judith Herman's *Trauma and Recovery* (1992) has inspired me for many years and is always in the background. And as always, I am forever indebted to my doctoral advisor, Martin Stokes. It was he who first pointed out to me that I habitually looked to survivors' visual art and other sorts of practices to inspire my writing about music. He encouraged me to ask myself why that was and encouraged me to think more broadly about the expressive life; this book is the result of that inquiry.

I wrote this book through the first eight years of my children's life, engaged in full-time work and childcare for the first six, and I finished it during the school closures of the coronavirus era; so I wrote it almost entirely at night. My conscious self took moments here and there to sketch notes about what my shattered nighttime self should do, and the latter obliged as best he could. Portions of the book have a rather hazy quality as a result, which is entirely the fault of my late-night assistant. I owe a deep debt of thanks to all those who supported this moonlighting and the work in general: first of all, my wife Yukiko, who made it possible, and inspired or outright handed me many of the best ideas in the book. My mother Bet Manahan is a constant inspiration and an amazingly meticulous line-editor. Thanks to Jay and Rachel, wonderful interlocutors and grandparents, and to Zeb Eaton for holding up the world. My brothers Ethan, Simon and Woody, Toby King, Casey King, Marié Abe, David Novak, Maria Mendonça, Daniel Anisfeld, Okamoto Tadanori, Michael Donahue, Han Jeongsun, Dongwon Kim, Rob Inglis, Colin Manahan, and many other interlocutors and supporters put pressure on my ideas and kept me going by starlight. I am grateful most of all to my children, Ren and Mari, for teaching me the meaning of life and love, without which I could not have written this book.

A NOTE ON TRANSLITERATION

Although I have tried to use English expressions wherever possible for ease of reading, I have used transliterations of Korean and Japanese where necessary. I use the system for transliterating Korean called the Revised Romanization of Korean, currently used by the South Korean government. The system has limitations, and conventionally academics use a different one, but I have chosen this one because non-Korean speakers, on journeying to Korea or visiting Korean English-language websites, will typically find place names, people's names, and other words romanized as they are here in this book. There are some exceptions: for instance, I use "Pak" instead of "Bak," and "Kim" instead of "Gim" (which would be accurate under the Revised Romanization system) because these are more familiar romanizations of these common Korean family names. Personal names of authors and artists are written using the romanizations they use themselves. I transliterate Japanese using the Modified Hepburn System. None of these systems is perfect; I encourage you to use the audio pronunciation guide for key names and terms on the book's website, and to take advantage of the sound and video recordings of speech and song on the website.

ABOUT THE COMPANION WEBSITE

www.oup.com/us/quietude

Oxford University Press maintains a website of audio-visual materials for this book. The website has three main parts. First is a collection of audio and video recordings of the people who feature in this book. Second, there is a pronunciation guide for personal names and for Korean and Japanese terms that appear often throughout the text. Finally, some of the photographs in the book were originally in color, but they are reproduced in the book in black-and-white. The website includes a gallery of these photographs so that the reader may experience them in color.

This is a book about listening—to singing, to people's voices, and to what they have to say. It is not a book, therefore, that is composed solely of text, but one of which the audio and video are indispensable parts. It is a book which is meant to be read, listened to, and watched. Please listen to and watch the recordings on the companion website as you read. The main text features translations of speech and song lyrics, and the footnotes include romanizations of those texts, allowing readers to follow along in real time.

Recorded examples available on the website are marked throughout the text with the symbol ▶.

CHAPTER 1

Introduction

Yi Suyong's father was one of tens of thousands of Koreans recruited for
munitions factory work in Hiroshima during the Japanese colonization
of Korea (1910–45). Her family moved to Japan in 1934, when she was
seven. She went through Japanese regular school and high school. In 1945
she was seventeen and had secured a position as a clerk at the Hiroshima
Savings Bureau, a massively difficult feat for a young Korean woman amidst
entrenched hierarchy and discrimination against non-Japanese. On August
6 at 8:15 AM, she had just sat down at her desk when the atomic bomb
exploded one and a half kilometers from where she sat, shattering the glass
of her window.

In mid-summer 2015, Yi Suyong was eighty-seven. She and I were in an
art therapy class at the Hapcheon Atomic Bomb Victims Welfare Center
(Hapcheon wonpok pihaeja bokji hoegwan), the Red Cross-run facility
in rural Southeastern Korea where she lived with about 100 other Korean
first-generation survivors of the atomic bombing of Japan. She was making
an incense burner out of a ball of clay (see Figure 1.1). She worked at a
steady pace for the better part of an hour, slowly transforming the material.
She spoke little as she worked; when she did, she spoke in her soft, slow,
steady voice. Her hands moved with skill, and with a speed that cut against
the pace at which she spoke and the planned tranquility of the session.

First, Yi Suyong spent a few minutes pressing the ball into the rough
shape of a bowl. Then she wet and drew her right forefinger around its circumference, smoothing and rounding the sides. After several strokes she
rotated the bowl slightly counterclockwise with both hands and started
again, always just shy of two strokes per second. As she worked, she pinched

Quietude. Joshua D. Pilzer, Oxford University Press. © Oxford University Press 2023.
DOI: 10.1093/oso/9780197615089.003.0001

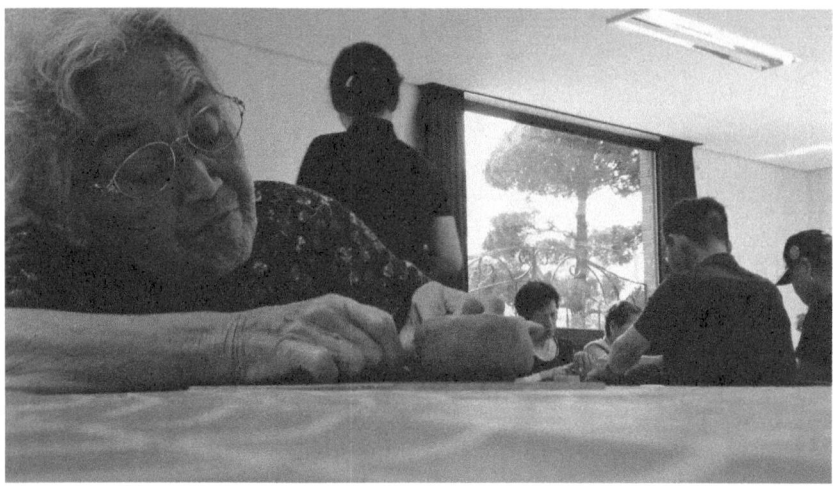

Figure 1.1 Yi Suyong working the clay, July 2015. Photo by the author.

the sides of the bowl with the thumb and forefinger of both hands, thinning the clay, squaring off the sides, and creating a flat bottom.

2

Changing tack, she began to smooth the inside surface of the bowl, all the while pinching the rim to give it an edge (see Figure 1.2). After about a half an hour, she had made a delicately circular, unadorned bowl with sides at ninety degrees to the flat bottom. She pinched the top three times to finish evening out the rim, and then laughed three times, echoing her hand movements. "How nice," I said. "Ha-ha-ha," she laughed again, three more times. She turned the bowl over and began to make its feet from a small reserve of clay she had set to the side.

Most of the twenty or so other participants, mostly women, finished the incense burner exercise in just a few minutes, with the speed customary of women who grew up in South Korea's latter-twentieth-century race for economic development and its contests for survival. But Yi Suyong was still working in her methodical and steady way when everyone else was done.

"Every day, I just bear up," Yi Suyong told me later, in her perfect Hiroshima Japanese. The steadiness, the rhythmic regularity, and the persistence of her working with the clay characterized other parts of her life as well. She took a daily walk in the early morning, counted the Catholic rosary on returning and once more in the afternoon, faithfully attended a weekly mass, and regularly participated in the activities of the

Figure 1.2 Yi Suyong smooths the sides of the incense burner. Image capture from video by the author.

welfare center. Whether in casual conversation or while testifying to her experiences of the bomb to the press and to researchers, she spoke at an even, unhurried pace, and in a somewhat inexpressive manner, almost documentarian in nature. Considering a minute or a year of her life you could find these similar, steady rhythms, these formal coherences (Feld 1988: 74) that were quiet ways of carrying on as well as a style of selfhood. But there were times when she allowed these rhythms of endurance to be eclipsed—by silences and the absences they marked, and by other things.

The director of the welfare center circulated around during the pottery session, helping the residents with various parts of the process. Towards the end he stopped behind Yi Suyong's chair and took the round bowl. Using a flower-patterned stamp, he imprinted the soft clay on the sides, making about twenty-five impressions. In this way the evenness and simplicity of Yi Suyong's work was partially obscured, just as the institutional constraints and transformations that conditioned her life were revealed. But one could see this evidence of her work and her style of endurance on the unadorned inside of the bowl.

Later that summer I sat with Han Jeongsun, president of the Hapcheon Peacehouse, at its small office table (see Figure 1.3). The Peacehouse was a community center for second-generation Korean victims of the atomic bombing of Japan. Han Jeongsun's parents had been in Hiroshima during

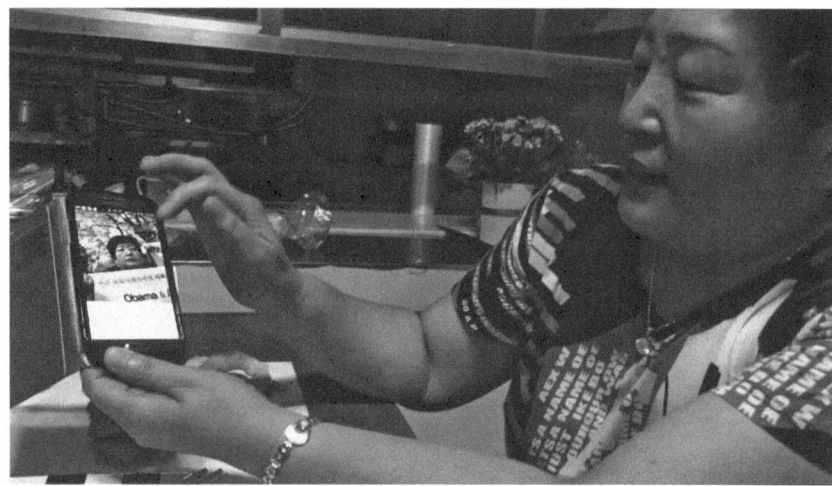

Figure 1.3 Han Jeongsun shows me a picture of herself at the protest outside the Hiroshima Peace Memorial Park on the occasion of US President Barack Obama's 2016 visit. Photo by the author.

the war, and she suffered from a debilitating bone and joint disease that she attributed to their radiation exposure.

We had just finished a dinner she had made of grilled fish, *banchan* (side dishes), rice, and *doenjang jjigae*—soybean paste stew. That staple Korean dish, made from soybeans roughly ground, salted, and aged, rather deliciously expresses something of the roughness of life. I have heard people say of music, art, people, and other things that are too pristine or too refined that they "lack the taste of soybean paste" (*doenjang mat*). The roughness and saltiness of Korean soybean paste, though, are themselves kinds of studied refinement, intentional gestures towards naturalness, and towards the vigor and unfiltered nature of life and experience.

Han Jeongsun told me about her many dietary restrictions, which caused her to give her version of the stew its singularly gentle low-salt taste. I have always thought that her lifetime of hunger and struggle contributed to it as well—the broth tasted of the toughness she had cultivated and the kindness she had learned through suffering.

As we were talking, Han Jeongsun began to sing a verse from the folksong "Arirang of Miryang":

> Hey, look at me, hey, look at me, hey look at me,
> as you would look at flowers in the depths of winter, look at me. . . [1]

---

1. *Nal jom boso, nal jom boso, nal jom boso,*
   dongji seotdal kkot bondeusi nal jom boso . . .

"Wouldn't it be nice if downtrodden people were seen and heard, admired and respected?" she said, with a long musical sigh, transitioning out of song into speech, weaving song and talk together into a seamless art of life.

The marginalized and forgotten have taken the measure of history and society; and they have created masterworks of selfhood in the work of survival. Han Jeongsun told me that others can learn many things from Korean bomb and radiation victims, if only they knew how to listen. But most of us don't know; so we begin, in ignorance, to learn to listen to others as one might look at flowers in the depths of winter.

Most of us, the world over, do not know much about the nuclear experience. We certainly don't know about the Korean victims of the atomic bomb and its radiation, or about their arts of life and survival, or about the tributes they pay to those who did not survive.

The Japanese colonial era in Korea was a time of mass population mobilization, which intensified during the Asia-Pacific War (1931–45). Korea was a source of raw human and agricultural materials, so many areas of the Korean peninsula were strategically underdeveloped. Poor agricultural prospects, colonial exploitation and underdevelopment, and proximity to Japan combined to make the Southeastern province of Gyeongsang the central ground for the volunteer and forcible recruitment of Korean laborers during the colonial era. People were taken or recruited as soldiers, military sexual slaves, and manual laborers. Often the Japanese colonial government employed a kind of patterned recruitment that took people from certain parts of Korea and placed them in enclaves throughout the Japanese empire—residents of Miryang were sent to Korean ethnic labor enclaves in Shimonoseki, and so on. Several tens of thousands of the residents of the Southeastern county of Hapcheon responded to recruitment drives and went to Hiroshima to work in munitions factories.

Most of us—in the English-speaking world, in Japan, even in Korea—have no idea that there were 70,000 Koreans in Hiroshima on August 6, 1945, the day of the atomic bombing of that city, or 30,000 Koreans in Nagasaki when the bomb fell there three days later. We do not know that 35,000 Korean civilians died in Hiroshima on that day and in the immediate aftermath of the bombing. And we do not know that there were another 35,000 Koreans who survived but were exposed to radiation, and that many of them and their children suffer the effects of chromosomal damage caused by their radiation exposure—congenital malformation, cancers, and other conditions. This ignorance, for most of us, is due to the fact that we have been led to believe that the atomic bombings were an exclusively Japanese tragedy, in part due to the postwar efforts of the Japanese state to remake itself as a victim nation rather than as an aggressor (see Yoneyama 1999). We then assume that the victims of the atomic bombings were

Japanese, with perhaps a few exceptions. Neither we nor the history books make room for the 100,000 Korean exceptions.

Imagine being banished from history in this way. What options for life remain?

Many governments have little interest in seeing the facts of Korean atomic experience becoming widely known. Japan would rather its people and the international community not know about Korean victims and their children, for it complicates the "victim nation" ideology. It is convenient for the United States not to know as well, for this allows many Americans to sustain the entirely false idea that the civilians who died in the atomic bombings were part of the Japanese war machine, and had in fact ceased to be civilians, thus making the rationalization of their deaths possible. This is an ideology of terrorism. To know that there were tens of thousands of Korean civilians in Hiroshima and Nagasaki is to know the profound falsity and immorality of this idea. So we do not know.

It is often convenient, too, for Koreans not to know, until such knowledge is useful to South Korean politics. When South Korea wants to make nice with Japan, the Hiroshima Koreans are utterly absent from public discourse; but when Korea wants leverage against Japan, they and other victims of Japanese colonialism are yanked to the center, like a yo-yo on a string. This, of course, neglects the rather important fact that it was the United States, not Japan, that dropped the atomic bombs, but that is typical in the whitewashing of US–ROK relations.

The push and pull of the attention given to the Japanese war legacy in Korean public culture is a schizophrenic experience for victims, who toggle between extreme social marginalization and the instrumental attention of public culture. The media typically draws attention to "Korea's Hiroshima" once a year, around the commemoration of independence from colonial rule on August 15. These days, with the deterioration of Korea–Japan relations, attention to Korean bomb and radiation victims is slightly heightened, but only in the interest of present-day geopolitical posturing and public-cultural identity work. A persistent few in South Korean social activist society have dedicated themselves to promoting understanding and social justice for these profoundly victimized and marginalized people. And the community of victims is itself active and has a large share in the leadership of the social movement on its behalf.

This book is about these overlooked and abused people, who have lived and died on the margins of East Asian modernity and the Asia-Pacific War. There is a small literature on Korean bomb victims and their children, which is mostly historical, political-scientific, and medical.[2] With this

2. On the historical dimensions of the Korean atomic bomb experience, see Ichiba Junko's work (1999, 2003 2005), the most comprehensive attempt to document the history of Korean victims of the atomic bombs. Forced labor scholar Hur Kwang-moo's recent research

book, I aim to add to that important work by contributing an account of how Korean bomb and radiation victims live now. This account is about particular people's remarkable work of selfhood and survival in the face of that massive erasure perpetrated by the United States, Japan, and Korea, and in the midst of a social movement on their behalf.

Recent estimates put the number of surviving first-generation victims in South Korea at around 2,200 (Hanguk wonpok pihaeja hyeophoe 2020). Many have fanned out across the country and the Korean diaspora, but a near majority of them live in the Hapcheon area, as do many members of the second and subsequent generations. Hapcheon has come to represent "Korea's Hiroshima" in South Korea and internationally, and has become a center of health care, social welfare, and activism on behalf of survivors and their descendants.

Three institutions central to the community of survivors and their children are located in Hapcheon, in the town that serves as administrative center of the county. The Hapcheon Atomic Bomb Victims Welfare Center is about a ten-minute walk from the town bus station. It lies on a hill above a small stream that flows into the Hwang River, which runs through town and through the county. The Center is operated by the Korean Red Cross, and it is the only health residence for first-generation victims in South Korea, with around 100 survivors in residence. The Korean Atomic Bomb Victims Association (Han'guk wonpok pihaeja hyeopuihoe), which monitors the health and whereabouts of first-generation victims and provides support services for them, sits at the foot of the hill in a new building, which opened in 2017, which contains the Hapcheon Atomic Bomb Reference Center and a small historical museum. The Hapcheon Peacehouse (Pyeonghwa ui jip), the center of community, welfare support, and political action for second-generation radiation sufferers, is also based in Hapcheon.

This book chronicles the ethnographic fieldwork I have done in Hapcheon since 2010, mostly at the welfare center and the Hapcheon Peacehouse,

complements this, focusing in particular on differences in the experiences of Hiroshima and Nagasaki Koreans (2011). Scholarship concerning the postwar is more scarce: Oh (2017) documents postwar activism in Korea and Japan by victims and their supporters; Kim Seung-eun (2012) describes how the issue of Korean bomb victims has played out in post-colonial Korea-Japan relations. From a social welfare perspective, Kang Su-han (2011) investigates the current situations of atom bomb victims in South Korea and makes recommendations for improving social welfare systems on their behalf. Several teams of medical researchers and scientists have produced studies on the occurrence of chromosomal damage, disease, and disability among Korean victims of the bomb and their offspring (Chung and Choe 1987; Ju et al. 2006). Lee Haeng-seon's article on Kim Ok-suk's novel Scar Flowers (Hyungteoui kkot) about Korean atom bomb victims is a rare outlier in literary criticism. As part of her project on the politics of memory surrounding the atomic legacy, Lisa Yoneyama has done invaluable work on discrimination against Korean victims in the memorialization of the atomic bomb experience (1995, 1999).

including a half-year stretch in 2011 and a four-month stay in 2015, in addition to about six or seven other shorter visits. I worked with about forty first-generation bomb survivors and their children, in the end focusing on about ten people. I took a broad interest in their expressive lives—as arts in themselves, as windows onto their identities and experiences, and as means by which they have sustained life and selfhood through the long years since 1945. We talked, walked, ate, sang, swam, played games, did arts and crafts, and went to places of worship together. I observed their testimonies and other kinds of participation in the social movement on behalf of bomb victims and the antinuclear movement. I tried to listen to stories and songs as a corrective to the enduring, multifaceted neglect and marginalization they have faced. I listened and watched not because they need "our" help, but because they have much to teach others about war and nuclear experience; about the social, cultural, and political life of illness, suffering, and disability; about discrimination; about survival; about social membership; and about peace and happiness. And I listened for what they have to teach us about the social utility and power of singing, talking, dancing, walking, and the other expressive arts that make up the performance of survival.

What I listened for most of all were the arts of survival and self-making by which particular Korean bomb and radiation victims in this book have survived. This involved trying to understand what sense they made of their experiences and themselves, and—an issue particularly important for survivors of traumatic experiences—things that are "beyond sense making but still affect . . . us" (Ochoa 2014: 34), either because they are unreachable by sense or because we have enshrined them beyond sense. My own ideas about ineffability do not line up with the inscrutable aspects of traumatic experience, or those of which victims refuse to make sense. In order to come closer to these things one must tune into silences, mutings, omissions, refusals, absences, and the fine balance between these things and the realms of sound and sense that I will refer to as *quietude*.

———

I blundered into this project thinking it would be like my former work with Korean survivors of the Japanese "comfort women" system (Pilzer 2012), and that I would work among a community of Korean survivors who looked to singing as a life resource.[3] I thought rather nebulously that the first generation of bomb victims would be a community of mostly elderly Koreans similar to others I had worked with, some of whom expressed themselves

---

3. I am grateful to Tom Turino for suggesting this language of "music as resource" at a personal meeting in 2008.

in song as an alternative mode of expression to speech, as a means of identity, as a way of narrating the past and the self, as a practice of social connectivity, and as a daily work and an art of survival. But as the months and years went by in Hapcheon my recordings of songs and stories about them accumulated much more slowly than before. I was struck more and more by the quiet of "Korea's Hiroshima." Among the more than a hundred Korean survivors of the bomb whom I met there were no loud voices raised in blunt songs of experience. There were no strident voices overwhelmed by emotion, even in testimony. Bomb and radiation victims rarely raised their voices even during protest, where such behavior is conventional. In Hapcheon there are many voices, but they are quiet. Rather than fret about the scarcity of music, I begin to listen to that quiet. I have inquired into the nature of that quiet for eleven years now.

The quiet of "Korea's Hiroshima" is not a quiet of defeat or resignation; rather it is one of many kinds of quiet that are intensely productive and even political ways of making do (Sprengel 2020: 246). The quiet of Hapcheon is a quietude, a kind of structured poetics of quiet.

That quietude has many sources. It is the habituated quiet of a community which has learned over many years to keep its head down, to stay out of trouble, and to get on with life as best as possible. Letting it be known that one was a survivor of the atomic bomb or the child of a survivor led to different forms of discrimination in postwar South Korean society. First-generation bomb survivors and their radiation sufferer children have long been accustomed to secrecy about their atomic experience. In recent decades, although many have come forward to proclaim their experiences through testimony and activism, that long-practiced reticence colors much of their expressive lives.

For some the quiet of "Korea's Hiroshima" is one of vocal disability. Thyroid cancer is one of the most common illnesses that those exposed to nuclear radiation suffer, and many live with what they feel are compromised voices as a result of thyroid surgeries. Yun Sugi, Jeong Hoyeon, and others at the welfare center were survivors of thyroid cancer; their voices were soft and raspy, and they had difficulty speaking or singing loudly. Bae Ilmyeong also had experienced thyroid trouble, and felt her voice was not what it used to be.

Quietude is also a cultural value: some first-generation survivors identify with the *otonashī* (mild) cultural style of Japan, where they spent their childhoods. The Japanese word *otonashī* can connote meekness, but more often it suggests self-control and a settled character, qualities which are generally valued and associated with maturity. Indeed, the word is reminiscent of the word for "adult"—*otona*—and one way of writing the word in Sino-Japanese characters uses the same characters. For first-generation bomb victims this is an identity, but also a marker of distinction, a way of sustaining their identities as Korean Japanese vis-à-vis notions of Korean loudness and its supposedly attendant civilizational backwardness. In this way they take part in a long tradition of civilizationalist discourse in Japan and Korea that disdains forceful rural voices as emblematic of the past and contrasts them with various genteel "voices of modernity" (Harkness 2014).[4]

Yun Sugi told me that he admired the Japanese *otonashī* style. He contrasted this with the noisiness of Korean emotional expressivity. Like many others, he associated quiet Japanese sociality with modernist progress, and the relative loudness of Korean society with backwardness. Kim Imseon told me that she was more comfortable talking quietly and that Korean society and people in general were too outspoken and noisy. Some among the first generation of bomb victims connect this style of quiet with the wartime spirit of self-restraint (*gaman*) they learned as children and young adults in Japan; first- and second-generation victims also absorbed the stiff-upper-lip spirit that the South Korean state promoted after the Korean War, which is another quiet on behalf of national progress. Yun Sugi and others associated this sort of quiet with masculine toughness, although it was prevalent among women as well.

Some first-generation bomb victims spend a lot of time reading, and this contemplation of novels, religious texts, newspapers, magazines and web pages is another source of the quiet of "Korea's Hiroshima." Literacy makes the many survivors who learned to read in Japanese primary school— especially women—rather unusual among others of their generation in rural South Korea, and people take pride in it as a mark of distinction. Bae Ilmyeong and Kim Iljo showed me collections of Japanese song lyrics which they kept in their rooms. Bae Ilmyeong's professor son gave her a folder of Japanese song lyrics and poetry which he had written in calligraphy; she took these out to read through in the evening, and she showed them to guests, demonstrating her written literacy, her knowledge of Japanese literature and song, and her son's calligraphic ability and high social status all at the same time.

Another source of quiet in Hapcheon is the finely wrought and precarious peace, or truce, with the past that survivors have cultivated over the years. When I approached victims early in the project and asked them

---

4. Nicholas Harkness's *Songs of Seoul* is a fine exposition of notions of the "clean voice" vis-à-vis traditional Korean voices among contemporary Korean Christians (2014). This is reminiscent of the discourse of softness and civility as a key value in modern Turkish popular music and society (Stokes 2010: 58). Similar twentieth-century transformations of the voice can be observed in many other places throughout the globe—Japan, China, India, and elsewhere.

about singing, many survivors told me they had no need to sing. Kim Imseon remembered singing popular songs while at school in Japan, but she told me that she didn't like singing at her age, as it served no purpose. Bae Ilmyeong told me that advanced age brought a desire for a simple life, for contentment with the fulfillment of basic needs, and that putting herself forward to sing publicly would cut against this and be unseemly. She preferred prayer. Among the many sources of survivors' quiet we find also resignation, truces with the past, and even the contentment of age.

The many-layered quiet of "Korea's Hiroshima" is made more complex by the fact that the Hapcheon Atomic Bomb Victims Welfare Center promotes the contentment of age whether one has found it or not. "Institutional quiet," as we might call it, is manifold. The prohibitions on drinking alcohol and general loudness legislate quiet on behalf of others, as do prohibitions on activities after hours. Residents respond by breaking the rules quietly, continuing a long tradition among bomb and radiation victims of avoiding the notice of those in power.

The quietude of "Korea's Hiroshima" is compounded further by the silence of traumatic experience—acoustic absences that represent lost people and dreams, mark the felt presence of injury, or signal the impossibility or undesirability of expression. These silences are personal, but they are touched by several contrasting discourses. One is the transnational political discourse surrounding the bombing of Hiroshima, with its language of silence as the acoustical shape of trauma, loss, and death. Here silence is a still aftermath in which the sound of the bomb and the cacophony of war echo, and the immeasurability of loss is given its affective measure. This notion of silence shows up throughout the Japanese and international artistic representation of the bomb and in its literature (see, for instance, Linner 1995; Naono 2010; and Pinguet 2006).[5] Its most famous performance is the Silent Prayer and Peace Bell (*mokutō to heiwa no kane*) minute that commemorates the bombing in Hiroshima at the Hiroshima Peace Memorial Park and throughout the city of Hiroshima. "At 8:15 on the morning of August 6th, marking the exact moment when the atomic bomb was dropped, bells ring out at temples, sirens wail throughout the city and the citizens of Hiroshima observe a solemn moment of silence in remembrance," Hiroshima Prefecture's official travel site tells us.[6] The "silence" of

5. Sociologist Naono Akiko describes "areas of silence" within testimony that survivors use to deal with the incommunicability of atomic bomb experience (2010: 510). Catherine Pinguet writes about silences that "demand respect" in her article about the literature of the atomic bomb (2006: 116). Rachel Linner named her monograph about her work with bomb victims in Hiroshima *City of Silence—Listening to Hiroshima* (1995).

6. See visithiroshima.net. One can also hear a recording of the Peace Memorial Park bell at http://www.stevenfeld.net/hiroshima.

the annual minute is one in which human voices are silent, and the distressed sounds of war are recreated for people to hear in solemn reflection. It is a sacred silence as well, for the tolling of temple bells and the bell at the center of Hiroshima Peace Memorial Park evoke the Buddhist tradition of ringing bells for the dead, often done a few days later during the Japanese festival of the dead (*obon*), at the New Year, and at other times throughout the year.

The idea of sacred silence is found in the anti-nuclear movement and public cultural discourse, but it is also found relatively independently among many survivors, for whom silence plays an important role in expressing the nature of traumatic experience. We shall see this later when we encounter moments of silence in memorial ceremonies and when we listen to testimony. This trope of silence as loss and death has informed the general style in which victims memorialize the bomb, and also the manner in which they give testimony, encouraging a muted, unemotional, documentary style of witnessing that contrasts with much more expressive testimonial culture in South Korea. This restrained style of testimony embraces the failures and silences of language to express the incomprehensibility of atomic war and traumatic experience.

In Japan, the discourse about sacred silence in the anti-nuclear movement coexists, sometimes violently and sometimes harmoniously, with another conversation about the importance of *breaking* silence about the atomic bomb experience. For decades in the postwar, victims were discouraged from speaking about their own suffering, which was often criticized as selfish. Instead, they were supposed to keep silent and pull together for the sake of national renewal. Victim-activists and others were therefore forced of necessity to break through this blanket of restraint and suppression (see Naono 2010: 509–10; Yoneyama 1999: 87–8; and Zubek 2016).[7] One reason for the flatness and unemotionality of testimony is that survivors have long wished to deemphasize the personal to shore up the sense that testimony is given without selfish motives.

The Japanese discourse of breaking silence about the atomic bombs resonates with the discourse of forced and broken silence that lies at the center of South Korean social movement culture, which has spent the last thirty years trying to undo half a century of authoritarian silencing in the Korean peninsula. That repression and the discourse that responds to it have had far and away more influence on Korean victims than Japanese conversations about silence, for they are conditions under which the quiet

7. Zubek investigates the way that atomic bomb literature—including testimony—challenges the silence imposed by the bombs and postwar Japanese and transnational peace discourse, which she calls "atomic silence."

of "Korea's Hiroshima" has grown, whereas Korean victims have had much less contact with Japanese society and its social movements.

South Korean democratization, which began in the late 1980s, brought the reexamination of the colonial, wartime, and authoritarian pasts out of the closet and into public discourse. As the pressure on survivors under authoritarianism to suffer silently on behalf of the nation faded, the "comfort women," other victims of forced labor, forced military conscripts, and those who suffered the red purges of war and authoritarianism have come forward to assert the injustice of their victimization. Social movements and national historiography have produced a common trope of silence and its breaking.[8]

The "silence broken" trope encourages victims to speak or act out in spectacular performances of suffering and injury, asserting a personhood and a particularity that cuts against years of silencing. As they do, their suffering is often coopted by the nation and the state, as a metonym for Korea's struggle for self-realization and as a source of moral authority vis-à-vis Japan, the USA, and others. For this reason, the performance of suffering—the performance of breaking the silence—involves attempts by victims of colonial and post-colonial violence to hold on to their own suffering or wrest it back for their own purposes. Victims who embrace the opportunity afforded by public attention to their suffering must play push and pull with the national narrative (Morris 1997: 41),[9] which affords them a listening public while rendering them as sacrifices to the nation, taking their suffering and losses for its own ends, in the continual reforging of what Jo Mina (2020) has called "victim nationalism" (*pihaeja minjokjuui*).[10]

These spectacles of broken silence conflict with the sacralized and canonized memorial silences of anti-nuclear discourse and traumatic

---

8. Examples of broken silence discourse in Korea are many. Anthropologist Kim Seong-nae (2007) has spent much of her career examining the enforcement and breaking of silence about the leftist uprising and the counter-insurgent state massacre that followed on Jeju island in 1948, focusing in particular on shamans' roles in breaking silence and envoicing the dead. Historian Yi Imha's *War Widows Break the Silence of Modern Korean History* (2010) borrows the trope of broken silence for her oral history of the many neglected widows of the Korean War.

9. Anthropologist David Morris describes the process by which victims constantly reinvent suffering by variously extending and contracting the borders of moral community, consequently reinventing such moral communities in the process (1997: 41).

10. Jo applies Ulrich Schmid's (2015) discussion of victimization in the founding of twentieth-century European nationalism to contemporary South Korea. Kim Seong-nae explores similar Korean national histories that take the pain of victims of the Jeju Island massacres as necessary evils of state self-actualization (2007: 201). Hwajun Lee shows how memorial halls devoted to displaying the colonial past mobilize suffering on behalf of a national "victim consciousness" (2014). In a similar vein, Dominick LaCapra describes the common process by which others' suffering is appropriated in his "Trauma, Absence, Loss" with particular reference to the Holocaust (1999).

experience; and victims are caught between pressures to keep the silence of trauma and death and to break it. Some part of the quiet of "Korea's Hiroshima" is the artful navigation of this seemingly impossible situation: victims have forged quietude as a means to give voice to silence, to enfold silence within expression, and otherwise allow silence and sound to coexist.

Finally, some part of the quietude of "Korea's Hiroshima" arises from victims' efforts to escape the compulsions to memorialize traumatic experience, and instead "to let it go, to forget it, to at least partially contain the wounds of victimization and carve out a world in which to live with dignity" (Sheriff 2001: 75, quoted in Quintero 2019: 149). This means attaching new meanings to silence, reclaiming silence from lofty discourses and social pressures, and resituating silence in everyday life for purposes of one's own. Yi Suyong, the subject of Chapter 4, marks silence in a twofold gesture when she ceases to speak: she acknowledges the limits of language and expression, and she turns towards me and others, foregrounding the richness and complexity of being together. Bae Ilmyeong, the focus of Chapter 5, refuses to testify but does not refuse to speak.

So victims' quiet springs from many sources: notions of Japanese soft-spokenness, vocal disability, the quiet contemplation of texts, religion, the changes to the human heart as one grows older, the experience of war, social marginalization, and traumatic experience, various institutional and social movement discourses, and personal relationships with and deployments of silence. The quietude of these survivors is an important and revealing effect of their history and experience as former Koreans in Japan and as victims in present-day South Korea. Although it is markedly different from the various discourses of "silence," it is often rendered to or mistaken for those discourses. It is the stylistic zone in which most Korean bomb and radiation victims in Hapcheon get on with the art of living. Quietude is quiet as a space of possibility, where voices, memories, and sentiments may emerge and recede, and where presence, absence, expression, and restraint can coincide. Quietude is my shorthand for a collection of ways of making do (de Certeau 1984), a site of the ongoing struggle for life.

So this is a quiet book. And although I am an ethnomusicologist, a scholar of music and culture, it is not always or even mostly about music. There are some people in the book who are quite devoted to songs and singing; and instrumental music makes an appearance or two. But much of the time there is not much that we would conventionally call music or musicking, and I focus on other kinds of expressive practices—speech, walking, arts and crafts, and others. Sometimes I find those practices situated in webs of expression which include music, such as the continuum which links speech and song, patterns of intertextual reference that connect expressive arenas, and the ways that music conditions and inspires everyday movement and vice versa. But at other times, there is little music; indeed, many victims were averse to music and singing. And since this book is about people and what they care about, I often set music aside and focus on other practices.

Nonetheless I listen, observe, and write as a music scholar, because that is what I am, and because I find the perspective fruitful. This book is thus an effort to encounter the broad expressive lives of Korean bomb and radiation victims musically. The phrase "musical anthropology," elaborated by Anthony Seeger in his 1987 *Why Suyá Sing: A Musical Anthropology of an Amazonian People*, holds out the possibility of a kind of ethnomusicology in which music is a perspective, not an object of study. In the present book I try to make good on the largely unrealized promise of that phrase.[11] Ethnomusicology was long conceived of as the study of *music in culture*, and then as the study of *music as culture*. But more and more, as scholars broaden its purview, the field might be characterized as a way of *studying culture musically*—a mode of musical inquiry, not an inquiry about musical objects. Much recent work in ethnomusicology is dedicated at least in part to considering non-musical practices musically, such as J. Martin Daughtry's *Listening to War: Sound, Music, Trauma, and Survival in Wartime Iraq* (2015), Ben Tausig's *Bangkok is Rising: Sound, Protest, and Constraint* (2019) and Yun Emily Wang's work on sounds of the everyday in her dissertation "Sonic Poetics of Home and the Art of Making Do in Sinophone Toronto" (2018). The perspective of ethnomusicology, in short, reveals much about expressive and social life even in the absence of musical objects.

Ethnomusicology, as a way of studying culture musically, may and often should focus on musical artefacts and practices. But it just as easily may not, and be ethnomusicology without music. That is largely the case in this book, and no doubt that will frustrate many readers in my field. But I would hope that they will reflect on the implications of my claim—that while we are free to study music as we like, we are just as free to turn our attention elsewhere and have just, or almost, as much to say. In this book I listen, observe, describe, and analyze everyday life with a musical sensibility.

First of all, that means that I am attuned to rhythm, timbre, pitch, dynamics, reverberation, and many other parameters often associated with music. These parameters, of course, have their own origins and trappings,

---

11. I am grateful to Lee Veeraragavan for suggesting I use this phrase in this expanded sense. Seeger's fine book and other work that employs the phrase "musical anthropology" (Lomax et al. 1976) typically remain attached to musical objects, using music as a lens to understand the broader cultural life.

as Kofi Agawu famously explains in his critiques of European and American ethnomusicologists' fetishization of rhythm in the musics of Africa, based as it is in the embrace of neo-primitive essentialisms of blackness as rhythm (1992, 2003). Similarly, the mostly European theorization of everyday life (Lefebvre, de Certeau, etc.) is overrun with essentialisms about rhythm as a primary structuring principle of social life, to the exclusion of almost every other perceptible sociopoetic parameter of the things people do. An ethnomusicology of the non-musical needs more parameters, to keep any one from becoming an essence. And crucially, it should remain at a more provisional level of analysis, less dedicated to the conceptual vocabulary, allowing the different parameters to interact, conflict, and fail when they should, and reconceptualizing them in more appropriate ways.

One key way of doing this is to invoke culturally and socially rooted aesthetic sensibilities and values that cut against those abstract parameters of expression and replace or refine them. This is the second method of my "studying culture musically." I turn often to Korean and Japanese aesthetic sensibilities and values, which have arisen in specific social and cultural circumstances in modern Korean and Japanese life, and which have their own fractures, contradictions, circulations, intersections, and limits. These limits are particularly important for this book, as the first generation of Korean atomic bomb victims have long lived between the two cultures and have been fully accepted by neither. To explain aspects of their experience and identities with exclusive reference to cultural values and concepts like shame, restraint, or quiet would be to force their experience and identities into tidy boxes of national identity into which they do not entirely fit, although many have struggled for decades to belong. Their experience of the bomb and its aftermath and their totality of life experience—much of which has been traumatic—cannot be rendered to national identities and cultures or excluded from them. And at the same time each victim can be said to have a culture of their own, which enfolds experiences of social marginalization and trauma.

Indeed, the Korean community of bomb and radiation victims force a rethinking of the whole notion of the "culture" in "studying culture musically," which coincides with and draws inspiration from the rethinking of the concept of culture in anthropology and ethnomusicology. Culture has long been described as a web of meanings, the schemes of thought that people use to understand the world. Although people who have had profoundly traumatic experiences do much work to make sense of them, one cannot do so completely. And rather than make sense of everything, many construct shrines to the sense-shattering aspect of traumatic experience, or aspects of experience which are not comprehensible or that they deem off limits to rational explanation. To accept culture to be a tidy web of meanings is therefore to attempt to erase the character of traumatic experience, to obviate experiences of trauma, and to repress histories of violence. Selfhood is not an entirely sensible thing in this book, although it is inextricably bound up with the desire for the self to make sense. And culture, too, must necessarily refer not solely to coherent systems of belief by which the world is given sense, but to the complex connections and disconnections between sensing, sense-making, and the insensible.[12] If the reevaluation in anthropology of the culture concept has taught us anything, it is that the coherences of culture—the bonds of thought and feeling that hold people together as individuals and as groups—are more things that people struggle for than durable entities which exist whether they wish for them or not. Culture, in other words, arises from a desire to cohere, and is a practice of coherence, on both group and individual levels.

The "culture" of Korean bomb and radiation victims is not just complex due to the extent of traumatic experience. The first generation of Korean victims of the atomic bomb have lived in several distinct cultural arrangements that do not easily reconcile with one another. Both the first and second generations have been subject to massive discrimination and social marginalization, actively excluded from membership in various human communities: Japanese and South Korean nations, the community of "normal" human beings. To attempt to explain everything about this community with reference to normative cultural concepts would be to flatten out that history of exclusion, and to erase the particularities of their experiences. Many victims in the social movement do this, in an effort to attain full membership in South Korean society by redrawing the boundaries of moral community (Morris 1997: 41), demonstrating the way that their experiences are archetypally Korean. That effort is important to many survivors and should be respected, even as it overwrites certain kinds of difference. But histories of marginalization produce their own cultural forms, however transitory and changeable, and these are an important part of what counts as culture in the following pages.

My version of "culture" throughout this book therefore includes how people understand the world, the conflict of competing schemes of understanding and selfhood, and the zones people partition off as outside understanding, sensed but not sensible. It is a shorthand for the senses and feelings and the work of coherence and disjuncture that guide people through life. Invoking cultural concepts, therefore, is only a partial strategy, another beginning like the investigation of abstract parameters of the

12. I am inspired in this investigation by Brian Massumi's *Parables for the Virtual* (2002), which attempts to shift inquiry into the nature of experience away from sense-making and towards that vast majority of experience which is felt but not rendered to schemes of understanding.

expressive life—rhythm, pitch, timbre, and so on. Cultural concepts must be allowed to fail, merge, or transform when they cease to explain, and to be supplanted or complemented by others that bomb victims have forged themselves in the crucible of life.

Finally, when the various expressive parameters and cultural concepts fail to explain the expressive behaviors of bomb victims and their children, I listen musically to people's deployment of silence. Silence in conversation draws one's attention to those aspects of experience and identity that cannot be described, or which people choose not to explain. But with the same gesture, it draws people into confrontation with one another as living things, and as presences and identities. In so doing it also draws attention to the social relations that bind or divide us. Silence and the doors it opens and closes are a fundamental part of the arts of life that I am struggling to understand by studying culture musically, a piece of the puzzle that points out the basics of human social relations and draws attention to the fact that culture itself extends beyond what is known.

These are some of the strategies involved in my version of "studying culture musically." Those who are familiar with linguistics and linguistic anthropology may sometimes notice the similarity of my means of study to those fields' analysis of prosody, the non-semantic aspects of spoken language. I am inspired by and indebted to many such studies, such as Jane Hill's "Voices of Don Gabriel" (1995), perhaps the classic account of the narrative uses of non-lexical aspects of speech, and the work of Nicholas Harkness, especially those aspects of it that concern timbre (2011, 2013, 2014). But whereas most linguistic anthropologists study prosody to understand how it complements speech's communicative function, I concede no such priority to communication, and pay as much or more attention to expression and collective experience. I have cultivated these foci through a lifetime with music; and I find them particularly appropriate for listening to the verbal art of bomb and radiation victims, who so often reach the point in describing their experiences beyond which communication is impossible or undesirable.

My perspective is also different from work in linguistics and linguistic anthropology for another more obvious reason: my musical attention extends beyond speech to the expressive and affective uses of many other practices— walking, pottery, drawing, calligraphy, swimming, and sport, among others. We learn much about the utility of these activities in victims' lives through tuning in to their rhythmic, amplitudinal, and textural dimensions. These aspects of everyday activity are part of the means by which people manage the time of life—a high-stakes practice by which victims lay claim to the present in a South Korean public sphere that consigns them to the past, and an important struggle for anyone approaching the end of life. The way people move, the choreographic aspects of these activities, also has much to teach us about the way they organize themselves as physical beings, social actors, and identities.

―――

For survivors and people living with traumatic experience, social marginalization, and discrimination, those efforts of wishing and working for sense, of guarding and feeling and mourning its absence, are all species of arts of survival. The purpose of this book is to chronicle these by focusing on talk and testimony, song, crafts, walking, and other diverse social behaviors which make life possible and preferable.

The most fundamental arts of survival are focused on sustaining life— mitigating violence, finding or making places of safety, and securing the means of life. Most of the first-generation and many of the second-generation Korean victims of the atomic bomb died unassisted by any state; and those who have survived are engaged in a fight for the means of life—relief from the burdens of poverty, and health care specific to their special needs. In the midst of this, victims use forms of self-expression to establish social connections and the security that comes with them. They sing and engage with various media to perform memberships in fandoms and communities of cultural literacy that allow them to fight social marginalization. First-generation bomb victims Yi Suyong, Kim Iljo, and others testified to their wartime experiences in an earnest attempt to elicit the consideration of fellow Koreans, and hence be granted full membership in South Korean society. Second-generation radiation sufferer Han Jeongsun leveraged pop cultural tropes of illness and suffering to connect South Korean popular culture with her experiences as a second-generation radiation victim.

The arts of survival have to do with forging and sustaining such relationships; at the same time, and often with the same strokes, they are forums for self-making. Expressive activities like speaking, testifying, and singing are techniques of identity, arenas in which one can create a story of one's life that coheres around oneself as its main character. This involves the complex harmonization of personal experience with social expectations.

These arts of survival also involve organizing and energizing the self for social action—they are means by which people find and sustain the ability to function socially. This often involves the difficult and ongoing work of mastering traumatic memory and emotion. These are opportunities to design one's voice, which can be used throughout life in situations both mundane and extraordinary. People cultivate singing voices that they use in political speech, and they cultivate witnessing voices that they employ outside of testimony. People with movement-related disabilities sing to access the danced movements to which song refers, to modulate the structures and energy of its movements for everyday mobility.

The design and ornamentation of everyday life are part of these arts of survival as well. People with disabilities, the chronically ill, and the elderly take care not to hurt themselves in the course of their daily activities. People manage time carefully, keeping to mindfully thought-out routines. People negotiate the spaces they live in with just as much care. In the institutional environment of the Hapcheon Atomic Bomb Victims Welfare Center people count their steps between points. They squirrel away alcohol in special hiding places to be brought out when the coast is clear. They craft exquisitely detailed exercise routines for physical and mental fitness. The art of managing the everyday is an art of laying claim to the present, which people feel slipping away, and which public culture would deny them by quarantining them in the past.

And at the end of this roster of the arts of survival, we come to the pursuit, through religion, art, philosophy, and other means, of reconciliation with the past, and with one's lot in life. The denizens of "Korea's Hiroshima" who pursue such ends do so indefinitely. Some are ambivalent about the whole idea of reconciliation. Many feel that states—the USA and Japan in particular—hold the keys to resolution and have locked them away, and that in any case, many things cannot be resolved even if justice were pursued to its limits. Losses cannot be bought off or otherwise compensated. Radiation's genetic inheritance cannot be "overcome"—it persists through generations.

Some bomb and radiation victims thus try to be content, while others abhor contentment. For most, it is a balancing act required to make life work. "I have to be content in and of myself, despite my suffering, in order to get by in life; but I am not content with the lot of others, of my community," Han Jeongsun told me, splitting the difference. Throughout the following pages, first and second-generation victims employ the arts of survival to thread these narrow passages between outrage and contentment, between personal experience and social expectation, between functioning and psychological or physical collapse, between schemes of sense-making and that vast majority of experience and existence that is exterior to sense. In these arts we find much ingenuity, and many resources for life. And we also find great grief, strength, and hope, inexorably intertwined.

CHAPTER 2

"Korea's Hiroshima"

Hapcheon County lies west of Daegu in the mountainous Southeast of the Korean peninsula. It is bisected by the Hwang (Yellow) River, flowing east out of the mountains into the Nakdong River, which vertically divides Southeastern Korea. Most of Hapcheon's landscape is made up of mountains, rising to elevations of around 1,500 meters, with rivulets running down valleys into rivers. To live there is to be surrounded by low mountains on all sides. The effect is of living in a bowl, which traps heat in the summer and cold in the winter. Residents often say Hapcheon is both the hottest and the coldest place in South Korea. The first time I climbed up the mountain edge of one of these bowls I expected to see some far distance, or a city, or a plain; what I saw was another bowl, and another, and another, as mountains upon mountains piled up in the distance, in an endless chain of mountain passes (see Figure 2.1).

About 60,000 people live in Hapcheon County, with about sixty-one people to a square kilometer. This is rather sparse in a country where the population density rises as high as 16,000 per square kilometer in Seoul. About 12,000 people live in Hapcheon town, which is the heart of the community of Korean survivors of the atomic bomb.

In summer 2010, on my first visit to Hapcheon, activist Kang Jesuk and the activist Buddhist monk Hyejin brought me downtown to the multi-use general Hapcheon Welfare Center to visit the Hapcheon branch of the Korean Atomic Bomb Victims Association. We sat across a coffee table drinking instant coffee with the branch's towering director, Shim Jintae. Everyone had recommended I meet him, a central figure in the Hapcheon bomb victims community, a scintillating personality, and an essential entry

Quietude. Joshua D. Pilzer, Oxford University Press. © Oxford University Press 2023.
DOI: 10.1093/oso/9780197615089.003.0002

Figure 2.1 Hapcheon town, viewed from the top of Mt. Galma, 2011. The Hwang River is visible in the foreground and the Hwang River County People's Park lies just to its left. Photo by the author.

point for outsiders wishing to learn about "Korea's Hiroshima." He had long served as director of the Hapcheon branch of the Victims Association, perhaps its most important branch, and he was a fount of local, national, and international knowledge about the Korean experience of Hiroshima and its aftermath. He was born in 1944 and spent the first year and a half of his life in Hiroshima, before his family returned to Hapcheon. That put him well past his *hwan'gap*—the Korean sixtieth birthday which signals one's assumption of elder status—but he strode about town like a young man thirty years his junior.

When we sat down across the coffee table that morning he had already been up for hours. He owned a large country farm, where he and his wife cultivated their own rice, kept a large garden and orchard, raised cows and kept bees, made soy sauce (*ganjang*), soybean paste (*doenjang*), red pepper paste (*geochujang*), red pepper powder (*geochugaru*), charcoal, and countless other things (Figure 2.2). "Human beings are meant to get up and go to sleep with the sun," he told me. He had worked on the farm this morning and passed the time of day with other residents of his village. He gave villagers free reign to use the *yukgak jeongja* (open-air hexagonal pavilion) that he had built out front of his house overlooking the rice paddies for socializing even when he wasn't there.

Figure 2.2 Shim Jintae in his orchard, October 2011. Photo by the author.

As director of the Hapcheon branch of the Victims Association, Shim Jintae kept track of the many survivors in Hapcheon, looked after their welfare, and offered advice and made connections when people had difficulty receiving their welfare allowance from Japan, healthcare, or funds from the South Korean state. He knew the names of almost every bomb victim in Hapcheon, where they lived or where they had died, and many of their stories. He met the press, researchers, and other visitors, and made trips to Daegu and Seoul for meetings, protests, and testimony. He officiated at various public meetings, and he made speeches at the yearly memorial ceremony and concert that took place surrounding the annual commemoration of the bomb on August 6 in Hapcheon. In general, Shim served as a guide to the Hapcheon experience of the atomic bombs.

Since starting fieldwork in earnest in 2011 I have spent many mornings with Shim Jintae in his office at the Victims Association's Hapcheon branch. Encountering this charming and cheerful man in this austere office—with its rows of black-and-white photographs depicting the horrors of the atom bombs—was like watching the sun break through clouds. He was possessed of a seemingly boundless vitality, which energized his virtuosic flow of oratory and conversation, whether speaking about the Hiroshima Koreans, discoursing on Korean folklore, or just entertaining in his office, at the Hapcheon Atomic Bomb Victims Welfare Center, at home, or elsewhere. At official times he spoke slowly to make sure he was understood, in his pleasant tenor voice. When at play, he spoke very quickly, pouring joke upon joke, anecdote upon anecdote, shaping each sentence in arcs of emphasis and volume. Encountering Shim in the atmosphere of Hapcheon, part of the rural southeast where male speech is typically spare and rather retiring, I got the feeling that he had taken it upon himself to counterbalance that reticence all by himself.

Shim Jintae was generous with his word but also with his deeds. Over all the years of my fieldwork, he has been my foremost guide to Hapcheon as a place and as "Korea's Hiroshima," as he has been for countless others. He took me with him to political events, festivals, and testimonies. He took me to Hapcheon Dam, to the nearby movie theme park, to the tombs of the Gaya Dynasty, and to many other sights around the county and nearby. He would call suddenly in the early morning and ask "What are you doing?" before taking me off to traditional funerals, to lunch, or to the famous temple Haeinsa for the day to escape the summer heat. We had dinners at the pavilion out in front of his house, and there we shared evenings of conversation and the occasional song.

Shim Jintae's conversation ranged from traditional folk tales to episodes from Hapcheon's history to philosophical musings on the nature of society and politics. His songs were typically folded into story or conversation, such as those he told to appreciative guests on those nights in his pavilion, and arose from or sparked conversation. They were usually part of his educative project—he sang military songs about the region, the anthems of local schools and other school music, regional pallbearers' songs (*sangyeo sori*), local folk songs (*tosok minyo*), and pop songs that bore on the conversation at hand or that prefaced stories. When singing popular songs, he sang in the smooth tenor with which he spoke, minus the expressive raspiness that he often let in to his informal storytelling. He carefully articulated text, and sang concisely, loath to monopolize the occasion or break the momentum of conversation. Song was just one of the vocal arts which he folded together to enliven his social scene and pursue his activism, together with story, public speechmaking, and testimony. He brought his extensive knowledge of Hapcheon, nuclear history, and folklore to bear on these modes of verbal art. And he modulated the pace, dialect, and timbre of his speech and song to suit the repertoire and the occasion. As director of the Hapcheon branch of Korean bomb victims, he brought his verbal artistry to bear on looking out for the well-being of Hapcheon's bomb and radiation victims, making outsiders such as myself feel welcome in Hapcheon and working towards his goal of turning Hapcheon, "Korea's Hiroshima," into a city of peace.

Shim Jintae was a year and a half old when he left Hiroshima and came with his family to their home in Hapcheon in the winter of 1945. Although he escaped injury or noticeable aftereffects at the time, he had mysterious chronic pain and ailments that he later suspected were related to his experience of the bomb. His legs swelled up, and in lieu of medicine his grandmother fried human excrement to make poultices for him. His legs got better eventually, although they still bothered him now and again.

The Korean War did not skip over Hapcheon. One day when talking about the war Shim Jintae sang me a local folk song about the tearful farewell of South Korean soldiers amidst the sound of the bombing of Hapcheon. He sang not with his typically smooth voice but in a rasp, gesturing towards folk song practice and the depth of experience and sorrow. On one of our rambles around his neighborhood he pointed out the hillside where his father had been killed by North Korean troops during the war. He told me how his father had been a village elder and a property holder of some stature, and how he was singled out and executed under the pine trees.

He took a deep breath and exhaled. "After that, in fifth grade, I had to leave school and go to work," he told me. In the morning before school his grandfather had him study the *Thousand Character Classic*, the sixth-century Chinese poem which people all over East Asia long used to learn Chinese characters. His grandfather had often complemented him on his brightness; Shim Jintae insisted to me that these complements were intended to encourage him, not based on any exceptional qualities he possessed, something I found unlikely. In any case, his studies were cut short. He found himself so preoccupied with making a living his whole life that he had never been able to finish reading a single book. One evening as we sat around the dinner table, he and Han Jeongsun sang for me the popular "Graduation Song" (*Joreopsik norae*), sung at graduation ceremonies. Shim Jintae told me that since he had been unable to graduate, singing that song made him cry. It also reminded him of his father's death, the reason he had been forced to leave school. But when Han Jeongsun faltered, he carried on singing strongly through the last wistful couplet of parting: "As streams meet each other in the ocean, let's meet again next time."

Shim Jintae eventually took charge of the family farm. He married and had three sons and a daughter; but his daughter died as a baby of a wasting sickness, which Shim Jintae suspected was due to his radiation exposure. He worried about his sons and grandchildren, concerned that the legacy of the bomb would reassert itself and claim them. Shim Jintae rarely spoke of these personal experiences of the bomb and its legacy—his breeziness and energy enfolded deep silences, and he made little attempt to hide them, wearing his status as a first-generation bomb victim on his sleeve. He refrained from speaking of such things, but his own suffering, his own losses and concerns, bound him to his work.

I have heard Shim Jintae describe the plight of Hiroshima's Koreans to Korean and Japanese school children, to the press, scholars, activists, and officials of the South Korean government. In 2016 I heard him speak to a small gathering of Korean victims and others in front of the gates of the Hiroshima Peace Memorial Park as we waited for the arrival of Barack Obama, the first time a standing US president had visited Hiroshima. The small group had made the trip by overnight boat from Busan to save money, and even so the expensive nature of the trip meant that only eight people were able to go. "We have come here to stand with other atom bomb victims," he said, "and to demand that President Obama and the Japanese government give us their sincere, official apology." He spoke loudly and clearly, punching out with a voice made more than usually raspy by its volume. All the same it was almost subsumed by the noise of the street and the many spectators. He held a sign that said "Obama! Abe! Apologize to Korean A-bomb Victims!" (Figure 2.3). In both hands above this he held a manila envelope containing a letter addressed to President Obama on behalf of the Victims Association. We saw Obama's motorcade flash by, but we couldn't get in to hear the speech. In any case, he didn't apologize—to Korean victims or anyone else—and Shim Jintae was unable to deliver the letter.

Later in the day we visited the Hiroshima National Peace Memorial Hall together, and the Cenotaph for Korean Victims located nearby within the Hiroshima Peace Memorial Park. Shim told me the story of the cenotaph,

Figure 2.3 Shim Jintae (fifth from left) speaking at the protest outside the Hiroshima Peace Memorial Park on the occasion of US President Barack Obama's 2016 visit. Photo by the author.

a large black stone monolith on the back of a granite turtle. It was built in 1970 by the community of Koreans living in Hiroshima but was not permitted inside the Peace Memorial Park until 1999, after years of controversy and protest

Shim Jintae told me he was glad that Obama had mentioned Korean victims in his speech, although the President had understated their numbers. But without apology, Shim Jintae said, these things are relatively meaningless. He believed that apology was the first step towards healing the wounds brought about by the double victimization of Hiroshima Koreans by Japan and the United States. People have to care about one another, he said. Without that, we are nowhere.

As an activist, Shim Jintae merged the goals of social welfare and political activism together, devoting himself to the project of making the world more peaceable and livable for victims and others. He saw a US apology in the combined light of the pursuit of justice and social welfare—it was important for posterity, it would be a comfort to the souls of the dead, and it would be a salve to the wounds of those who have suffered the American nuclear legacy. And yet he didn't lose sight of the basic needs of that community either, as often happens among activists driven by political aims, however righteous.

Shim Jintae was an activist and a community leader; but he was also a philosopher, who brought a wealth of experience and study of nuclear experience to musing on the nature of life and human social and political organization. He spoke of the nature of power and its instruments. The existence of nuclear weapons, he told me, even if they are meant to not be used in the compact of Mutually Assured Destruction, nonetheless embeds the possibility they will be used. And the fact that human political organization has infinite possibilities, he said, implies the inevitability of their eventual use.

Shim Jintae contemplated depravation and war and how they shape human beings. He spoke of the nature of nations and political divisions. When the perennial subject of the reunification of the Korean peninsula arose, he told me that "We had better try to unify the world, not just the two Koreas," adding that Korean unification was one among many starting points in this effort. When the subject of the Asia-Pacific War arose, Shim Jintae, despite having been raised in the militantly pro-US and anti-Japanese atmosphere of late twentieth-century Southeastern Korea, spoke with crystal clarity about the moral transgression of the war, equally critical of Japan and the United States. He saved his most virulent criticism for the Korean government, and its tepid and intermittent interest in the Korean victims of the atomic bombs.

Over the years Shim Jintae and I talked often about the book I was planning to write about Hapcheon. I told him that I didn't want to write a fly-on-the wall historical introduction to the place and to Korean experiences of the atomic bomb. Instead, I would make the book about different people and their different versions of that experience. To give readers the sort of broad context that such chapters usually provide, I asked him to narrate the first version based in his depth and breadth of knowledge. Shim Jintae agreed, and he sat down with me in his office one late July afternoon in 2015 to tell me his story of "Korea's Hiroshima."[1]

I began by asking him why Hapcheon was the scene of recruitment for labor in Hiroshima, and why so many locals went. He spoke slowly and in standard Korean throughout, quite differently from his blisteringly fast and colloquial way of speaking when socializing. He spoke about the lay of the land in Hapcheon, the systematic impoverishment of the Hapcheon area during the colonial period, and its proximity to ports in easy reach of the Japanese archipelago.

Hapcheon's terrain of mountains and rivers made life exceedingly difficult, Shim told me. When it rained too much, the Hwang River flooded and the crops were washed away. When there was a drought, the heat trapped in the valley killed everything. Either way there was famine. Hapcheon was this way until 1984 and the completion of the Hapcheon Dam, a project which dictator Chun Doo-Hwan, a native of Hapcheon, pushed through under his reign (1980–88).

Compounding this already difficult situation, towards the end of the Japanese colonial period the colonial government began its policy of *kyōshutsu*, the unpaid plunder of colonial agriculture, and the area became entirely destitute. "[The Japanese] took away not only our rice and barley but all the food products. They even plundered what we call *solgang-i* in Korean—needled pine branches, which, when rotten, produce an oil that ignites. Japan took it all, and so the people of Hapcheon were hungry, despite being farmers."

So Hapcheon residents who could afford to were inclined to leave, making for colonial centers of industry on the Korean peninsula or abroad. When a recruitment drive began in the county, men and then their families flocked to Hiroshima in massive numbers. Unlike elsewhere in the peninsula, labor recruitment from Hapcheon was not typically forced; but many saw the alternative to be starvation. Around seventy percent of the 70,000 Koreans who were in Hiroshima on the day of the bombing were recruited

---

1. I supplement Shim Jintae's narrative with my own research for corroboration and for relative completeness.

in this way, Shim Jintae told me. Another 30,000 had been brought to Nagasaki by similar means.

The proximity of Hapcheon to the Southeastern port city of Busan also made it a prime location for recruitment, Shim told me. It is just a night's ferry ride from Busan to the Japanese port of Shimonoseki, connected by rail to Hiroshima. It was the same route which Shim Jintae, Han Jeongsun, and others took to get to Hiroshima for Obama's visit. I mentioned that I had taken this trip many times myself, mostly to save money on plane fare; never had I thought I was traveling in the wake of Korean labor migrants to and from Japan, following the lines traced by many who never returned.

The main industry in Hiroshima was the manufacture of munitions, and that is where most Koreans worked, making weapons and bullets and packaging them for transport. Both Korean men and women worked in the munitions factories, although men were more likely to have full-time jobs. This extremely dangerous work—like mining, railroad construction, logging, and other high-risk vocations—was largely done by Korean and Chinese laborers in the war-time Japanese empire. Even some Korean schoolchildren in Hiroshima spent part of the day working in munitions factories.

Shim Jintae stood up and went to a map on the wall. "If you look at that map of Hiroshima, where the river runs downward, Koreans could not afford to live there, so they mostly lived together on the outskirts, on the riverside," he told me, pointing to the southern district of Ebamachi, on the banks of the Ota River in the Hiroshima Delta (Figure 2.4). "Koreans built long wooden shacks and one person or family lived in each room," he said, referring to inexpensive and ramshackle versions of Japanese *nagaya* (longhouse) architecture.

Living on the margins ended up saving many Korean lives. The poor areas of town near the port and the Seto Inland Sea were the most vulnerable to typhoons; but they were also between six to eight kilometers distant from the center of the city, and hence on the day of the explosion many women, children, and elderly Koreans were far from the blast. "The area within a two-kilometer radius of the epicenter was completely enveloped in flames," Shim told me. The Korean area escaped this level of devastation, but many people were also injured and exposed to radiation. "Many houses and shacks were blown down in the wind. Elders say that some fires broke out there as well."

Factories and military facilities were often located in the southern, coastal areas of Hiroshima near the ports, so they lay at some distance from the epicenter of the explosion above the largely administrative and commercial city center and its residential periphery.[2] Nonetheless, a combination of proximity to the blast, fires, and building collapse meant that

---

2. The choice to drop the bomb on downtown shows that its main purpose was not to destroy the military industry of the city, which is often given as the reason why Hiroshima was chosen

Figure 2.4 Shim Jintae pointing out Ebamachi on a map of Hiroshima in his office. Photo by the author.

a great number of Korean and other munitions workers died that day. In addition, many schools were closer to the center of town in residential areas, and thousands of schoolchildren died that day, including many Koreans. All told, the Korean Atomic Bomb Victims Association estimates that 50,000 Koreans died in the two atomic bombings of Japan (Hanguk wonpok pihaeja hyeophoe 2020).[3] They estimate that 35,000 Koreans died in Hiroshima on August 6 and soon after—half the Korean population of Hiroshima. Korean victims therefore accounted for one-fifth to one-third of the total casualties, which are estimated to be between 90,000 and 146,000.

In 1945, Shim Jintae was a baby and too young to remember the bomb. He was at home in Ebamachi, several kilometers south of the epicenter. But

as a target, but to demonstrate the power of the bomb by killing civilians and military alike and destroying a whole major city.

3. This number and others are estimates, because the effort to record Korean fatalities and victims was neglected until decades after the war. Kang endorses the current Victims Association figure, stating that 50,000 Koreans died of injury or acute radiation sickness (2011: 9). Other studies have put the numbers somewhat lower: the Victims Association's 1972 survey states there were a total of 50,000 Koreans in Hiroshima and 20,000 in Nagasaki, and that a total of 40,000 died (see Korean Ministry of Foreign Affairs 1972–3: 5). Yoneyama puts the number of Korean fatalities in Hiroshima at 20,000 to 30,000 (1995: 502).

in our interview he told me stories he had heard from his family and from the many elders he has worked with over his long years of activism in the atomic bomb victims community. They are familiar stories if you have read accounts of the aftermath of the bombing such as John Hersey's *Hiroshima* (1946). Shim Jintae told of people burned black walking along Hiroshima's many rivers in search of water. He related survivors' accounts of seeing people with their flesh hanging from their bodies like loose robes, and of rivers filled with dead as if schools of fish had suddenly died. He spoke of the black rain. We shall hear more accounts later.

Among the 35,000 surviving Hiroshima Koreans, rumors circulated that in the chaos of the postwar period, Koreans would be massacred as they had been in ethnic cleansing campaigns following the Great Kantō earthquake of 1923.[4] Stranded in the devastated city without a home or a means of life, and fearful for their very existence, 30,000 of the Korean survivors made the passage from Japan to Korea in the months following the end of the war.[5] Most of them came first to Hapcheon.

Shim Jintae didn't speak of this as a "return" to Korea, a phrase which you often hear among survivors, in scholarship, and in public culture, which speaks of the Hiroshima Koreans "repatriating" (*gwiguk*).[6] Shim avoided this term because many of these so-called "returnees" were children who had been born in Hiroshima, including himself and many of the first-generation survivors in this book—and so they came to Korea for the first time. Thus Shim Jintae spoke of how the Hiroshima Koreans "came to Korea." He spoke of the treacherous means by which many passed the strait of ocean that separates Japan and Korea. It was cold as the year wore on, and people buried themselves in the salt fields in Shimonoseki to avoid the cold while waiting for passage. Most crossed by ferry. Some attempted the passage on private boats, and many of these died.

"How glad people must have been when they met their families and siblings who were thought to be dead," Shim told me. They were doubly happy, he explained, because families in Hapcheon, like elsewhere throughout Korea, were powerful in proportion to their size. But joy turned quickly to worry because of the necessity of feeding everyone in underdeveloped Hapcheon. Many were hungry and some even starved. He

4. False rumors that Koreans were rebelling against Japanese authority, poisoning wells, and other things spread in Tokyo and surrounding areas in the aftermath of the earthquake. Gangs and police massacred around 6,000 Koreans in Tokyo and neighboring Kanagawa Prefecture, and countless more elsewhere (Ryang 2003: 732).

5. See Hanguk wonpok pihaeja hyeophoe (2020) and Yoneyama (1999: 152).

6. For example, the title of Ikeda Junko's 2005 monograph, *People Who Brought Hiroshima Home: What Gave Rise to "Korea's Hiroshima?"* (*Hiroshima o mochikaetta hitobito: "Kankoku no Hiroshima" wa naze umaretanoka*), uses this language of return.

told me how some, including himself, went to the mountain and stripped the inner bark of pine trees to eat, a common Korean survival strategy in times of lack.[7] People ate *ssuk* (mugwort), which nowadays is a rarely eaten and abundant weed, and people ate dirt. Locals began to refer to the influx of Hapcheon returnees and their children as *uhwan dongpo*—anxiety-inducing compatriots.

The Hiroshima Koreans were not just mouths to feed. Many of them were wounded or had chronic illnesses. There was little medical help available, and none of this was tailored to the victims of the atomic bomb and its radiation. In the wake of the war Japan slowly evolved a healthcare system and legal provisions for the care of survivors of the atomic bombs, many of whom suffered from physical injuries, as well as numerous radiation-related illnesses: radiation sickness, leukemia, lung cancer, breast cancer, thyroid disease and cancer, heart disease, angina, cataracts, and other conditions. In 1957 the Japanese government promulgated a special law to see to the medical treatment of survivors, granted they could prove their presence in Hiroshima or Nagasaki during the bombings. It created a social welfare law in 1968 to provide monetary stipends, health checkups, and other amenities to survivors. But only victims living in Japan were eligible for these different kinds of support. People living in Korea only became eligible fifty-eight years after the bombings, in 2003, with a legal victory in the Osaka High Court.

Most Korean atomic bomb victims therefore lived entirely without specialized care until very recently. Shim Jintae told me that "people who suffered the atomic bombs. . . if they had received medical treatment it wouldn't have been that way, but even after coming to Korea their wounds kept weeping." In lieu of medical treatment, he said, the wounded made recourse to local ethnobotanical remedies, squeezing potato, taro, or peonies on their wounds in the fields. Down the decades many survivors died due to lack of treatment; others had to make do with available resources. Many turned to religion, seeking the acceptance and security of religious community and hoping that prayer and devotion would help secure the good will of divine protectors.

The social and cultural adjustments for Koreans who came from Hiroshima to South Korea were not easy. Bomb survivors were treated with suspicion in South Korean society, which has long held prejudiced views against Koreans in Japan. Many treated Koreans returning from Japan as national traitors, assuming they went to Japan to get rich, and suspected them

---

7. Mun Pilgi, a survivor of the "comfort women" system, told me a similar story (Pilzer 2012: 3). Investigative and testimonial accounts of life in North Korea show it to be a common practice: see, for instance, Demick (2009: 201, 237, 238, 242, 264, and 289).

of collaboration with the colonialists. Young children came to Hapcheon speaking little or no Korean and became outcasts at school. They would face more severe discrimination as they grew older. "When survivors went to get married," Shim told me, "many bore the wounds and scars of the bomb, so they were known to be victims of radiation. Rumors started spreading that exposure to radiation would pass on to the next generations." So many first and second-generation victims were marginalized and prevented from marrying. This discrimination continues to this day.

In the face of this discrimination, Shim Jintae told me, "the victims who were highly educated, people who had learned, people who were propertied, people who were able to eat and survive have not told their descendants that they experienced the bomb. We took the atomic bomb and hid it away, and we have hidden it away until now . . . we lived by quietly burying it away. There was no benefit in revealing the facts." This atmosphere of secrecy—of burying the past, of keeping one's head down—was a foundational tactic of survival and, together with many other factors, helped to inaugurate the quiet of "Korea's Hiroshima." Like so many other kinds of secrecy about the colonial and wartime pasts, it was encouraged by South Korea's long string of postcolonial authoritarian governments, which for numerous reasons discouraged the reexamination of the colonial and wartime pasts,[8] and political activity in general. Authoritarian regimes buried the issue of Korean atomic victims assiduously until forced to do otherwise, when Korean victim Son Jindu successfully sued the Japanese state in the Japanese Supreme Court in 1978 (see Kim Seung-eun 2012).

I asked Shim Jintae about the community and institutional history of bomb survivors and their children. If there were so many Korean bomb victims, couldn't they bond together, help each other, and not hide the truth at least amongst themselves? He told me that it took a long time for community and networks of support to develop. This was in part because of the practices of keeping experiences of the bomb secret; but the lack of work and arable land in Hapcheon caused the majority of Hiroshima Koreans to spread throughout the country after coming to Hapcheon. But survivors pressed for state support and the Korean Atomic Bomb Victims Association was founded on July 10, 1967 as an official governmental organization.

Following on the activism of the Japanese Red Cross, the Korean Red Cross became involved in the issue of Korean survivors of the bombs. It made a survey of Korean survivors in 1968, which put the total number

8. Among these were authoritarian leaders' own history of participation in the Japanese colonial government and the South Korean state's pursuit of rapprochement with Japan, which fueled the country's post-Korean War recovery.

remaining in South Korea at 2,054, a number which is now considered to have been much too low. The Victims Association followed this up with a survey of its own in 1972. A few years later, chronicler Pak Subok published what is perhaps the first book about Korean victims, *Without Sound or Name: A Record of Korean Atomic Bomb Victims' Thirty Years* (1975).

The founding and activities of the Victims Association and the early Red Cross involvement signaled the beginning of the social movement on behalf of Korean atom bomb victims and their descendants, and the beginning of Korean state and social welfare organizational involvement. But Shim Jintae told me that few survivors took an interest in community organizing and social action until the late 1970s. They just got on with their lives as best as possible. The majority of Koreans in Hapcheon and else-where kept their heads down and focused on the practicalities of survival in post-Korean War, authoritarian South Korea. But solidarity, a social move-ment, and state support continued to develop quietly in fits and starts.

These efforts were bolstered by support from Japan, where anti-nuclear activists, survivors, doctors, and artists began reaching out to Korean survivors in the 1960s. The Mayor of Hiroshima, Hiraoka Takashi, began activism on behalf of Korean victims of the nuclear bombs in the mid-1960s (see Oh 2017). In 1972 Maruki Iri and Maruki Toshi depicted the Korean dead in Hiroshima in the painting "Crows," one of the fif-teen paintings that became famous as the *Hiroshima Panels*.[9] In the late 1970s the Japanese Association of Citizens for Supporting South Korean Atomic Bomb Victims was founded to assist survivor Son Jindu in his efforts to sue Japan to improve Korean access to Japanese bomb-related health services. The organization continued its work by visiting Korea and attempting to help other Korean survivors receive the Japanese bomb victims health booklet (*boshi techō*) that entitled them to health services and stipendiary support. The association's director, Ichiba Junko, went on to publish articles and books about the Korean victims of the atomic bombs (1999, 2003, 2005), which are among the first scholarly publications on the subject.

The Korean Atomic Bomb Victims Association demanded redress from both Japan and the United States from its founding until the late 1970s. Pressure from the authoritarian government of South Korea caused it to drop its demands vis-à-vis the United States in the late 1970s. In 1986, at the peak of the people's movement (*minjung undong*) for democratiza-tion, labor rights, and reunification, the authoritarian tide had begun to

---

9. The artists gave the painting this name because it depicted how Japanese authorities had left Korean bodies in the streets of Hiroshima to be fed on by crows.

ebb, and the South Korean government's Ministry of Health and Social Affairs began a program for the domestic treatment of Korean victims of the atomic bomb. With the democratic transformation of South Korean politics over the next decades, South Korean society began to revisit its colonial, wartime, and authoritarian pasts. Social movements arose on behalf of the many victims of colonialism, war, and dictatorship—sexual slaves, forced military conscripts, and laborers of the Japanese military; victims of the red purges of post-WWII South Korea; victims of American atrocities in the Korean War; victims of the brutal suppression of the Gwangju Uprising of 1980; Vietnamese victims of Korean atrocities in the Vietnam War; and others. A growing sense of the moral authority of victimhood and the potential for real social welfare support brought many people out into public to testify to their experiences. In this atmosphere, many Korean victims of the atomic bombing of Japan began to come forward. In contrast to many other South Korean social movements, led by progressives or nationalist activists on behalf of others, Korean atomic bomb victims were always central to the organization of the movement on their behalf. This remains so until the present—most movement leaders are themselves victims.

In this new atmosphere of foment, disclosure, and organization, the Korean Red Cross, with Japanese support, built the Hapcheon Atomic Bomb Victims Welfare Center (see Figure 2.5). In 1996 the center opened as a residence, health center, and memorial to Korean experiences of the bomb. It quickly

Figure 2.5 The homepage of the Hapcheon Atomic Bomb Victims Welfare Center, March 31, 2020.

attained its maximum capacity of around 100 first-generation victims. The center built a memorial hall, in traditional Korean style, to display the names of deceased victims who wished to be remembered there.

The 2003 Osaka High Court victory that allowed residents of Korea access to Japanese bomb-related medical services and stipends was the next major event in the history of the Korean atomic bomb victims movement. It was a major leap forward for survivors living in Korea, who now could obtain the all-important A-bomb health book from the Japanese government. The book now entitled them to health and social welfare benefits without traveling to Japan to receive them, a trip many had long been unable to make due to poor health or lack of financial resources.

Specialized medical care and social welfare systems have become progressively if belatedly available to first-generation atomic bomb victims in Korea, but Shim Jintae told me the situation of their children is considerably worse. Some studies have shown that anemia, heart disease, depression, asthma, and other conditions occur more frequently in the children of atomic bomb victims. Unusually high rates of congenital malformation, Down syndrome, avascular necrosis, skin diseases, immunoglobulin deficiency, leukemia, various intellectual disabilities, and other conditions have also been linked to the second generation.[10] Around 2,300 known members of the second generation suffer from disabilities and health conditions that the Victims Association links to their parents' bomb experiences. Many, like Kim Hyeongryul and Shim Jintae's daughter, have already died.

Shim Jintae told me that the heart of the movement should be with second generation of radiation sufferers. "The first generation is near its end. And the problem of the second generation is huge and complicated to solve." States are afraid of looking to the second generation's problems because of the immense expense it might entail; meanwhile, the second generation is reluctant to participate on its own behalf. "As the second generation is young, they have to make a living by going out into society. This prevents them from gathering. As it is hard to gather, they lack unity." Like the first generation before them, with no perceptible benefit to coming forward, many find it best to avoid the spotlight and make do as best they can

10. There are conflicting opinions about the idea that there is increased risk of medical conditions among offspring of radiation sufferers, but a large amount of evidence supports this. Jordan (2016) finds no evidence of increased abnormalities among the offspring of Hiroshima and Nagasaki bomb survivors, but Busby (2016) criticizes his findings as based on historical studies rooted in a number of flawed assumptions and methods, citing a study of the offspring of Chernobyl victims (Schmitz-Feuerhake et. al 2016) that found increased risk of a variety of conditions including congenital malformation and Down syndrome, among others. See also Chung and Choe 1987.

with available resources—their own social networks, health resources, and disability stipends from the South Korean government.

Nonetheless, a group of children of bomb victims came together in the early 2000s, led by Kim Hyeongryul, and formed the Korean Atomic Bomb Second Generation Sufferers Association in Daegu in 2002. Several years later, in 2009, the Second Generation Sufferers Association founded the Hapcheon Peacehouse as a shelter and center of activism. The staff of the Hapcheon Peacehouse, most of whom are second-generation victims themselves, monitor the welfare of the more precarious and drastically affected members of the second generation in the Hapcheon area, participate in activities at the Red Cross Center, and work together with Shim Jintae and others in the Hapcheon atomic bomb victims scene to raise awareness of the plight of the second generation in Hapcheon, elsewhere in Korea, and abroad.

For some, activism on behalf of the second generation also involves participation in the movement for disabled rights. This struggle has been a long one in South Korea as elsewhere. For a long time there were no special accommodations for the disabled, and the nation-building project wished, above else, for the disabled to go away. Although much has changed, contemporary paternalistic attitudes render disability as something to be overcome rather than something that belongs to particular human beings and is part of identities. This outlook romanticizes visions of pre-disability pasts and cured futures, casting actual disabled people as defective and foreclosing the possibility of disabled agency (Kim Eunjung 2017). Second-generation radiation sufferers with disabilities, like other activists in the broader accessibility movement, are constantly placed in the position of having to remind the world that they exist, and that in many case "cures" are not possible or desirable. This kind of erasure compounds with the marginalization and erasure they face as radiation sufferers, discriminated against in the marriage market and otherwise held suspect as the children of Korean returnees from Japan. One way in which radiation sufferers claim agency is by connecting their experiences to the long South Korean tradition of casting the effects of colonialism as debilitating (ibid., 19–20). Radiation sufferers, unlike many others, are able to attribute their disabilities directly to colonialism and war. Outspoken activists in the second-generation community therefore emphasize their connection to the colonial and wartime pasts and assume the conditional agency granted to them as symbols of Korea's national suffering.

In general, sustained public interest in the bomb and radiation victims movement is difficult to maintain and a constant source of frustration, Shim Jintae told me.[11] The atomic bombing of Japan is generally held in South Korean nationalist narratives as a key event in the liberation of Korea from

11. On this general neglect, and the way that bomb victims are cut out of South Korean nationalist historical narratives, see Oh (2017: 306).

Japanese colonial domination, and the idea that it too victimized Koreans is at odds with the national narrative. With some difficulty, it can be revised and added to the national story as another instance of the suffering which inaugurates Korean modernity and identity, and another instance of exploitation at the hands of colonial power. But it is difficult to sustain interest in the plight of bomb victims and the nuclear legacy beyond the season of Independence Day and other times when anti-colonial sentiment rises to its peak. And activists need consistency to mobilize for change, as they must create and fight for real support systems on behalf of victims, rather than merely creating paternalistic rituals of "helping" that make states and individuals feel good about themselves and allow them to forget.

Ending our interview, Shim Jintae told me that his greatest hope was for a cure to this episodic amnesia, and for national and international publics to acknowledge his community. His answer reflected a lifetime of marginalization and neglect that continues into the present.

———

The year of our interview, 2015, was the seventieth anniversary of the atomic bombs. As the bomb victims community had grown and its institutions flourished, Hapcheon had become a place where social welfare and medical professionals saw to the needs of first and second generation bomb victims, where victims reckoned with the nuclear legacy and the struggles of daily life, where activists pursued the political goals of the anti-nuclear movement, and where bomb victims and others memorialized the nuclear experience. Hapcheon was a nexus of social welfare, survival, activism, and memorialization—four practices that often came into conflict and which residents sought to balance in the practice of everyday life.

A few weeks after our interview I met Shim Jintae at the Hwang River County People's Park,[12] which runs along the river through town (see Figure 2.1). It was August 5, one day before the anniversary of the Hiroshima bombing, and the annual concert commemorating the bombings was about to begin. The concert was part of the Hapcheon Anti-Nuclear Peace Festival, two days of events that gather victims and others together to memorialize the dead, commemorate the bombings, and build awareness about nuclear victims at home and abroad. In these few days one encounters many of the keynotes and players of the Hapcheon bomb victims community, its social movement and its social welfare infrastructure. One also observes

———

12. The park is also known as Ilhe Park, after the literati name given to dictator Chun Doohwan (Jeon Duhwan), a Hapcheon native; most members of the bomb victims community do not use this name, however.

how institutions, activists and others represent the bomb and its legacy. Throughout the next chapters of this book, in the shadows of this sea of representations, particular victims reclaim the experience of the bomb and its aftermath and make representations and identities of their own.

The concert on the 5th and the memorial ceremony at the Hapcheon Atomic Bomb Victims Welfare Center on the 6th are the centerpieces of the Anti-Nuclear Peace Festival, always held in that order. Over the course of the festival there is no patterned transformation from somber memorialization to rejoicing in the present. The solemn memorial comes last, and the sound and energy of music, dance, and performance of the concert give way to the quiet of "Korea's Hiroshima."

The annual concert was organized and run by the Hapcheon Peacehouse, the center for the second generation, whose staff had been busily preparing for months. Han Jeongsun, president of the Peacehouse, told me that the concert was meant to provide entertainment for victims and the broader Hapcheon community as a complement to the staid memorial ceremony the following day. Few of the performers are bomb or radiation victims: outside entertainers are brought in. Despite its entertainment function, however, it is not an unreservedly light-hearted event; the Peacehouse searches for the right balance between solemnity, education, and entertainment. The concert walks the fine line between the social welfare goals of the Hapcheon bomb victims community, its interest in memorialization, and the political goals of the anti-nuclear movement. The tensions between these different aims are always present in the daily lives of Hapcheon's bomb victim community, but they peak in events such as this.

I sat with Bae Ilmyeong and other residents of the Hapcheon Atomic Bomb Victims Welfare Center to watch the concert. The singer Jang Imsun, who was MC for the evening, walked out on the broad stage of the riverside amphitheatre and opened brightly. She spoke of the deep significance of the Anti-Nuclear Peace Festival and mentioned rather opaquely that this meaning was a cause for joy. She encouraged the audience to enjoy themselves, to cast off the tiredness induced by the hot weather, and to clap and dance. She introduced notables in the community who had come—a representative of the county government, the director of the Bomb Victims Welfare Center—and mentioned those not in attendance who sent their regrets. Then she introduced Shim Jintae and invited him to come up and speak.

Shim Jintae came to the stage to the accompaniment of pre-recorded eighties-rock synth "walk on" music. He greeted the audience as his "Hapcheon Atomic Bomb Family" and spoke of the size and significance of the event for Hapcheon. He noted that people had travelled from all over Korea, from the United States, Japan, and Canada to attend the event.

He thanked all the people and civic groups who had come from all over to help the Korean bomb victims community. He spoke hopefully of an upcoming trip to the UN to ask the United States to apologize to the victims of the atomic bombs, of plans for the construction of the Hapcheon Atomic Bomb Reference Center, of the plan to move the Korean Atomic Bomb Victims Association central office to Hapcheon the following year, and of plans for a Peace Park, still unrealized. All of this, he said, was aimed at making Hapcheon a "city of peace," and that goal grew closer and closer. That was a reason to hope and to celebrate. The possibility of justice after all these years and the transformation of "Korea's Hiroshima" into a city of peace were astounding and hopeful things. Shim Jintae thanked everyone for coming out in the heat, wished them health again, and walked back into the crowd to the *Rocky* soundtrack-style synth accompaniment.

After more introductions and greetings, the performances began. Sculptor and calligraphic artist Kim Daehyeon, from neighboring Uiryeong County, bowed to the audience before a large, blank canvas. To the accompaniment of an impressionistic soundtrack combining rock guitar, EDM beats, and Korean traditional instruments, and carrying two large calligraphy brushes, Kim wrote the word *"gieok"* (memory)— from the festival motto "We Remember You"—on the upper right of the canvas in black ink. As electric guitars and traditional *daegeum* (flute) soared and crisscrossed against a background of synthetic beats and *jing* (large brass gong), he danced before the canvas drawing three faces. First, he painted a bearded humanoid face, perhaps a Korean traditional goblin (*dokkaebi*). In the middle he painted a skull wearing a radiation-sign mask. Finally, at far left, he drew a large mushroom cloud. Gradually the stem of the cloud revealed itself as the face of another fierce goblin with blazing eyes, which wore the bell of the mushroom cloud as a hat.

This black and white backdrop, this grim gesture of memorialization, provided the background for the rest of the several hour-long concert. It was a species of memorialization hardware quite common in Hapcheon; similar art objects provided the backdrop to victims' lives in general.

The Hapcheon Nature School Children's Chorus came on next, and the painting jarred against the brightness and optimism of their songs and voices, just as austere statues jarred against the commonplace events and the energy of victims' everyday life in Hapcheon. The Nature School brings urban teenagers to the Hapcheon countryside to farm and learn about the environment and social issues, and the singers in the choir were participants in the school's week-long "Peace Camp." In the course of the week leading up to the concert they had listened to testimony from bomb victims and radiation sufferers, including Shim Jintae and Han Jeongsun, visited the Red Cross Center, and released sky lanterns as prayers for peace and justice. The school organized a chorus for the concert and memorial each year and sang songs of peace composed during the week with their teachers Hwang Se-gyeong and Pak Jinpil, as well as songs from elsewhere in the anti-nuclear movement. "Let's make it, let's make it, a world without nukes," they sang in unison, swinging their arms at their sides as Principal Hwang conducted from the grass beneath the stage. Whether by coincidence or design, the children stood in a solid wall, blocking the three menacing faces of Kim Daehyeon's drawing from view for those in the first rows of seats (Figure 2.6).

The concert continued for more than an hour. There was a folk duet that performed sweet songs of melancholy and optimism, channeling the social movement history of folk music during the democratization, labor, and re-unification movement of the 1980s. A magician came out, asking children up to help with his various routines, and the crowd laughed and wowed in appreciation. This was the first moment in the concert when the crowd was not asked to remember the nuclear legacy.

But the work of memorialization resumed quickly. Dancer Seo Jiyeon took the stage wearing a billowy pink neo-traditional dress. While a recording of *buk* (traditional barrel drum) and *piri* (double-reed oboe) played, she performed an original take on the dance form *salpuri*. This dance was created and evolved throughout the late nineteenth century by professional dancers as a staged version of Southwestern Korean shamans' ritual funeral dancing for the dead, which is meant to ease the passage of the dead to the next world. The performance followed the evolution from

Figure 2.6 The Hapcheon Nature School Children's Chorus performs at the 2015 memorial concert. The mushroom-cloud goblin is visible on the far right. Photo by the author.

quiet perambulation to the ecstatic performance of release that is the culmination of the *salpuri* performance, rising to a whirling fever as the music exploded from the quiet into a metal mashup of Bjork's 1995 "Army of Me" and a male voice singing a traditionesque[13] melody in the style of Korean traditional Buddhist chant.

The *salpuri* dance is based on traditions from Southwest Korea, and might seem out of place in Hapcheon, which is in the Southeast. But in the twentieth century the folk arts of the Southwest became super-symbols of Korean tradition, and particularly of Korean traditions of suffering and sorrow (see Willoughby 2000).[14] So the dance brought the concert out of the spaces of relaxation and entertainment established by the magician and back to the work of memorializing atomic suffering and death. That memorialization was harnessed to the pattern, near-universal in Korean traditional performing arts, of first dwelling on and then overcoming sorrow. This narrative of overcoming jarred against the way that many bomb victims and radiation sufferers in the audience felt about the idea and the possibility of overcoming. The legacy of the bomb—its traumatic memories, the intergenerational handing down of radiation suffering—is not so easily overcome. Yi Suyong was far from the only victim who saw every day as another test of her ability to bear up under the weight of life.

Next, MC Jang, who was a singer of traditional Southwestern song and *pansori* (Southwestern epic story-singing), took the stage for her part of the performance. She taught the audience the playful, musical exclamations called *chuimse* that listeners typically use to respond to traditional Southwestern singing and asked them to shout out to encourage her as she sang. She clearly intended to keep her performance light and entertaining. Her first song was the up-tempo "Sarangga" ("Song of Love") from the *pansori* epic *Chunhyangga* (*Story of Chunhyang*). Several other singers joined her onstage for a folk song medley of several variants of Korea's near-ubiquitous folk song "Arirang" from around the Southwest and Southeast of the peninsula. They pointedly including the Arirang from nearby Miryang in the Southeast, and the characteristic Southeastern folk game song "Kwaejina chingchingnane," whose title is an onomatopoeic rendering of the sound of the small brass gong (*kkwaenggwari*) of farmers' drum and dance music (*pungmul*). The group did not linger in the sorrow

---

13. A term invented by scholar of new Korean tradition-related genres Andrew Killick (2001).

14. The fertile, heavily exploited Southwest was a fount of Korean traditional culture throughout the late Joseon dynasty, fueled by agrarian wealth and a complex agrarian bureaucracy that supported many professional musicians, dancers, shamans, and others. Much like the southern United States, its culture was long appropriated by Northerners for their own ends, and in this way Southwestern cultural forms became emblematic of Korean tradition and Korean suffering in the twentieth century.

that has become identified with the sound of Southwestern folk singing. It is not easy to keep a performance of Southern Korean traditional folk song that light, and the effort was notable and obviously intentional.

The singing troupe's onomatopoeic reference to drum troupes set up the closing act, a rousing performance by a traditional drum and dance group. Many in the audience rose from their seats to dance and clap along. Farmers' bands and groups channeling the itinerant professional drum and dance band tradition often include acrobatic dancing and are often used to create a festive and dynamic ending for variety performances of traditional music. The last moment of the performance was its loudest and most dynamic crescendo.

The concert had passed through phases of bright entertainment, politically charged contemplation, and sorrowful remembrance before seeming to arrive at the energy on the other side of sorrow. The organizers had lined the acts up into this story. But the discomfort which lay between the different goals of the concert—memorialization, overcoming, attending to and enjoying the present—lingered in its aftermath just as it permeated the social life of Hapcheon. And so did the unease of survivors with the notion of overcoming.

It was getting late. The residents of the Hapcheon Atomic Bomb Victims Welfare Center left in phases, although some stayed on until the end. They were thinking ahead to the memorial ceremony and the early start the next day. I made my way back to my little room in the Prince Motel in downtown Hapcheon, joined by other international and Korean participants who had come to participate in the festival.

The next day I walked the fifteen minutes from the motel to the Hapcheon Atomic Bomb Victims Welfare Center for the memorial ceremony. The long, three-story red brick building came into view just above the small tributary of the Hwang River as I walked. A banner hung from the trees along the road asking drivers to exercise caution because the center's elderly residents crossed the highway on foot to walk by the river. The hill above the center was red with the blooms of crape myrtle trees—known in Korean as "trees that are red for 100 days" (baegilhong namu)—which bloom all through the months of summer.

The ceremony was formally called the "Atomic Bomb Victims Memorial Ceremony," although it changes from year to year. In 2015 it was put on by the Victims Association, the county, and the Korean Second Generation Atomic Bomb Sufferers Association, with additional support from the welfare center, Hapcheon Peacehouse, and the Korean branch of Sōka Gakkai, the international Japanese Buddhist organization. The name of the ceremony does not specify that it is dedicated to Korean victims, as it is held on behalf of all bomb victims. Japanese victims, victims of American nuclear testing in the Pacific, and others have traveled to Hapcheon to partake in the memorial ceremony. Activists and others come from across South Korea and the world to participate, and members of the national and international press come as well.

The service is held every year in front of the memorial hall behind the welfare center, a traditional Korean building with traditional latticed doors. These are open throughout the event, revealing a memorial shrine with wooden name plaques of deceased Korean bomb victims.

On the steps of the hall is an altar where participants pay ritual respects to the ancestors (*jesa*), here specifically to the deceased victims of the bomb. The altar was covered with fruit, dried fish, traditional cakes and candies, and other gifts for the departed. Around the altar in front of the memorial hall there were mourning *heonhwa*, chrysanthemum and lily flower offerings, with messages of condolence and the names of senders on display. A special tent for honored guests stood beside the memorial hall.

The ceremony started well after 8:15, the time of the Hiroshima explosion, at the usual 10:00 a.m. start time. Each year nothing is planned for 8:15—no stentorian bell, no moment of silence. The time is reserved for survivors and other victims to do as they please, kept separate from the memorial ceremony with its banners and sponsorships and inevitable gestures to Koreanness and South Korean identity politics. It is a private moment.

The residents of the center and other survivors spent the morning before the memorial ceremony quietly. Many came to the altar and performed the gestures of the *jesa* ceremony for the ancestors (Figure 2.7). They lit incense, poured drinks for the deceased, and bowed, pressing their foreheads to the mats spread across the stone floor. Not everyone participated: some were confined to their beds, some were asleep, and some were Christians prohibited or discouraged from taking part in ancestral rites, which they or their religious leaders considered a form of idolatry.

I watched Shim Jintae at the altar, dressed in traditional white funeral robes and a black hat. After taking his turn at the altar he stood with other similarly clad elders towards the front of the proceedings, in a place of honor, waiting for the formal service to begin around 10:00 a.m. and watching people arrive.

I have attended the ceremony four times, in 2011, 2015, and 2016. My recordings of the 2011 ceremony are the most complete, beginning just prior to the start of the service. The recording begins with a brief soundcheck of pre-recorded music to be used during the service. Soon the garden was filled with the somber sounds of an album of new compositions for the Korean traditional *haegeum* (spike fiddle) with synthesizer accompaniment. Despite the heat of the August morning the cicadas were quiet, and people talked as they gathered for the service against the background of

Figure 2.7 Shim Jintae pays his respects to deceased Korean atomic bomb victims at the altar before the start of the memorial ceremony. Photo by the author.

the haegeum's reedy voice, which conveyed Korean tradition and seriousness at a somber and unwavering ninety beats per minute. Cicadas began to sing, a solid mass of sound. An electric guitar took the lead for a moment, only to be supplanted by a breathy, synthesized Peruvian panpipe solo. The *haegeum* returned to restate the main melody at the end, thus bookending the piece with gestures to Korean tradition. Another track, this time featuring a *gayageum* (twelve-string zither) in a similar arrangement, succeeded this one. In between tracks the cicadas sang their buzzing song "*maem maem maem mae-aem*" over the sound of the garden's bubbling fountain.

A huge banner was hung high across the span of the memorial building, with the name of the ceremony—the 2011 Atomic Bomb Victims Memorial Ceremony (2011 wonpok huisaengja chumoje)[15] on the top (Figure 2.8). In the center, in much larger font, it read "We Will Not Forget the Pain of the Atomic Bomb or Your Sacrifice."[16] The words "*huisaeng*" (sacrifice) and "*huisaengja*" (sacrificial victim), which appear in the title of the ceremony

15. This name is not used every year. For instance, in 2016, it was the *Wonpok pihaeja yeongryeong chumoje* (Memorial Ceremony for the Spirits of Atomic Bomb Victims).
16. *Uri neun wonpogui apeum gwa dangsin ui huisaengeul itji aneul geoshimnida.*

Figure 2.8 The monk Hyejin speaks at the memorial ceremony, August 6, 2011. Photo by the author.

and its 2011 slogan, refer to great loss and the victims of great loss, respectively, and are distinct from *pihe* and *pihaeja*, which are more close correlates of "victimization" and "victim," the last of which is in the name of the welfare center. The term *huisaengja* is the preferred term to refer to victims who have lost their lives, and its use in the title made it clear that the ceremony was for the dead and not for living victims, many of whom were in attendance.

The slogan "We Will Not Forget" is common in activist culture, and is meant as a gesture of empathy, and often inclusion, where victims and supporters become the first-person plural "we." But it has trouble avoiding entirely the patina of a paternalistic South Korean public culture that conventionally proclaims, in its acts of memorializing past trauma, that an unspecified "we" (*uri*) will not forget the pain and suffering of others, all while appropriating that pain and suffering for "our" own purposes—to consolidate national and other identities around a supposedly shared history of suffering, and to claim different kinds of moral legitimacy. By making clear that the memorial ceremony was for the dead, the organizers of the event, many of whom were themselves victims, made it clear that there was no line that excluded living victims from the work of remembering. They were included in the ambiguous, changeable "we" which is so important to South Korean identity formation and nearly ubiquitous in everyday speech—Korean is conventionally called "our speech" (*uri mal*), Korea is "our country" (*uri nara*), and so on. Indeed, here "we" is first and foremost the living victims of the bombs, a "we" that wishes that the wider world will come to know and remember the sufferings of the Korean victims of the bombs.

A first step in accomplishing this is convincing Korean publics that the experience of the bomb is a Korean one, and that the atomic bomb is part of the colonial and wartime history of the Korean people. For this reason, among others, before and throughout the memorial ceremony music and dance were deployed as solemn signifiers of Koreanness.

The fading of the neo-traditional background music signaled the beginning of the ceremony, which opened with another gesture to Korean tradition. Traditional dancer Yi Mihwa stood before the memorial hall. She was dressed all in white, the costume of a *salpuri* dancer, which is a stylized imitation of the white clothing of southwestern shamans. She carried the long white sash that *salpuri* dancers always use. This is a reference to the shaman's white cloth, which symbolizes the path to the afterlife.

This *salpuri* was a yearly feature of the memorial ceremony. Beginning the memorial ceremony with it stitched Hapcheon to the nation and connected "Korea's Hiroshima" to national funeral traditions and traditions of sorrow. Yi Mihwa danced to a recording of a traditional *sinawi* instrumental ensemble, which proceeded in a series of rhythmic patterns of increasing tempo. The dance, following convention, narrated the movement of the spirit towards release from this world, and created an atmosphere in which spectators could move from sorrow to solace, and from isolation to togetherness.

As Yi Mihwa ended her performance House of Peace Director Yi Namjae, who MC'd the event, formally announced the ceremony commemorating the sixty-sixth anniversary of the bombs in his orotund baritone. Then he asked everyone to stand for a moment of silence for the dead (*chumo mugnyeom*). "Let us now have a moment of silence in memorial of the souls of those bomb victims who gave up their lives," he intoned. His voice gave way to the cicadas' roar.

⏵3

About three seconds later the cicadas were joined by a recording of cello and piano played over the PA system. The piece was "Wolfgang's Tune," in D minor, from a 2001 album by spike-fiddle (*haegeum*) player Kang Eun Il and cellist Wolfgang Schindler. In this selection, the Korean instrument was silent as the cello spoke over piano accompaniment. In postcolonial South Korean modernity, Western art music is often given this pride of place, assumed to have universal value born out of Western liberal and rational modernity. The cello marked the solemnity of the occasion and its proximity to the absolute. In the recording the Korean instrument answers after about a minute, but it was not played at the ceremony.

Many events called "moments of silence" have sonic accompaniment—even the minute of silence at the memorial ceremony in Hiroshima Peace Memorial Park features the ringing of the park's famous Peace Bell and sirens sounding throughout the city. At the Hapcheon ceremony I had resigned myself to another "moment of silence" with background music, where the only thing that stopped was the human voice, where the music covers the unexpected, the unknown and the insensible.

But something happened then that I had not expected. Twenty-five seconds into the moment of silence the sound engineer suddenly faded the music out in the middle of a passage and in the middle of the minute. I think he had been given a signal from one of the organizers, who struggled each year with professional event planners and presenters to obtain the right atmosphere of solemnity. The sacredness of the occasion, it seemed, demanded an unbroken silence. The silence continued for another thirty-five seconds. Towards the end the cicadas' tymbals swelled into the foreground, rising in a broad-spectrum wall of clashing overtones. I heard hushed exchanges and some laughter among center residents—many had little investment in the formality of the ceremony, having already paid their respects to the dead in the early morning.

Everyone resumed their seats at the request of the MC, who read a long list of important attendees—political figures, Shim Jintae and other heads of the various organizations, the local police chief, the Japanese director of the film *Hiroshima and Pyongyang*. Yi Yongsu, a survivor of the Japanese military "comfort women" system with whom I had worked often, had come from her home in Daegu and was introduced to warm applause. A long parade of notables then gave short funeral addresses (*chumosa*). After the speeches the Peace Camp children's chorus sang their songs from the previous night again.

Then Shim Jintae walked to the podium. He told of the progress in the South Korean National Assembly towards the Special Act for Support of Korean Victims of the Atomic Bombs (*Hangugin wonjapoktan pihaeja jiwoneul wihan teukbyeolbeop*) that he and others were fighting for, which went into effect six years later in 2017. The law, he said, would promote an accurate survey of the contemporary situation of victims, support social welfare, and institute various commemorative projects. He and others, he continued, were fighting for it to include provisions for the next generations of bomb victims, who suffered from the genetic inheritance of radiation exposure. "Although we are victims, not aggressors," he said, "the severity of the second generation's plight is such that the first generation neglects it at the risk of doing them harm." Without seeing to them, he said, the first generation cannot die in peace. And he spoke of the importance of preserving the history of Korean victims and others, and of the pursuit of a world free of nuclear weapons.

When Shim Jintae retired to his seat, the MC led the participants in several political chants. He shouted the call and the group answered, in the style of Korean political protest chanting:

"A world without nukes, a peaceful world!"
"A world without nukes, a peaceful world!"
"We pass despair down the generations and seek to pass on hope!"
"We pass despair down the generations and seek to pass on hope!"

To close the ceremony, the participants released several hundred blue helium balloons into the sky. They rose up in in a great cloud, against the backdrop of the red brick welfare center and the hill red with crepe myrtle blossoms. The event was over.

The memorial, like the concert, walked a fine line between memorializing bomb victims who had died and attending to the welfare and preferences of living survivors. The desire for silence and solemnity out of respect for the dead contrasted with the activist impulse to shout and show, to draw attention to those in the present who still suffer from the nuclear legacy. The structure of the ceremony reflected this balancing act. The shamanist spirit-cleansing dance and the moment of silence emphasized a kind of memorialization not quite harnessed to the goals of the political movement and so they occurred at the beginning. But the latter half of the ceremony made a rather clear transition to the discourse of the international anti-nuclear movement and Korea-specific discourses of the political movements on behalf of the multiple generations of victims, although reference to the dead was still made.

Because of this formal transformation the ceremony can be understood as a process by which the dead were appropriated for the political movement's ends. But it can also be understood as a process by which the dead were consoled, honored, and sent on their way before the living got on with the business of trying to make the world a better place. Both are true. The ceremony, like so many other politicized acts of remembrance, is designed to both keep and release the dead. It is a dramatic turn away from the fine-grained letting go of the shamanic tradition and its dance of ritual emancipation. The bomb victim community in Hapcheon is, for the most part, unable or unwilling to let go, despite the desirability of peace. There are still knots tied in the cloth that prevent them from doing so. One of these is traumatic memory, which never goes away. Another is the knot of injustice.

And finally, there is the legacy of radiation, which holds onto them whether they let go or not, making itself felt down the generations. The result is another sort of dance, the impossible dance of memorialization.[17]

The tension between the welfare of victims and other political ends—commemoration, the quest for Japanese and American apology and compensation, anti-nuclear efforts, and so on—characterize the institutional life of the Hapcheon atomic bomb victims community in general. The pursuit of social, psychological, and physical welfare for others and for oneself is, of course, political. But it is often cast as otherwise in South Korean social welfare circles, who resent some political movements' tendencies to appropriate and instrumentalize suffering for their own ends at the expense of victims' welfare. The tensions between welfare and activism, memorialization of the dead and care for the living, overcoming and remembering, and remembering versus attending to the present and its futures characterize the bomb victims community and its institutions in general. In Hapcheon—the nucleus of these tensions—the survivors of the bomb and their children go about their artful work of survival. After the memorial ceremony was over the residents of the Hapcheon Atomic Bomb Victims Welfare Center walked back into the building and back to life as usual, but they did not leave these tensions behind.

17. Marié Abe (2016) describes a similar act of memorialization in the wake of the 2011 Fukushima nuclear disaster, which also recalled deceased victims without relinquishing them entirely. Participants in a summer anti-nuclear festival invoked the Japanese *bon-odori* festival of the dead to turn memorialization into an act of political solidarity and imagining alternative futures.

CHAPTER 3

Between Worlds

The Hapcheon Atomic Bomb Victims Welfare Center

After the memorial Shim Jintae and I headed into the welfare center for lunch. We walked around to the front entrance and entered the main lobby, a social area and meeting place. On other days, residents came down from their living quarters on the upper floors to read the newspaper there and waited chatting before meals, as the lobby was adjacent to the cafeteria. Male residents drank coffee there and stepped outside for an occasional cigarette under the arbors across the parking lot. Residents waited here for family members and other visitors, who visited them in a special room just off the lobby before sometimes going upstairs with them. One survivor with progressed Alzheimer's was often here, waiting for the older brother from whom she had gotten separated in the bombing.

The first floor also held administrative offices, laundry, meeting rooms, and other multi-use rooms. These were used for physical therapy, exercise, and art classes for residents, as well as interviews and testimony, film screenings, meetings, and other events. The second and third floors were made up of residence rooms and common areas. The men's residence was the east wing of the third floor; women occupied the whole of the second floor and the west wing of the third floor—because of differences in life expectancy and the disproportionate number of men who died in the bombings, there were always more women than men in residence at the center. Between east and west wings on both floors were two common rooms where events and performances were often held and where residents gathered to watch television, play *hwatu* (flower cards), exercise, and talk.

Quietude. Joshua D. Pilzer, Oxford University Press. © Oxford University Press 2023.
DOI: 10.1093/oso/9780197615089.003.0003

The welfare center was a place where residents spent the final years of their life. There they pursued regimens of mental and physical health, and other routines, attuned to the importance of that phase of life that resident Yun Sugi referred to in Japanese as *tasogare no jiki*—one's "twilight season." They chose from the options at the center to compose a suitable everyday life, attending such events as they liked—volunteer performances, field trips, art therapy classes, Bible study. They met up with friends in the common areas to read, watch television, play cards, board games, or table tennis. They rode the exercise bikes in the third-floor common room. They caught the center bus to town to visit the library, the market, the post office, and various hospitals and clinics. They walked to churches on Sunday or were picked up by fellow parishioners. A few men had their own cars and drove to the athletic center down by the river or to nearby restaurants.

In this way the center was much like other residences for elderly people; but the specter of the Korean atomic experience cast a long shadow. Each of the one hundred or so residents was in some way injured during the bombing, more or less severely, and healthcare was organized around the after-effects of the bombing as well as around the general health issues of elderly people. The center drew members of the press, researchers, students, and others from Korea, Japan, and elsewhere who had an interest in the atomic bomb experience or in nuclear issues and wished to meet survivors or support them in some way. The residents were put in a spotlight, cast as survivors, witnesses, and victims—roles which they embraced or avoided for different reasons. Some wholly embraced an activist role, which generally meant giving interviews to scholars, students, activists, conscience tourists, and the international media, and giving speeches and other performances in concerts, memorials, and other related events. Many were glad of the attention and the sense of belonging that came with it. Others embraced the role more partially, giving testimony only in Japanese, for instance, or speaking with Japanese visitors but not giving formal interviews, in the hopes that private matters would not reach the press. Others refused participation entirely aside from offering thanks to the well-wishers and donors who visited to show their support. Each one of these attitudes reflected different attitudes towards the value or danger of exposure, the ownership of experience, and ways of coping with the wider social world. The welfare center was a unique place, perched on the thresholds of many worlds; and here, through everyday talk, song, play, and a host of other artful activities, residents balanced these worlds, weaving tapestries of survival, selfhood, identity and history.

———

"All in all we've been lucky," said bomb victim Kim Iljo, a prominent figure in the social life of the welfare center. She was speaking with friends in the large room they were sharing temporarily as new air conditioning was installed in their rooms. They were playing solitaire with decks of flower cards—*hwatu*, a slightly modified adoption of Japanese flower cards, *hanafuda*. Flower card solitaire and go-stop, the most popular game, were ways some residents at the center passed the time and exercised their minds. Kim Iljo, Yun Sugi, and others at the center spoke of the importance of the flower cards and other games—*baduk* (checkers) and *janggi* (Korean chess), particularly popular among male residents—for keeping the mind and memory functioning properly.

Kim Iljo was counting out the cards out in her urbane Hiroshima-dialect Japanese, all the while talking about fate in her fast, rural, Southeastern Korean, keeping two streams of speech in two languages going. She passed seamlessly back and forth between the two, never crossing or mixing the streams.

Jeong Ilbun, a quiet but insistent presence at the center, was sitting nearby. Knowing I was a music scholar, she mentioned to me that there was a folksong about the flower cards. She began to tell me about "The Ballad of the Flower Cards" ("Hwatu taryeong"), a Korean traditional song composed in the twentieth century after the importation of the cards from Japan during the colonial era. There are quite a few regional variants throughout the Korean peninsula. Her version used the melody from the verse of the Seoul-area folksong "The Ballad of the Traveling Entertainer" ("Changbu Taryeong"), which was wildly popular in the Southeast in the first half of the twentieth century, and which has been adapted for other songs as well.[1]

Jeong Ilbun walked me through the lyrics to her version of "The Ballad of the Flower Cards" before beginning to sing. Her energetic friend Jeong Hoyeon enthusiastically joined the conversation; she loved singing and knew the words rather better. The song, which has no refrain, walks through the traditional lunisolar New Year to year's end, describing the cards' seasonal imagery. I asked Jeong Ilbun to sing it, and Bae Ilmyeong, sitting nearby, laughed and suggested that if she didn't want to, she should sing something else—anything else. We were entering the social space of song, where people of their generation cajole each other to sing. Kim Iljo stayed where she was, counting the cards in Japanese.

Jeong Ilbun sang through the first half of the year in her soft and smooth voice, telling of the cherry blossoms and loving hearts of March, the

1. The song "Haebangga" ("Song of Liberation"), which commemorates the end of Japanese colonialism and Korean Independence Day, is one example.

dancing peonies of June. Then she hesitated, and Jeong Hoyeon jumped in. She started back at the beginning, singing us through to the maples of September. Jeong Hoyeon sang enthusiastically, despite a hoarse voice that bore the traces of the nerve damage to her larynx she suffered in her struggles with thyroid cancer. She raised the key to suit her range, which was higher than her friend's, and sang forcefully. The room grew quieter as everyone listened to her. Jeong Ilbun joined back in after a while, at the same pitch level that she had before, so that they rolled along together in a glorious, uncontrived harmony, where the voices didn't blend but contrasted in their togetherness.

The melody of "The Ballad of the Flower Cards" begins at its highest point, and settles downward in a descending contour, and so both women started to sing with bursts of intensity; the first words of each line cut repeatedly through the placid soundscape. Those vocal explosions of energy intervened in the quiet of institutional life and contrasted with the even intonation of Kim Iljo's Japanese counting, two very different ways of using the voice and of marking and passing the time.

4

Flower cards, when played alone, are often more than a game: they can also be a kind of fortune-telling. Kim Iljo was playing solitaire, one of the means of fortune-telling with the cards. She set out the row of cards following the months of the lunar year from start to finish. She added three cards below each month card, forming twelve columns. Each column of four cards tells one what a month may bring—calamity, hunger, love, bounty.

As she worked the cards, Kim Iljo and her roommates were talking about the war and the circumstances that brought them to Hiroshima. They spoke of the miracle of surviving the bomb and about fate in general. Kim Iljo arranged the cards over and over into columns for each month of the year, considering different versions of this year's fortune, still counting in Japanese and talking to her friends in Korean. "*Ichi, ni, san, shi* . . . so as I say, all in all we've been lucky. That's what I think." The even, level Japanese counting contrasted with the dynamic rise and fall, push and pull of her Korean speech, and we were given a glimpse not only of Kim Iljo's mastery of both languages, but of the different speech styles and personas that she brought to each.

Kim Iljo and many other older residents of the welfare center lived substantial parts of their childhoods and early adulthoods in Japan and are profoundly bilingual and bicultural. The constant mixture of Korean and Japanese language, song, experience, and identity is one of the defining characteristics of the welfare center. Part of the weaving that constitutes the art of life here involves rehearsing those composite if often unsettled selfhoods. Many outsiders to this community take residents to be "broken" Koreans, or people whose selves are split between Korea and Japan, but the reality is far more complex. Some feel they belong comfortably to both societies and are proud of their bilingualism and bicultural literacy. Others feel at home nowhere. These are just two extremes in the myriad of identifications one finds among Korean first-generation bomb victims.

Bilingual practices of speaking, singing, reading, writing, and self-presentation are a principal way that residents manage these complex selves. Survivors may talk and sing about very different things in the two languages, or they may seek continuity between the two. Likewise, their methods of voice production and self-presentation may be radically different or relatively consistent.

Many Japanese guests come to the center, and so there are many occasions for residents to speak and even sing in Japanese. But there is also the palpable atmosphere of disapproval—a post-colonial disavowal of things Japanese—which pervades the Southeastern countryside and finds its way into the center. Many residents embrace this attitude after coming to Korea and through the long years of the post-colony and avoid the Japanese language. Others who remain fluent are averse to public displays of Japanese fluency, although they may read or speak in Japanese in the right private circumstances. Survivors embrace or reject opportunities for using the Japanese language and engaging with Japan and their Japanese pasts as suits themselves, the atmosphere, and the occasion.

In October 2011 an amateur choral group from Hiroshima visited the welfare center (see Figure 3.1). The Hiroshima Children's Song Preservation Society (*Hiroshima dōyō aigokai*) came to sing children's songs for the amusement of the residents as a gesture of trans-national solidarity among those impacted by the bomb. Among them were first-generation Japanese victims of the bombing.

About forty residents gathered in the second-floor common room. The choir stood in front, flanked by PA speakers. I sat next to Bae Ilmyeong, who provided running commentary throughout, explaining each song as it came up. She translated the Japanese introductions for me, although she knew I spoke Japanese, perhaps for the pleasure of doing so. She moved smoothly between Japanese and Korean in our brief exchanges between songs.

After polite introductions the director told us that the group would first perform the iconic new folksong (*shin min'yō*) "Sakura, Sakura," a late nineteenth-century composition about the famous cherry blossoms of

Figure 3.1 The Hiroshima Children's Song Preservation Society performs at the welfare center, October 18, 2011. Photo by the author.

Japan's spring. She told us that the cherry blossom was a symbol of Japan. She played a brief note on a harmonica to set the key, a Japanese *in* pentatonic A-minor scale. She then signaled to the group to begin. Most of the residents joined in the singing.

> *Cherry blossoms, cherry blossoms*
> *Across the spring sky,*
> *As far as you can see.*
> *Is it a mist, or clouds*
> *Fragrant in the air*
> *Come, now, come now,*
> *Let's go to see them!*

5

"Sakura, Sakura" is so well known that the choir certainly chose it so that most of the residents of the welfare center would be able to sing along. The song is about *ohanami*, cherry blossom viewing, and it invoked survivors' childhood memories of springtime in Japan. Cherry blossoms are a national symbol, one imbued with considerable pathos. The cherry blossom season is very brief, lasting at most a few weeks, so the flowers are symbols of evanescent beauty. The bloom corresponds with the beginning of the school year and is associated with school entrance ceremonies and the ephemerality of youth. In the wartime cherry blossoms were used to aestheticize Japanese militarized masculinity—soldiers were told they would "fall like a beautiful cherry petal for the emperor" (Ohnuki-Tierney 2002: 131). Unwittingly, the song's performance at the Red Cross Center juxtaposed an aestheticized, naturalized Japaneseness with the fraught biculturalism of Korean bomb survivors, who are excluded from any notion of a "natural" Japanese identity.

The director continued this thread of nationalist song with the next song, "Fujisan" ("Mount Fuji"), introducing the song about Japan's iconic mountain. The choir presumably sang "Fujisan," like "Sakura, Sakura," because it is known to most people of the survivors' generation, and they wanted to sing songs that would remind people of the better parts of their childhood.

These two fantastically nationalistic songs may seem an odd choice for such a fraught post-colonial audience as the residents of the welfare center. The ability of a progressive group, interested in improving Korea–Japan relations, to stand before Korean bomb survivors with no ill intent and sing such nationalist Japanese children's songs is a measure of the extent to which nationalism is naturalized by children's music and in Japanese life in general. It is also a measure of the strength of Japanese activists' paternalism vis-à-vis Korean survivors based in the sense of ownership of the nuclear experience which the Japanese state has cultivated for many years as part of the reframing of Japan as a victim rather than an aggressor nation (Yoneyama 1999).[2] The Japanese proprietorship of the nuclear legacy long placed Korean victims beyond the periphery—quite literally outside the bounds of the Hiroshima Peace Memorial Park until the monument to Korean victims was relocated inside the park in 1999—thus erasing them from historical consciousness. Now it locates them firmly on the margins of the nuclear experience, here in Hapcheon, and arrives to minister to these castoffs of the Japanese empire.

The choir clearly had no intention of performing such an act of marginalization of the Korean experience. As if to make that clear, they ended

2. The Japanese state and the municipal government of Hiroshima have long put tremendous effort into claiming and curating the atom bomb experience, even as the state neglected its survivors. The state leveraged the atomic experience to transform itself from an aggressor nation to a victim nation; and the victimology that resulted energized financial recovery and legitimated a new round of sacrifice on behalf of the nation. This alchemy also allowed the Japanese state to deemphasize its history of exploitation of colonial subjects and its own people.

their performance with a Japanese version of the Korean children's song "Spring in my Hometown" ("Gohyang eui bom"), a song from the 1920s with special significance to the many Koreans who were displaced from their hometowns in Korean colonial modernity. Bae Ilmyeong and others sang along, mostly in Korean. It made a nice bookend with the song of the spring that had begun the concert. And yet the Japanese proprietorship of the nuclear legacy and its well-meaning paternalism hung in the air, shading towards what Chérie Rivers Ndaliko has called "charitable imperialism" (2016: 26–27).

The residents of the Red Cross Center quietly contested this proprietorship. Bae Ilmyeong's comments as she narrated the concert to me had been a kind of claim to cultural literacy, placing her firmly in the middle of the story of wartime Japan. Others commented on the stark contrast between the songs the choir had performed and the musical life of wartime Japan.

After the performance the center staff set out tables and placed on them sliced watermelon and snacks that the choir had brought. For the next twenty minutes or so the older residents of the center—who were more fluent in Japanese—sat with choir members at around five tables and sang one war-era Japanese song after another. A great tapestry of three or four songs at once from the different tables, accompanied by rhythmic clapping, overwhelmed the room with sound. It was a great uprising in the general atmosphere of quiet at the welfare center and "Korea's Hiroshima" in general.

I sat with residents Kim Iljo and An Wolseon and several of the visitors. The two women conversed easily in Japanese with the visitors. Then Kim and An started, in the style of the concert, to sing canonical children's songs. They sang "Haru ga kita" ("Spring Has Come") and "Yūyake koyake" ("Sunset and Its Afterglow"), the iconic song about going home from school and work around sunset. But they followed these up with film and military songs, and the choir members, who had been singing along, grew silent as they encountered songs they had never heard before and others they associated with a time which sits uneasily in Japanese cultural memory. The two children's songs had been in a pentatonic major mode; the turn to wartime film and military songs landed them squarely in the plaintive minor pentatonicism of most mid-century Japanese popular music. Likewise, the subject matter turned from the exuberance of youth and the rhythms of days and years to solemn but stalwart reflections on love, loss, and loyalty.

An Wolseon sang Takamine Mieko's wartime pop hit "Kohan no yado" ("The Lakeside Inn"). The song explores the loneliness of a young woman sitting by a deserted lake mourning for a love far away, presumably at war. She—the "Blue Queen"—tries to read their future with a pack of cards.

In the background at another table residents and guests gave another rendition of "Spring Has Come." Kim Iljo listened in and commented: "at that time . . . rather than this kind of song, we were encouraged to sing war songs." She used the expression *sensō no uta* (songs of war), rather than the genre name for military songs (*gunka*).

An Wolseon continued to hold the table with Kikuchi Akiko's 1943 "Kohan no shōjo" ("The Lakeside Maiden"), another song set on the side of a lake. It describes a young girl longing for her hometown, and struck a chord in Japan during the war, due to the practice of evacuating children from cities to avoid American firebombing. An Wolseon was stringing songs together into thematic chains. She finished by pointing out to the choir members out that most of the songs she sang were unknown to young Japanese people. So as the two women sang, they gave evidence of their presence in Japan at the time of the bomb, and of their considerable knowledge of Japanese music history, which ran deeper than that of many of the choir members. In so doing they put themselves on the map of war-time Hiroshima and claimed a place in the nuclear story, and even a proprietorship over it. This effort was reminiscent of Korean residents of Japan's long struggle to move the marginalized memorial to Korean victims of the atomic bombing to the inside of the Hiroshima Peace Memorial Park.

The two women continued to sing songs one after another, sometimes overlapping, with little discussion in between. Kim Iljo sang in a bright, slightly nasal voice, reminiscent of the popular music of Japan's mid-century. Her voice became suddenly rough in low cadential passages, and she ornamented her melodies with little "cry breaks"[3] that added pathos. An Wolseon made use of these ornaments as well. Her voice was fuller and handled the melismatic passages a bit more smoothly—she was a fond singer and hence more in practice.

Aside from Kim Iljo's comment about singing military songs, the pair refrained from talking about how they had learned the songs, the contexts in which they had sung them, or what they were about. An economy of silence and sound marks first-generation bomb victims' remembrance of Japan. Kim Iljo and An Wolseon's singing enfolded different kinds of silence—about origins, about contexts, about the extent to which one identifies with a song's main characters or does not. This is one of many ways in which bomb victims' quiet expression envelops, conceals, and protects withheld things.

3. I borrow this term from Aaron Fox's discussion of cry-like effects in country music vocalization (2004: 280–3).

For many first-generation bomb victims living at the Red Cross Center, focused reminiscence about childhood in Japan is a decidedly ambivalent affair. The uncomplicated optimism of many children's songs sits uneasily with traumatic memories and opens up doorways to memories of war and its horrors. And there is the general air of disapproval that greets speaking and singing in Japanese among Koreans of their generation, although this is lifted sometimes in the atmosphere of the welfare center. When an opportunity such as this arises, songs and reminiscences pour out with a rush of enthusiasm; but quite soon they crash back into the ambivalence of memory, and the songs and their accompanying talk return to the quiet.

It is not a silence, but a hush full of language and song. Kim Iljo and Bae Ilmyeong—both of whom were enthusiastic participants in the singing and reminiscing—showed me Japanese song texts that they kept stashed in their rooms and looked through often. Kim Iljo showed me a book that a Japanese visitor had sent to her after learning of her love of old Japanese pop and children's songs. She read through it for me, pointing out the many songs she remembered. She often looked at it, she said, and hummed the melodies and the words to herself, a kind of quiet singing that circumvented the post-colonial disapproval of things Japanese that infiltrated the welfare center, and that meshed with the center's atmosphere of quiet. Sometimes she just looked at the lyrics while remembering the songs in her mind, singing silently and rustling the pages. Bae Ilmyeong showed me some sheets of calligraphy of Japanese song lyrics that her son had written for her, which she would occasionally bring out and sing through quietly or just read. And numerous residents read books in Japanese. They had learned how to read Japanese in elementary school in Hiroshima, and many were deeply proud of this literacy, which set them apart from other Koreans of their generation. This profoundly bicultural community did much of its Japanese singing and speaking quietly, on the thresholds of silence.

———

The number of bilingual and formally educated people at the welfare center contrasted dramatically with the averages for the Hapcheon area among people born before 1945. In Hapcheon, as in many other places in the Korean peninsula, universal education did not become a reality until long after the colonial period. Education for girls was particularly rare. In 1940 only around thirty-three percent of all Korean children between the ages of six and twelve were in school, and only around eighteen percent of girls (Chang 1975). Shim Jintae told me that in his elementary school class of forty-three there were only five girls, out of about forty in his village. During the colonial era, all children who were fortunate enough to attend school went to school primarily in the Japanese language; and many of those who could not go to school nonetheless picked up Japanese words and phrases in the course of everyday life.

Most of the older residents of the welfare center were native Japanese speakers, however, born in Japan or having lived there from a very young age. Some of them had used Japanese rarely since coming to Korea at the end of the war but others kept it up, especially those who traveled to Japan often for medical care or to see family and friends. Some remembered Japanese songs more readily than they remembered how to speak; others spoke and sang fluently, and despite their long absence their Japanese was often indistinguishable from that of other people from the Hiroshima area.

The variety of experiences of Korean children in Hiroshima accounts for some of this diversity of language recollection and ability. Some lived in Korean enclaves; others lived among Japanese and may even have been the only Koreans in their primary schools. Some spoke Korean at home; others, like Bae Ilmyeong's family, spoke Japanese. Many ate Korean food, took Korean lunches to school, and considered themselves Korean. However, many told me they were treated like Japanese people, and even that they had considered themselves to be Japanese.

At the time of the bombing most had dreams and plans for futures in Japan. Yi Suyong was in her late teens and working in a savings bureau—a rare instance of a Korean securing a job in a government position—and planned on working her way up through the ranks. Kim Pan-geun was training to work on the railroad. "If Japan hadn't lost the war, I would have become an engine driver," he told me.

The futures of these Koreans in Japan were ended by the bomb, the end of the war, and their parents' decisions to return home to Korea. But for many residents of the welfare center dreams of these lost futures lived on. Kim Pan-geun, now in his eighties, sat every day in his room at the center perusing Japanese books and pamphlets about train routes and steam engines which he had acquired after the war: the D-51 and D-52 freight engines, and the C series of passenger trains especially (see Figure 3.2). He traveled to Japan in 1988 and met a friend whom he had studied with who was still working for the railway. Yi Suyong dreamed of her lost Japanese future at the bank, which she revisited (see Figure 3.3), and years later sought out her school friends to attempt to create a new Japanese present for herself.

Many survivors did not abandon their identifications with Japan and Hiroshima but kept them quietly, adding to them new identities as members of postwar South Korean society. The once-possible futures became permanent dreams, and these dreams grew in meaning and intensity against the harsh backdrop of life in the post-colonial, postwar devastation

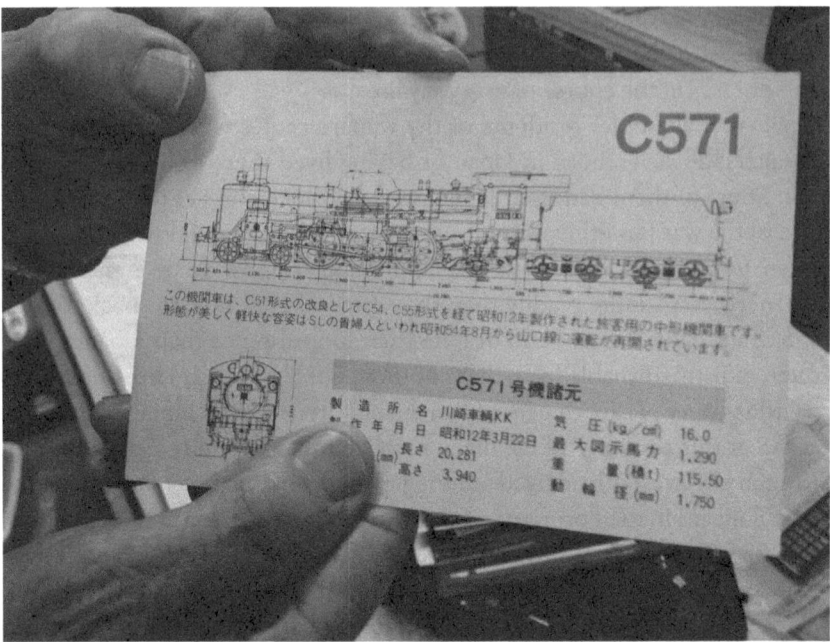

Figure 3.2 Kim Pan-geun shows me a sheet of specifications for the mid-century Japanese National Railroad steam engine C571, August 2015. Photo by the author.

and struggle of South Korea and its underdeveloped Southeast. The senses of self that survivors had cultivated in Japan remained as well. These selves were modulated into Korean selves or compartmentalized and kept with varying degrees of concealment.

Everyday life practices like speaking, singing, and reading were key opportunities for residents to negotiate these complex bicultural identities. The voice, in particular, was one central locus of this unending practice of selfhood. The volume and expressivity of both languages vary considerably according to region, both in Korea and Japan. Natives of the Hapcheon region of South Korea are generally more reserved and less forward in speech than people from the cities, for instance. But even in Hapcheon there is rather more outright emotional expression in public in Korea than in most parts of Japan, and more occasions where you need to speak up if you wish to be heard; and there are more occasions in Japanese life where one seeks to avoid standing out by keeping one's voice to a respectful level. Over the course of entire lives bilingual survivors have negotiated these different styles of voice production and expression. Upon coming to Korea after the war their Korean speech, which many but not all used in the home in Japan, became a public language. Some survivors who had spoken Japanese at

Figure 3.3 A photo of Yi Suyong (center) posing with staff outside the new location of the Hiroshima Savings Administrative Center, 1990s.

home in Japan told me that they continued to do so after immigration to South Korea.

Survivors faced a bind: should they have two markedly different voices, one for each of the two languages they spoke or sang in? Some bomb victims, such as Kim Iljo, reformed their Japanese somewhat to suit the outspoken vocal style of Korean life, speaking like the same person in two languages. Others, like Yi Suyong, maintained two dramatically different voices and expressive styles in the two languages, always speaking quietly in Japanese but often speaking loudly and forthrightly in Korean. And others who considered Japanese soft-spokenness to be central to who they are, like Yun Sugi and Kim Imseon, recreated the soft voice in Korean, and thus practiced the tension between their selves and their society every time they spoke. In the very voices of survivors one can hear the life work of balancing and managing the two major social worlds of their experience, the Japanese and the Korean.

There was a propriety of bilingual speech in daily life at the welfare center that was part of the work of balancing these two realms and cultural styles. Yun Sugi, who had left Japan for Korea at fifteen, generally spoke with me in Japanese only when we were alone or with other Japanese speakers, including his roommate Kim Pan-geun, who had wanted to be an engine driver. We'd talk in Japanese in front of the computer while he played *baduk* (*go*), which he did every day; but he'd switch to Korean if someone came into the room. He spoke Korean with his best friend at the center, Gu Gyeong-won, who was six years younger and had lived in Japan only until he was nine (see Figure 3.4). His economy of speech was governed by consideration for others, and by the atmosphere of disapproval which surrounded the speaking of Japanese. He ignored that, however, among close friends, and would pepper his conversations with Gu Gyeong-won with Japanese phrases, deliberately needling his nationalistic friend.

"*Kankoku wa dame!*" (Korea is no good!), Yun Sugi vociferated loudly to Gyeong-won and me one day in Japanese, smiling at Gyeong-won during a heated argument about the relative merits of South Korea and Japan. He went on in Korean: "If you get three people together they fight right from the start."[4] He went on to comment on the preponderance of factions and in-fighting in South Korean politics and social life. Gu Gyeong-won answered by saying that the sufferings of Koreans at the hands of the Japanese empire left society devastated, and people had no choice but to fight, habitually, for every scrap of livelihood and status. Korea never wins, he said, and so it evolved a culture of fighting over the leftovers. Gu valued his reputation as the only center resident to have gone to college, and he reminded people of this with trenchant commentary like this. Yun Sugi said this was no excuse, as Korea wins now and again—look at Yi Sunsin, for instance, Korea's greatest military hero, who defeated Japanese invaders throughout the late 1500s and died undefeated and victorious in battle. Gu shrugged and smiled. "Well, anyway, we've got to ship you off to Japan," he said.

Yun Sugi told a lot about himself in moments of bilingual play like this. He let fall his admiration for Japan, quite taboo among people of his generation. He told me that he admired Japan for being quicker to develop as a modern society, for its convenience, and for what he called the gentility of its people. One of his brothers had remained there after the war, and he visited often until quite recently. Most of all, he liked Japan because it was a more comfortable place to be—less competitive and precarious than the daily struggle of life in post-colonial South Korea, and a place that prioritized the

4. "*Sesaram isseumyeon meonjeo puteo ssawa.*"

Figure 3.4 Yun Sugi (right) and Gu Gyeong-won, 2018. Photo by the author.

enjoyment of everyday life. He thought of Japan as a kind of second life that would have been preferable to the postwar life he had actually lived.

In moments like this Yun Sugi also showed his pride in his own bilingualism, which he and other bilingual residents let slip when they felt it would be well received. He considered it a sign of educatedness, of cosmopolitan sophistication, and he, like other residents, walked the minefield of post-colonial Korean anti-Japanese sentiment in search of opportunities to practice and be recognized for it. Testimony in Japanese was another occasion where the austerity about Japanese language was relaxed. There the language was used for a good cause, and it was another source of pride. Yun Sugi rarely gave testimony, but he met often with Japanese visitors and conscience tourists and reveled in playing the host in Japanese, as he did with me.

The older residents of the welfare center went through life scrabbling for chances like this, as they were not generally able to be openly proud about what they had accomplished as cultured beings. The quietude of survivors is a quiet that veils experience and selfhood, and bears witness to the repression that quiets, although not to the point of silence—they speak of these things quietly. Yun Sugi's quietude was also inflected by thyroid trouble and surgery. But that vocal disability was overwritten with pride in his softspokenness, which was for him a marker of distinction and culturedness.

These were some facets of Yun Sugi's version of the layered quiet of "Korea's Hiroshima" that manifested in his speech.

———

Kim Imseon was about ninety when I first met her in 2010. She lived in the East wing of the second floor, which is set aside for people in need of constant care. There she shared a room with four other women. Until she grew too physically weak and took to her room, she was an active participant in the social life of the center, taking part in arts activities, attending performances, and spending time in the second-floor common room watching television. She was a keen participant in the political activities of the center, giving testimony for Japanese guests in her immaculate Hiroshima dialect. She was deferred to and honored by her fellow residents and the staff as one of the center's oldest residents.

Kim Imseon and I chatted often in the afternoons, and I visited her daily on my trips to Hapcheon once she had ceased to leave her room. She spoke animatedly of her time in school in Japan, and about everyday things, especially when asking me about my young children, whom she also asked for pictures of. She showed me a few treasured photographs of her trips to Japan which she kept in a drawer in her bedside table. She told me stories of her travels, always in her steady, strong, imperturbable voice, which seemed to have stopped aging sometime around 1970. She spoke more quietly and haltingly of the wartime. She always spoke to me in Japanese.

Kim Imseon was born in 1922. She had a keen memory but couldn't tell me whether she was born in Japan or Korea. She told me that from a young age she had lived in Hiroshima with her working-class family, who had been brought there to work in the munitions factories. She went to elementary school in Hirose, in central Hiroshima, and learned to read and write. She was the only Korean girl in her school. She swam in Hiroshima's many rivers, especially the Tenma, which was next to her school. She swam competitively for the school, and she ran in track races on the annual sports day. She fondly remembered her walk to school, the prepared lunches (*obentō*) she took to school, and the many parks of Hiroshima. "Those were good times," she told me, laughing, and then descended into silent thought. We spent a fair amount of time sitting together without speaking.

She told me that some of her happy memories of youth were difficult to disentangle from her traumatic experiences of the war. Hirose, where she lived, was less than a kilometer from the hypocenter of the explosion in the center of town. In the bombing she lost her parents, her husband, and all but one of her siblings, who died soon after. She never told me the story of how she survived, and I never asked.

After the war Kim Imseon remarried and relocated to Southeastern Korea, settling in Daegu. She had five children from her second marriage, although she outlived two of them. One became a nurse, married a German, and now lives in Hamburg. Kim Imseon visited her several times. She also made yearly trips to Hiroshima for meetings of her school alumni association and for travel until sometime in her eighties, which is a likely reason why her Hiroshima-dialect Japanese was still so perfect.

She exercised regularly at the center, taking walks with a walker down the hill to the road and the river beyond. But in 2015 she stopped walking or leaving her room, and spent her days in bed, taking her meals there and watching television (see Figure 3.5). She watched Japanese TV sometimes, flipping the television to NHK (Japanese public television) when she thought she could get away with it without rousing the ire of her roommates, who often complained that they didn't understand.

Kim Imseon told me that "I've suffered so much in life that I can't say it with my mouth." She spoke in a way that tucked her sorrows and sufferings into the corners of language, into silences and absences. She used language and speech to explicitly mark the inadequacy of language and speech to express her experiences; and in so doing she drew attention to the quiet, and to silence.

One day in 2015 in Kim Imseon's ninety-third year, a few weeks after the seventieth anniversary of the bombing, she was thinking about August 6,

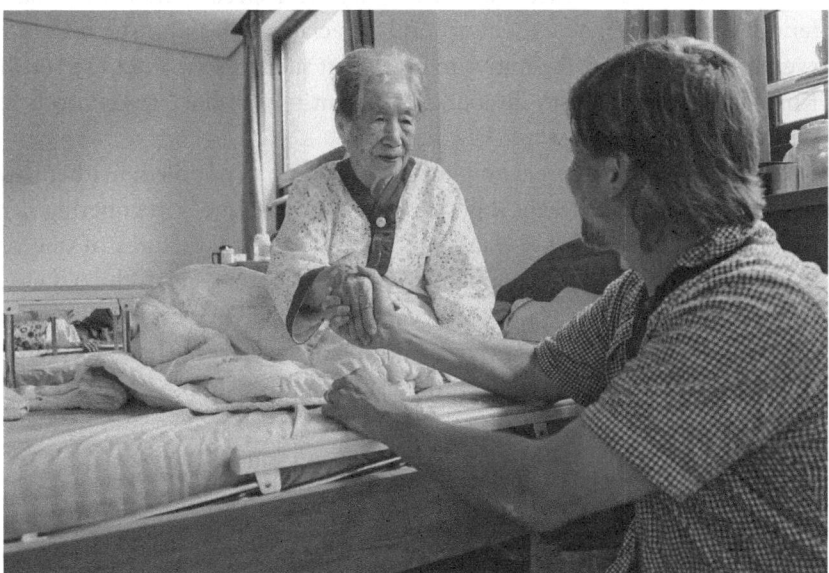

Figure 3.5 Kim Imseon and the author in her room at the welfare center, August 2015. Photo by David Novak.

1945. As we sat together, she spoke, leaving plentiful silences between her words.

The atomic bomb is . . . scary.	*Genbakuwa . . . kowai.*
My father, mother, siblings—	*Otōsan, okāsan, kyōdai—*
they all died in the atomic bombing.	*minna ga genbaku de nakunatta.*
I've forgotten everyone.	*Zenbu wasuretta.*
They all died in the bombing.	*Zenbu genbaku de nakunatta.*

I wasn't recording, but I guess that she paused for anywhere from five to ten seconds between each sentence. She spoke slowly, and weighed her words, and paused to find the right ones, or to mark their inadequacy, like when she paused before calling the atomic bomb "scary." Her calculated understatement marked the failure of language. She placed two long silences after her first two sentences and a shorter one after "I've forgotten everyone," as her brief story gathered momentum towards her final line: "They all died in the bombing." That sentence could have no following.

The ensuing silence was crowded and empty and terrible. It seemed to stretch on forever. I broke that silence eventually just to reintroduce something like a regular sociality back into the room. Kim Imseon seemed to have had no intention of doing so herself.

Kim Imseon's expressive life was as close as I came to the silence of the Hiroshima bomb, and the silence of atomic bomb discourses. She juxtaposed the blank spaces beyond language and speech with her own suffering, with unspeakable memory, and especially with those she lost, lost even in memory. The imperative to break that silence, so manifest in South Korean social movement discourses, was entirely absent. It was too late. One cannot break that which has died.

Yet Kim Imseon, approaching her 100th year, had not died; neither had she broken or fallen irrevocably silent. She sat with me remembering her travels in Europe with her daughter. She showed me pictures of one of her visits to Hamburg. She remembered the quaint streets of the old city. She recalled seeing the water of the canals of Venice that came right up to the front doors of houses. "I can see it if I close my eyes," she said. "What can you see?" I asked. "The port, the canals, and the houses," she replied. But, she said, "I've forgotten everything. Even the languages." But then she looked up brightly: *Danke schön!* she said, and smiled.

CHAPTER 4
Yi Suyong

A few weeks after the pottery session that begins this book, Yi Suyong and I were sitting together in her room on the second floor of the welfare center. It was a hot summer day a few days after the seventieth anniversary of the bombing and its memorial ceremony. She spoke to me, as she always did in her room, in her flawless Hiroshima Japanese. She mixed formal and informal speech, balancing respect for my position as a professor with familiarity and friendship, and her seniority to me.

"*Mainichi gaman shite imasu*," she told me: Every day, I just bear up. "When things are tough, I bear up. And when things are comfortable, too, I just bear up." I thought of her persistent work with the clay, the consistency with which she prayed the rosary (see Figure 4.1), the sameness of her daily routine.

The Japanese word she used, *gaman*, connotes restraint, patience, and endurance, and embodies an ethos which Yi Suyong encountered in her wartime childhood as a cultural style of bearing up under hardship. When she returned to Korea she encountered a different kind of restraint, the stoic nationalist work ethic of postwar South Korean authoritarianism. In these two phases she had been trained for self-sacrifice and endurance throughout her whole life, and she had made a style of living out of these things.

Some residents of the center spoke to me of being content with their current situation, oftentimes comparing it to the terrors, trials, and "bad luck" of the past. But Yi Suyong told me many times that life was not a source of pleasure for her. It was only something to endure. She practiced an art of growing old without forgetting traumatic memory and loss, and without the contentment of old age. She said she was resigned to dissatisfaction;

Quietude. Joshua D. Pilzer, Oxford University Press. © Oxford University Press 2023.
DOI: 10.1093/oso/9780197615089.003.0004

Figure 4.1 Yi Suyong shows me her rosary, November 2011. Photo by the author.

but she had resolved to continue in the service of others—her children and their families, her fellow bomb victims, and the rest of us.

As one of the few perfectly bilingual residents of the Red Cross Center, Yi Suyong was sought out from early on in her residence to give testimony to the Japanese press, and she found purpose in this work. She began to speak to Korean journalists and researchers as well. When I met her, she lived in an intermittent spotlight of newspaper articles, television spots, and the occasional research project. Both in this public eye and in the everyday she evoked and honed her practice of quiet endurance in sociopoetic performances of bearing up under life's weight. She practiced and performed endurance in testimonial and casual speech, in crafts, in prayer, and in exercise. It was a continuity at the center of identity, and a means of securing the empathy of her various publics and relations. It was also, partly by virtue of her own activism, a central feature of the movement culture and the press surrounding Korean bomb victims, a mediated quietude selectively amplified and heard.

I met Yi Suyong soon after I started work in earnest at the center in 2011. We were put together because of my Japanese language ability. Speaking in Japanese was one of the few things she ever expressed real enthusiasm to me about, saying that she found it more comfortable, despite the flawlessness of her Korean. On that first long trip I stayed for half a year, longer than the typical day visits or weekend stays of interested Japanese-speaking foreigners at the center, and our relationship developed over that time. I was a bit of an anomaly for her, a Japanese-speaker who nonetheless was not Japanese, and who therefore did not share in the fictions of Japanese ethnic homogeneity or the burdens of Japanese imperial history.

For my part, I was drawn to her mildness, gentility, and grace, and to the obvious enjoyment she took in our time together. I found her Hiroshima Japanese easier to understand than her Hapcheon-area Korean, but in any case, we had two languages in which to speak and had, then, at least four chances to get messages across. All that switching back and forth was a kind of play by which she navigated the relationships, nationalisms, and economies of cultural literacy at the welfare center. Yi Suyong was also resolutely uninterested in anything having to do with music, and rarely employed musicalized speech; and she, above all else, inspired me to try to study culture musically in the absence of music.

We spent a great deal of time together. I went with her to Sunday Mass, ate with her in the cafeteria, and went with her to memorial concerts and field trips. I followed her to interviews with members of the Japanese and Korean press. Most afternoons I sought her out in her room on the second floor, and we passed the time in conversation (see Figure 4.2). In the course of these conversations she told me much of her life story. And she showed me much of her art of endurance—the artful ways she used quietude and perseverance as means of forging social relationships and navigating the expectations of the people, institutions, and publics she encountered as a Korean victim of the atomic bomb.

Yi Suyong was born in 1928 in Goryeong, the district adjoining Hapcheon to the Northeast. Goryeong was the site of the Goryeong Gaya chiefdom of the Gaya confederacy in the first half of the first millennium AD, an independent kingdom among many others in the as-yet ununified Korean peninsula. It became part of the Silla Dynasty when Gaya fell in the sixth century, but the giant earth mound tombs of its rulers remain, perched imposingly above Goryeong town. The area is, like Hapcheon, largely rural, mountainous, and bisected by a river. That river is the Hoecheon ("Gathering River"), a tributary of the Nakdong River, which vertically divides Southeastern Korea. The Hoecheon, although a smaller river than Hapcheon's Hwang River, has a broader river basin, which made the region an easier place to grow rice, as Goryeong was slightly less prone to flooding.

Figure 4.2 Yi Suyong shows me books and photographs in her room, August 2015. Photo by David Novak.

But the area was, like Hapcheon, radically underdeveloped in the colonial period, and a site of the same aggressive labor recruitment. Yi Suyong's father responded to a recruitment drive to work in Hiroshima, and soon after he left, she followed him to Japan with her mother and two elder brothers. She was seven. Her mother's elder brother was living in Nagoya, and they visited him before making their way to Hiroshima.

Yi Suyong's family lived among Japanese, not in a Korean ethnic conclave. They spoke Japanese at home, and she told me that she grew up feeling that she was Japanese. She attended Senda Elementary School in Hiroshima's Sendamachi district, just south of the center of town. While her father worked in the munitions factory, her mother did all sorts of work—cleaning and running errands in a bathhouse, cleaning factory living quarters—all the while raising her three children. Her father, she said, suffered much with the aim of giving his children an education. Her eldest brother graduated and became a construction worker. Her younger brother went on to study at night at Hiroshima University, a fact of which she was proud. Her family was given a Japanese surname, Yoshida, and she went by Chiyoko, shortened to the endearing diminutive "Chiyo-*chan*" by friends and family.

Upon graduating from elementary school, Yi Suyong attended a two-year, non-compulsory high school, and on graduation sought work in government at her teacher's recommendation. It was very unusual for marginalized Koreans, and even more so for a young Korean woman, to find work in government, where jobs were generally reserved for Japanese nationals. Her teacher had suggested she should work at City Hall or at the Hiroshima Savings Bureau (*Hiroshima chokinkyoku*); she told me that at the time she thought that the bank was a more appropriate job for a young woman. Her teacher recommended her for the post.

She had to take a test as part of the application. "My family members told me it would be impossible to get that job, and so there was no need to take the test." But she had made up her mind—she had, it seemed, been a rather persistent person from a young age. She tested and interviewed for the job, and was successful.

"I was Korean, and accurate and had a good head, it seems. So at the office I always got the hardest assignments," she told me, laughing. She had to deal with mistakes in materials submitted to the bank. She had to straighten out cases where patrons had given the wrong bank account number or written their name or number backwards, so she spent her time digging through records. "I would say to the boss, 'Boss, you should do this one, I'm not going to,' and he would say, 'oh, pleeeeeease . . .' and so that's what I did every day, although it was ended by the bomb. If there had been no atomic bomb I could have stayed in that post."

In 1945 Yi Suyong turned seventeen. She was in her second year of work at the bank. On the morning of August 6, she had just sat down at her third-floor desk by the window at the Hiroshima Savings Bureau. Although she was often late to work, for some reason that day she was on time. This is why she was not outside when the bomb exploded, one and a half kilometers away. Her timeliness that day saved her life.

The window next to her shattered. Shards of glass cut her all over her face, and she was covered in glass. Her leg was badly cut by the glass; she tied a *furoshiki* wrapping cloth—probably the one she had wrapped that day's lunch in—tightly around it, but it bled furiously. She went down to the second floor, where there was a bomb shelter, and stood outside it crying for her mother. But it was full, and she wasn't admitted. "So I walked," she told me, "looking like death . . . and I reached the river bank, and a bamboo grove there. There were many wounded and dead. People whose skin had fallen off . . . people drinking fire retardant. So I went among the burned and stayed there, waiting, hoping for death."

Finally soldiers arrived with a boat to evacuate the wounded to Ninoshima island in Hiroshima Bay. "I got on, covered in blood, my hair all messed up, and blood flowing from my leg . . . ." Yi Suyong stayed there among the wounded for five days with a coworker who had also been evacuated. They shared a blanket. "And there, every day, corpses were sent to the mountain, where they were doused in oil and burned."

On the fifth day she returned to the city. Her brother was waiting for her at the train station with a bag of food. He had gone to find her at the Savings Bureau but had gotten there after she had left and had assumed she was dead. Seeing the state of the bank and the severity of the destruction, Yi Suyong told me, he thought it wise to think that way. But he wandered around looking for her anyway and giving one mouthful of food to each ailing person whom he passed. And by luck or by fate he was waiting around the train station when she got back from Ninoshima.

They went together to their family home, which was half-caved in. She walked up, still covered in dried blood, with her hair matted and crazy, crying for her mother in Japanese: *"okāsan, okāsan!"* "When I called to my mother and went in, her eyes bulged, and my brother's eyes also bulged, and they were unable to speak" (*kotoba o ienakatta*). "After that it took a while. But eventually my mother figured out who I was, and she hugged me and cried."

Her brother and others felt it wasn't safe to remain in Japan once the war had ended, due to the rumors that anti-Korean purges were coming, and he encouraged her and the family to return to Korea. With the exception of her eldest brother, who stayed in Japan and settled in Nagoya, where he had family, Yi Suyong's family returned to Goryeong in November 1945. And so Yi Suyong, a young, urbane, working Korean Japanese woman, was transplanted to the deep Southeastern Korean countryside, unable to speak Korean, and with no job prospects other than farming, which she hadn't the first notion about.

She migrated from the country to Busan, the largest city in Southeastern Korea. There she found her way into agricultural wholesale, working for a company that sold fruit and vegetables to shops and restaurants, and so she managed to find some use for her education, her mathematical acumen, and her experience. She married and had three sons and a daughter.

Yi Suyong didn't visit Japan again for decades, until the mid-1990s, when she returned for surgery for uterine cancer related to radiation exposure. In the early 2000s, when the Japanese government opened up its system of healthcare, social welfare support, and compensation to atomic bomb victims living abroad, she found an elderly Japanese activist who promised to help her prove her presence in Hiroshima at the time of the bombing. This would allow her to receive the all-important victim passbook that entitled her to bomb victim healthcare and benefits. He looked for proof at the Savings Bureau, now renamed the Hiroshima Savings Administrative Center. He was shown boxes of wartime records and told to seek for evidence of Yi Suyong's employment by himself. He searched for many days and began to wonder if she had been lying. But he found the records on the third day. So Yi Suyong got her health book (*boshi techō*), which gave her access to a stipend and medical support for bomb survivors. For many years she visited Hiroshima yearly for treatment related to ongoing problems with the leg that was damaged in the blast.

The director of the bank had asked the activist to bring Yi Suyong for a visit, and she came on one of her first trips back to Hiroshima. The director showed her photos from the time when she worked at the bank, and of its rebuilding and relocation. She told him stories of her time working there and of the day of the explosion. And he expressed his sympathy and invited her to come back any time she was in Japan.

She also visited her school. "After fifty years I went to the school, and they gave me a book, which had lots of pictures and other things from the time when we were students. And they opened up the school, which had been all rebuilt, and I took a tour with the principal," she told me. The principal also looked her up in the enrollment ledgers from the years of her attendance. Early records show her Japanese name, Yoshida Chiyoko, with her Korean name in parentheses. The record from 1944, the year of her graduation, shows only the Japanese name, in line with the program of total assimilation and erasure of difference of colonial subjects that was one goal of the wartime Japanese empire. She asked the principal for photocopies of these records and kept them handy in a special envelope in her dresser at the welfare center.

Yi Suyong—with her story of survival and return, and her near-flawless Hiroshima-dialect Japanese—attracted the attention of Japanese progressives and the local press. She began to appear in newspapers and television spots in Japan. One of her first appearances was in an article about how she was looking for old schoolmates. This request was published in Hiroshima's *Chūgoku Shimbun* newspaper on December 11, 1996 as "I Want to Meet My Friends from Fifty Years Ago." Seeing the notice, a few came to meet her at Kawamura Hospital, where she was staying. One classmate brought her a bouquet of flowers, and another brought her a book about the school. She remembered those meetings as some of the happiest moments in her later life. She kept pictures of these meetings in her special manila envelope.

She moved into the center some years after the death of her husband. From the time I met her in 2011, she lived in the same room on the West wing of the second floor close to the nurses' office, a spacious room which she shared with three other women.

Next to her small bed Yi Suyong had a small bureau covered with ferns and flowering plants and various necessities—a cup for water, a pair of reading glasses. On either side of the window frame above there were two bouquets of cloth flowers, one tucked into the gathered curtain. Above one of these was a bronze Jesus on a wooden cross.

Yi Suyong lived a meticulous life. She took a walk every morning at 4:00 or 5:00 a.m., depending on the time of sunrise. She prayed the Catholic rosary once on returning from her walk and once again at four in the afternoon. She told me that she did so mostly out of respect to her mother, who had been Catholic. She took all three meals in the cafeteria. She walked, or caught a ride, to the Catholic Church in downtown Hapcheon once a week for Mass. In the midst of this patterned regularity she browsed the schedule of the activities of the center and took part in anything educational or art related. She declined to participate in the choir that was active in 2014–15, as she declined to take part in other public singing events, although she had taken part in the song party that followed the performance of the Hiroshima Children's Song Preservation Society, which had afforded an opportunity to speak in Japanese and with residents of her former hometown. She eagerly awaited the many Japanese visitors who visited the center—progressives, health professionals, conscience tourists, researchers, and reporters. She was, among other Japanese-speakers and activist residents such as Kim Iljo, An Wolseon, Kim Doshik, and a few others, the most likely to be asked to speak with the Japanese press and to give testimony to visitors. Her fluency not just with Japanese but with the interview and testimonial process made her one of the most politically active residents of the center, and she gave many interviews and testimonies for the Korean media and other visitors as well.

Yi Suyong and I had many conversations over a period of many years, mostly in her room before or after her afternoon prayer. I sat on the floor at the side of the bed; she sat on the bed but sometimes she joined me on the floor when she was showing me photographs and documents. These were mostly photos of her trips to Hiroshima, and photocopies of school registries and other papers that documented her presence in Hiroshima in 1945.

I asked few initiating questions when we spoke, because I wanted Yi Suyong to choose the direction of conversation. She brought the conversation ever round to the past, and to the days following the Hiroshima explosion in particular. While she spoke to me at length about the wartime without prompting, she did not speak about her childhood in Goryeong or her life back in Korea after the war. I broke my custom of not asking much in order to fill out the biographical sketch above.

It turned out that Yi Suyong was not unwilling to speak of these things, she just assumed that visitors were less interested in them than in her wartime experiences and her suffering due to the bomb. The conversations we had were deeply patterned by her sense of her role as a witness to the atomic bombing of Japan and the presence of Koreans in wartime Hiroshima. She had spent many years at the welfare center being asked by outsiders primarily about this.

It is terrible when people feel themselves reduced in the eyes of others to their experiences of suffering, or reduced to being windows on the past. Yet it is all too common in the reception of victims' narratives in South Korea and throughout the world. And yet many victims are glad to have an audience, however limiting its expectations; and the platform this affords becomes an arena to build an identity and to refine a poetics of self-expression, and a voice with which to speak. Like so many other victims of traumatic experience, Yi Suyong was immensely proud of her memory and of her expressive abilities. And as a witness she did more than report on the past. In the way that she spoke and what she chose to speak about, she told volumes about herself in the present. When she spoke, she set order, rhythm, and regularity against the devastating, fragmenting, incomprehensible things she had experienced. It was a formal rendering of survival, the consistency of her character, and her measured response to life. She had been cultivating this since long before she was called upon to serve as a witness to "Korea's Hiroshima." But now she derived satisfaction from the amplification of her quietude.

Listening carefully to Yi Suyong's talk, one can piece together features of the poetics of her practice of witness and selfhood, those cultivated arts of survival and expression that she put on display in talk and throughout her life. One afternoon in late July, 2015, I sat with her on the floor of her room. It was a hot day, and the windows were open, admitting the steady drone of cicadas in the trees outside. Yi Suyong had just been interviewed by a reporter for a Korean magazine, the *Jugan Joseon* (*Weekly Korea*, the magazine of the daily *Joseon Ilbo* [*Korea Daily News*]). The interview was for a story about Korean bomb victims that would roughly coincide with the seventieth anniversary of the Hiroshima bombing on August 6, as well as the seventieth anniversary of the end of the Asia-Pacific War and the Japanese colonization of Korea on August 15, Korean Independence Day.

Yi Suyong spoke to me in Japanese, as she always did when we spoke in private. She spoke to me mostly in Korean in the common rooms to avoid the disapproval of the many anti-Japanese nationalists at the welfare center, and she switched to Korean in her room when other residents complained. Bae Ilmyeong, who was also bilingual, took advantage of her seniority to chide her politely one day: "You're Korean, he understands Korean, you should speak Korean!" But Yi Suyong sought opportunities to speak Japanese amidst that atmosphere of censure, meeting reporters, researchers, and visitors as often as several times a week in the summer. She enjoyed the social aspect of these meetings, and she kept in touch with some

Japanese visitors to the welfare center long after they had stopped visiting. She also cherished the opportunities to revisit her life in Japan, that time of possibilities, a vision of a life and future in Japan that she compared to her actual postwar life. Her voice tingled with excitement as she recounted the difficulty and the intricacies of her work at the Savings Bank. It was a moment of time sealed in memory and not touched by what followed. Yi Suyong carried these moments and their lost future with her always, as wounds and treasures.

Today, fresh out of the *Weekly Korea* interview, Yi Suyong had the bombing on her mind. Without any prompting she began to speak to me about that day. She began with the immediate aftermath of the bombing, foregoing the moment of the explosion itself. I think she told me about that moment once soon after we first met; but since then, I have never heard her speak of the explosion to me or to others unless asked, and I have never asked. She didn't try to imitate the sound in onomatopoetic speech, like the canonical Japanese "*pikadon*," which describes both its flash and its sound, but just described it as sudden and extremely loud.

But she didn't speak of it today. She began the story covered in the glass of the shattered window. Yi Suyong spoke of leaving the bank building and wandering on the riverbank. She went on to describe her removal by military transport to Ninoshima. Throughout, she spoke in a soft voice and at a moderate and remarkably even pace. Whether in testimony or casual conversation with me, in both Japanese and Korean, she spoke at an unvarying pace of around 200 syllables per minute. The speed of her speech was much the same in testimony and conversation. Today she quickened ever so slightly when telling dramatic but less difficult parts of her story, such as the story of the search for records proving that she was in Hiroshima; but she always returned to her typical even and unhurried pace.

Yi Suyong's speech was remarkably even not just in tempo but in pitch and dynamics as well—she spoke in a timbrally diffuse, pitch-indeterminate voice, perambulating in the same narrow, low register, almost entirely without the expressive, "sing-song" gestures which shade towards definite pitch in speech—sighs, exclamations, emphatic prolongation, and others. She spoke clearly and quietly without notable amplitudinal shaping, and without raising her voice. Her speech downplayed expressivity.

Yi Suyong's quiet voice had many sources and many meanings. She used it to express her sense of self—she often told me that she thought of herself as a "quiet person" (in Japanese, *shizuka-na hito*). She said that when she was young "even Japanese people told me I was mild" (*otonashī*). For Yi Suyong, like Yun Sugi and Kim Imseon, this designation of *otonashī* was both a style and a marker of distinction. Like the others she spoke often with disapproval of the forcefulness and loudness of rural Southeastern Korean speech. She favored quiet restraint and persistence in the face of suffering, the combination of *otonashī* and *gaman* (endurance and self-control). Hers was a sounding and gestural practice of endurance, characterized by the regularity of putting one foot, or hand, or syllable, in front of another, without overly expressive gestures and with rare but important interruptions.

Yi Suyong's quietness and steadiness in speech also resonated with the flat, documentarian style of eyewitness testimony that is common among atom bomb survivors, redolent of *gaman* and a characteristic part of the atomic experience's cultures of witnessing and memorialization. The halls of the Hapcheon Atomic Bomb Victims Welfare Center, like those of the Hiroshima Peace Memorial Museum, are filled with these even-handed voices of testimony. The center's most prominent testifiers—Kim Iljo, An Weolseon, Yi Suyong, and others—speak to the press and to scholars in such steady and unemotive voices, without sing-song graces, without timbral variation or sudden increases in volume, as if reading from a transcript. Such voices can also be heard when residents speak with one another and visitors in the course of everyday life mixed in with other more animated voices. Other testimony in South Korea—that of the survivors of the "comfort women" system, for instance—often tends more towards emotional expression, tears, and dramatic vocal and physical gestures—those gestures of "breaking the silence"; but that is not common in the center.

The origins of this "documentary style" at the center are complex. In Japan, the seemingly selfless documentary style became convention as survivors, activists, and others came together to document the bomb experience. The atmosphere of postwar Japan disdained speaking of one's own suffering as opportunistic and selfish, and this disdain led the Japanese public to doubt the legitimacy of testimony (Yoneyama 1999: 87–8). Early bomb witnesses minimized the expressivity of their testimony to make it clear that they were not motivated by self-interest, a pattern also seen among Holocaust survivors: a "moral commitment to the depersonalized documentation of chronology and facts" that brought with it "a concomitant stigmatization of the personal voice" (Tresize 2001: 56). The documentary style was a way of speaking out against the social pressures to maintain *jishuku*, self-restraint (literally "quiet of the self") in the interest of the social whole, which came back to the fore in the wake of Japan's latest nuclear disaster in 2011, redolent of ideologies of wartime and postwar austerity (Abe 2016: 245).

Complaint was discouraged as well in postwar authoritarian South Korea, during the desperate rush to rebuild in the aftermath of the Korean War (1950–3), and this harmonized with the ethos of restraint in the interest of the nation with which Koreans who had been children in Hiroshima were raised. People were supposed to refrain from complaint in the interest of national advancement. In two distinct eras of their lives bomb survivors were educated against unrestrained self-expression. This likely explains why, despite decades of separation from Japanese public life and isolation from the discourse of the bomb and its culture of restrained testimony, Korean survivors spoke of the bomb in a similar inexpressive, documentarian fashion. Perhaps victims' traumatic disassociation from their own experiences—the psychological survival mechanism by which people experience and remember things as if they happened to someone else—contributed to that style of reporting as well. Recent decades of Korean survivors' contact with the international scene of bomb witnessing and memorialization may also have helped the documentary style to flourish further in Hapcheon and influenced Yi Suyong's and others' restrained style. The fact that Korean bomb victims' struggle for recognition and social welfare has been a literal struggle to document their presence in Hiroshima in 1945 and their existence in the present may be another reason for this documentary style.

Yi Suyong sought to create such an atmosphere in her testimony not only through inexpressive speech but also by bringing actual documents with her to show to listeners. She often had her manila envelope handy when we talked, and she always brought it to formal testimony. She showed me and interviewers copies of the school registries she had received on postwar trips to Japan and read to us from the published postwar history of her school she had received from a former classmate. She read from newspaper clippings about her return to Japan for medical treatment and her search for her old school friends. And she showed photographs from her postwar trips to Japan: pictures of her sitting with the current principal of her school in his office, standing in front of the rebuilt Hiroshima Savings Bank with its current director, on the street in Hiroshima in front of a hospital where she was treated, and at a class reunion. Her testimony tended towards the documentary in two complementary ways: flatness of expression and the foregrounding of actual documents that took precedent over speech.

Yi Suyong's style of restrained expression amounted to a version of the quiet of "Korea's Hiroshima" that differed substantially from both the discourses of silence of the anti-nuclear movement and the discourse of broken silence in South Korean public culture. She was not silent, nor did she break silence with extravagant expression. But she had her own kinds of silence, and her own uses for them—as did others at the welfare center—which she folded into her practice of quietude.

For one, Yi Suyong's inexpressiveness in testimony and other practices of restraint were techniques of omission—transcripts of things unsounded. Her steadiness was punctuated by absences, like the absence of emotive speech. She also omitted certain details of her story, by passing over things or letting her narrative break down and lapse into silence. We have already seen how she often omitted the moment of the bomb's explosion. She had marked her mother and brother's inability to speak when they saw her return from Ninoshima. She used the Korean expression "I can't speak" (*mal meotaji*) or the Japanese equivalent (*nani mo ienai*) often to mark the inexpressible and the insensible.

Such moments are, among other things, gestures to the nature of traumatic experience. Psychiatrist and trauma scholar Judith Herman describes how the shattering of schemes of sense-making is one principal effect of trauma. "Traumatic memories lack verbal narrative and context; rather, they are encoded in the form of vivid sensations and images" (1992: 38). Acts of omitting or refusing to explain can often be involuntary effects of shattered frames of reference, or deliberate ways of referring to the experience of that incomprehensibility.

In the unfolding of traumatic experience these memories at first appear unbidden and make the sufferer their object instead of a subject that remembers (Caruth 1995: 6). Yet for Yi Suyong these moments were folded into a long story about her life, her experience of the bomb, and her survival. In Yi Suyong's long narratives, she revealed her long work of what Herman calls "narrativization," the process by which people, in the wake of world-shattering traumatic experiences, take hold of inchoate sense memories and make them part of coherent stories. But as Yi Suyong performed the failure of language, her voice strayed into terrain which she chose not to explain, or could not explain, and she folded these things into her narrative without dispelling them.

Since the breakdown of sense is a key feature of traumatic experience, the ability to narrate one's experience without erasing the inchoate is an important part of representing traumatic experience, and of the unending work of traumatic recovery. Silences—omissions, pauses, endings—are means by which people accomplish this. Thought of this way, Yi Suyong's expressive deployment of silence was a complex aspect of her own voice, defying conventional notions of silence as the extinction of voice (see also Ochoa 2016: 183).[1] This silent voice was a prominent feature of her quietude.

As Yi Suyong continued talking that day, she came back to wandering the river bank in search of aid. "If I talk about that time, I really . . ." she said, and trailed off into silence. She sat still for about four seconds. I didn't say anything. We sat together with the difficulty of expression and the inadequacy of language, and with other things that I could not see.

---

1. In her seminal essay on silence and sound studies, Ochoa describes how scholars in recent psychoanalysis and linguistics have turned towards understandings of the relations of silence and the voice which move beyond opposition.

She picked up on the subject of her return to Korea. She told me about the rumors that circulated about anti-Korean pogroms, and of her family's decision to leave Japan. She told how she came back to Southeastern Korea after eleven years, eighteen years old, able only to understand spoken Korean, and quickly became literate and a fluent speaker. She spoke of marrying and having children, and of her work in agricultural wholesale.

Yi Suyong told me how her father, mother, and two brothers all died without receiving any government compensation or assistance, which she called "A-bomb money."

> "But it's good that everyone survived," I said.
>
> "Yes, they lived, but they came back to Korea and passed away."
>
> "They passed away soon?"
>
> "Mm."

A long silence followed. After about six seconds I broke it, fearing unnecessarily that the conversation would end if I didn't say something.

"But now in general things have become comfortable, no?"

This was a bland, stock question, drawn from the discourse of "comfort" (*allak*) in old age so omnipresent in Korean social welfare circles and at the welfare center, which described itself in print matter and online as a comfortable place for bomb victims to spend their golden years.

"Yes, now because I've grown old . . ." she laughed through the last word, adding three short laughs beyond it.

> "Grown, because I've grown old,
> and because I'm living here,
> but . . .
> though I move in here, *ne~* I . . .
> I don't [*laughing*] know what to say ha ha ha."[2]

She ended with three warm laughs and fell into the silence of the cicadas again. That silence lasted for about nine seconds, until I broke it.

---

2. *Hai, ima watashi toshi o totteru kara . . .*
   toshi totteru kara
   koko ni haitteru kara
   demo . . .
   koko ni haittemo ne~ watashi . . .
   do iu koto iuttara ii ka wakaran yo mo a ha ha.

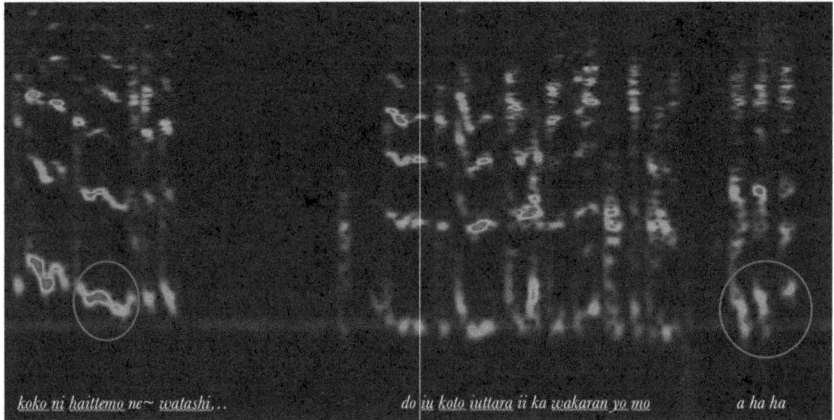

koko ni haittemo ne~ watashi...   *do iu koto iuttara ii ka wakaran yo mo*   *a ha ha*

Figure 4.3 A melodic range spectrogram of Yi Suyong's ending sentence. Created with Sonic Visualizer.

How shall we listen to these silences? First of all, we should listen to what precedes them, what echoes in silence. Here the conversation faltered, in part, due to my generic and rather thoughtless question about comfort. Although Yi Suyong began with a stock reply, her reversal and silence demonstrated a polite unwillingness to embrace the social welfare discourse of comfort in old age. She also expressed the general difficulty of finding the right words to explain how she felt, since "comfortable" was so unsatisfactory. She performed the limit of language, of speech, and of the sounding voice. That reluctance, and that limit, and the silence which represented them, were folded into the way she spoke prior to falling silent. Prior to the long pause, Yi Suyong had peppered her final sentence with pauses.

Rather surprisingly to me, as Yi Suyong performed the failure of language before falling silent she emphasized non-linguistic aspects of speech. This was something she rarely did in her even, inexpressive way of speaking. As she answered my question, her pitch rose considerably, well above her normal speaking range, and the sense of focused pitch sharpened. By her penultimate line—"though I move in here *ne~*" ("*Koko ni haittemo ne~*")—she was speaking with definite pitch. The line arced downward across just less than a fifth of pitch space, somewhere between around 465 to 330 hertz. The final "*ne~*" was a focused-pitch sigh that spanned approximately three semitones. Its fundamental frequency is circled on the left in the melodic range spectrogram in Figure 4.3.[3] The thickness and brightness of the line

3. I made this image with Sonic Visualizer and annotated it with Microsoft PowerPoint. The melodic range spectrogram emphasizes prominent frequencies and limits noise for ease of viewing. The lines above the fundamental frequency are the overtones (octave, fifth, and so on) produced by Yi Suyong's voice (overtones are multiples of a fundamental frequency which

show energy focused in the fundamental as opposed to in the overtones above it, which is one way of creating a sense of definite pitch. That sort of brightness is absent in moments when pitch is less definite, such as the beginning of the next phrase.

The Japanese phrase-ending particle "*ne~*" that Yi Suyong had ended on is an intense form of appeal, showing emotion and eliciting empathy. When it occurs as a sigh, it can be, among other things, an appeal that references emotions or experiences which are difficult or impossible to describe. But the appeal of "*ne~*" left open the possibility that those feelings and memories might be communicable or sharable through other means than language—copresence, the sound of the voice, the sound and rhythm of breath, the movement of the body in an acting out of feeling. Yi Suyong used the sigh to simultaneously circumscribe a zone of unspeakability and invite me into it as a space of affective encounter. Trauma theorists Atkinson and Richardson write that affect provides one means to "think about trauma in terms of present relation rather than absence or disconnection" (2013: 1); the space that Yi Suyong created with this expressive gesture seemed rife with such possibilities.

Yi Suyong followed the sigh's suggestions of unspeakability with an explicit statement of the failure of language and, perhaps, the limits of her own facility with language.[4] "But though I move in here, *ne~* I . . . I don't know what to say," she said, dropping about an octave, now well below her normal speaking range. She stopped speaking with definite pitch. And as she had laughed at the outset of her answer, she started laughing in mid-sentence, and laughed three more times after she had finished her sentence. The laugh, like the drop in pitch, counterbalanced the sigh, the brief moment of sentimentality in her previous phrase. Her final, non-lexical laughs were suddenly focused again pitch-wise in an ascending pattern, three laughs spanning roughly a whole tone in an even, terraced ascent, circled on the right in Figure 4.3. Laughing therefore also swung the balance of pitch back to her normal speaking range, walking up from the low utterance, and returning to her even-keel baseline from which she typically spoke without ornamentation.

Yi Suyong often laughed on the threshold of silence, and often with relatively focused pitch. She laughed while still speaking, and then continued to laugh beyond language. In this way her laughter literally bridged speech and silence, cushioning the breakdown of language.

---

are produced by it, and often called "harmonics"). The color image is easier to understand, so please view it on the book website.

4. An example of what linguistic anthropologist Michael Silverstein has termed "metapragmatics" in language (1976: 48).

The nexus of laughter and definite pitch was a means by which Yi Suyong continued to speak beyond the boundaries of language, if only briefly, as she laughed past the end of her last word. In the face of social theory that holds the ability to speak to be contingent upon the ability to be intelligible in language—in other words, within an existing discursive framework (Spivak 1988)—this was a positive instance of speech and the voice extending beyond language. Some might argue that from that theoretical perspective Yi Suyong's voice became noise, which is all that is supposedly left in the places beyond discourse, or it became inaudible. But it did not. Yi Suyong's voice passed the threshold of language as laughter with definite pitch—as a doubly articulate vocal gesture of affective encounter.

The ensuing silence was another highly articulate, expressive gesture. Predicted by her many pauses throughout the conversation, this long culminating silence allowed for quality, affect, and copresence to intrude upon the planned schemes of meaning of her narrative. Yi Suyong's use of silence here shifted the spotlight from narrative to feelingful exchange, prolonging the atmosphere of encounter between speaker and listener that the awkward laughter and the expressive gestures of speech had prepared.[5]

Yi Suyong's sigh and laugh echoed within the silence and set the tone for this affective encounter. When she had laughed, it was not because she was amused. Much laughter has little to do with humor. Like the sigh, the laugh seemed to me an appeal, which called for other means of communication and togetherness in the wake of the failure of language. It was a request for a certain kind of empathy, an attempt to engender copresence, that mutual recognition of being together that "renders persons uniquely accessible, available, and subject to one another" (Goffman 1963: 22). It was an appeal for me to experience with her the feeling of the breakdown of language and expression in the face of life, the unspeakability of experience, and the threshold that separates the things that we put into words and those that we do not. In this way she gave a social life to those aspects of life and memory which remained unexplained. "In its creative function, silence basically represents a way of being *with* the interlocutor," philosopher Gemma Fiumara writes. "It indicates, that is, a proposed interaction, an invitation to the development of a time-space in which to meet, or clash, in order to share the challenge of growth" (1990: 101). It was a space of shared experience, one of Yi Suyong's own making, in which she focused on mutual experience rather than communication.

5. Louise Meintjes notes the social potentials of "affective silences" (2017: 17) such as this one.

I can only speculate about what the quality of that experience might have been for Yi Suyong and what she hoped to get out of it. Perhaps she wished this to be a moment in which I shared in the feeling of her struggle and her social poetics of endurance. But ultimately, I do not know; and it seems to me that my role as an ethnographer here is not to know and explain, but to keep listening and to wonder. For me this feeling of sense falling away that Yi Suyong made part of her talk seemed to hold little terror amidst the sighs and laughter. It seemed to bring with it an atmosphere of possibility for mutual experience and the transformation of the world. The silence rang with the echoes of Yi Suyong's multiple voices—high and low, plaintive and sardonic, pitched and unpitched—as if each of these was or stood for a possibility. The silence had warmth and coolness, peace and uneasiness in it; but it was not austere, like the transnational discourses of memorial nuclear silence. Nor was it stifling, like the heavy silence of post-colonial South Korean victim nationalism, waiting to be broken. It was her own version of silence, retrieved from its public austerity and folded into her version of the quiet of "Korea's Hiroshima." Yi Suyong folded silence into her quietude and her social poetics of endurance, gesturing towards possibility and the limits of expression at the same time.

We sat for a while in silence and then began to speak of practical matters in the minutes left before dinnertime. Yi Suyong asked me if I was comfortable in my room in the Prince Motel and if I wasn't bored in the evenings. I told her I went swimming at the athletic complex most days and went for dinner with the staff now and then. She insisted that I eat at least lunch at the welfare center, which I did most days. She encouraged me to have dinner there too. She asked after my family, and we looked at pictures of my son, whom she would meet the following year. She went to the refrigerator and stuffed my little gear bag full of little boxes of milk. She gave me some fruit that wouldn't fit in the gear bag, telling me to enjoy it with the milk in the evening.

The magazine article Yi Suyong had been interviewed for before our long conversation was duly published a few weeks later in the August 10–16, 2015 edition of the *Jugan Joseon* (*Weekly Korea*), a product of the conservative *Joseon Ilbo* (*Korea Daily News*). It was titled "'Korea's Hiroshima': Hapcheon's Tears," and subtitled "Seventy Years after the Bomb, 2584 Surviving Victims—We Remember You!" The subtitle quoted the Anti-Nuclear Festival's motto, which had been written on the poster at the August 5 concert.

The article began with Yi Suyong's story:

8:15 AM, August 6, 1945. Yi Suyong, a second-year female employee of Hiroshima Savings Bank, had just arrived at the office. At that time it was as difficult for a Korean to become a financial officer in the Savings Bank as it is to pluck stars from the sky. Yi Suyong, who graduated a model student from high school, fortunately received a recommendation from her school and was successful in obtaining the job. The train was packed and it seemed she would be late, but luckily she arrived early at the office. She had just taken her seat by the window when there was a sudden flash of fire. This was just after the dropping of humanity's first nuclear bomb, "Little Boy," at an altitude of 580 meters above Shima Hospital in Hiroshima. The Savings Bank was one and a half kilometers from Shima Hospital. On that day, 96.5% of those within a half-kilometer radius of the explosion died; 83% of those within a 0.5–1 kilometer radius were killed; and 52.6% of those in a 1 to 1.5 kilometer radius lost their lives.

The next two paragraphs described the bomb experiences of welfare center residents Kim Iljo and An Wolseon, whom I had recorded singing together on the day of the Hiroshima Children's Song Preservation Society's visit.

The cover of the magazine bears a sidewise profile photo of Yi Suyong against a black background (Figure 4.4). Her face is brightly illuminated,

Figure 4.4 Yi Suyong on the cover of the August 10–16, 2015 issue of *Weekly Korea*.

exaggerating her many wrinkles. The bright light reaches some parts of her face and leaves others shaded. Her left eye is just visible but her right is black and shadowed. The photo is an instance of the common use of signs of age as visual indices of traumatic experience in the iconography of post-colonial South Korean victimhood (Pilzer 2012: 24).[6]

Several copies of the magazine did the rounds at the center. Bae Ilmyeong, who sat next to me during the choir's concert, and who flatly refused to do interviews herself, had a copy of the magazine and was studying the article eagerly. We looked at it with her roommate Baek Du-i. The two women both commented on how old the photo made Yi Suyong look. "*Neomu obāchan hae-natta*," Baek Du-i said, laughing—"They really made her look like an *obāchan*." She spoke in Korean but used the Japanese word for "grandma."

The table of contents shows a rather less dramatic and far more everyday photograph of Yi Suyong. She is sitting on her bed, holding up a photo of herself and the principal of her former school, taken during one of her mid-90s trips to Japan. In an inset photo in the article there is another photo of her against the black background; she is talking and gesturing with her right hand.

These are not the only images in the article: there are portraits of other survivors, a photo from the memorial shrine at the Red Cross Center, and a montage of paintings made by first- and second-generation victims for the memorial ceremony displayed on fences around the welfare center grounds. But Yi Suyong—or her "grannified" image—is the principal icon of the article, the only image on the cover and the only one that repeats, albeit in variation.

The black background in two of the photos was created for the purposes of the magazine, for there is no such place in the Red Cross Center. It serves as a kind of "visual silence" (Jaworski 2016).[7] Yi Suyong stands out against that backdrop just as the survivor's archetypal voice stands out against the background of broken silence. In the nationalist forum of this article, published in the season of Korean Independence Day with its waves of nationalist sentiment vis-à-vis the colonial past, Yi Suyong's quietude is thus rendered to the discourse of silence and its breaking that has characterized post-authoritarian South Korea.

Perhaps the image is also inflected by the discourse and iconography of silence in the international memorialization of the atomic bomb. In any

---

6. Signs of aging are used to represent victimhood in the narratives of youth stolen by imperialist exploitation found in the iconography of the "comfort women." The use of the trope in the present case is likely inspired, however indirectly, by this.

7. Jaworski describes the poetics and transductions that link acoustic silence and "visual silence."

case Yi Suyong is cast in the role of one who speaks for the dead and who speaks of the legacy of atomic suffering. Perhaps the article is meant to portray her breaking the silence which has long repressed that suffering. But as we have seen, if she breaks silence in speaking of the bombing, she does not do so entirely. Its traces linger in her voice, because she speaks of it, and enfolds it into her speech.

Articles like this cast victims in a double role of both breaking and envoicing or otherwise representing silence. One the one hand, this is rather true to the nature of post-traumatic testimony and recovery, and perhaps speaks to the way in which personal traumas have become public cultural traumas without changing this one aspect of their nature. But I also suspect that it is a means by which public culture domesticates those who do the silence-breaking, a means by which victims are permanently tagged by silence and denied the capacity to exist without it in the public eye. Yi Suyong and others are almost never asked about anything other than their experiences leading up to and on August 6, 1945, and its immediate aftermath. They are not allowed to have presents and futures, or to exist independently of the legacy of suffering.

It was therefore a fraught landscape in which Yi Suyong acted as a witness to her experiences. Media and public culture listened to her story only if certain conditions were met. But Yi Suyong made use of these affordances and found a sense of purpose as an activist, and she found in activism an avenue of participation in society. I was with her on August 5, 2015, one day before the seventieth anniversary memorial ceremony, when she spoke at the welfare center to a group of Japanese activists (see Figure 4.5). Mr. Okada, a Japanese schoolteacher who had quit his job in Japan and relocated to Daegu to teach Japanese and work for Japan–Korea reconciliation, facilitated the session, and a member of the group acted as interviewer. At the start he asked Yi Suyong to speak for about fifteen minutes, which was all the time that the group had before its next scheduled activity. He apologized for the rushed schedule. "Oh, that's alright," Yi Suyong replied, amiable but visibly disappointed. She punctuated this with a short staccato laugh and fell silent.

The interview began with detailed questions about how Yi Suyong came to Hiroshima, whom she came with, and the neighborhood in which she lived. Yi Suyong answered but moved quickly to discussing her job at the Hiroshima Savings Bank, mentioning that she had brought photographs and other documentation with her. The interviewer asked about the documents and Yi Suyong explained that they concerned her school, work, and other aspects of life in Hiroshima. He stopped talking, quickly shuffling through the papers and photographs. Other members of the team clustered round, snapping photographs of her and of her documents.

Figure 4.5 Yi Suyong gives testimony at the welfare center, August 5, 2015. Photo by the author.

Yi Suyong continued with an extended description of how she secured her job at the bank, leading up to the day of the bomb. The interviewer looked at his watch and steered the conversation towards the canonical questions of bomb discourse, ticking them off his mental list. He asked her how close she had been to the epicenter of the blast—the standard measure by which one's victim status is determined in the Japanese reparations and social welfare system for A-bomb victims. "One-and-a-half kilometers (from the center). I was wounded . . . I ceased to be human," she said, and laughed. She went on to describe her injury in detail as she had done with me. She described her removal to Ninoshima and her return to her family. The time ran out. She offered her cell phone number should the team wish to follow up. She told the group that "I have many accurate stories, it's a shame we don't have more time." This was one of her moments to shine, a moment she had prepared for over many years, and which she had looked forward to; and there was only time for this woefully incomplete recounting.

Yi Suyong's speech was remarkably consistent in content and manner of speaking in this interview, as it was in her conversations with me over the years. She spoke in testimony here and elsewhere in much the same way she did in our private conversations—in a low, steady range with very little pitch fluctuation, and without expressive devices such as sighs, interjections, increases in volume, or pauses in moments of emotion. Despite the rushed nature of the interview, her pace of speaking was not noticeably faster than elsewhere. She used many of the same phrases, and the information she conveyed was practically uniform, although less complete than what she had shared with me, due to the shortness of the interview. This consistency in testimony was one thing that made her an asset at the center, a reliable spokesperson on behalf of Korean bomb victims. It was also a sign of the extent to which her speech with me was not an informal event but a moment of her public life as a witness to the legacy of the bomb, and of how folded together her public and private lives had become.

And yet Yi Suyong pursued her own goals for the interview rather than passively playing an assigned part. She gave the team the information and the experience they wanted—demonstrating her legitimacy as a survivor through detail and documentation, and presenting her account of the day of the bombing firsthand for them to hear in her own voice and words. But she also spent a substantial portion of the fifteen minutes telling the remarkable story of her securing her job in the face of structural discrimination. In this way she turned the rushed and regimented format, with its stock questions, into something personal. She stepped into the generic shoes of the victim role afforded by her listeners, but she made them her own in this small way. She demanded an attention which stretched the specifications and limitations of the role granted to her and challenged the limits of her audience's willingness to listen. She asked people to listen to the life she had and lost, and to the woman she had become.

As when we spoke, Yi Suyong laughed and fell silent in the pursuit of this copresence and its affective encounter. But the interviewer anxiously filled all silences, collapsing the intervals, the pauses in the system, the potential for transformation that silence afforded. Yi Suyong's quietude could be heard if one was listening, despite the interruptions. And it could be seen in the image of her patiently bearing up under the stream of stock questions.

But the possibilities of Yi Suyong's quietude and its silences were not listened to by this group, as they were rarely listened to at all. The sanctified silence of the Japanese discourse of atomic experience is, typically, only listened to in touted and highly conscribed performances—moments of silence at memorials, the breath before the pause at bomb-themed memorial performances, renderings in poetry, the season of Independence Day. In those moments, people listen for the voices of the dead. They listen to survivors, in the main, as mediums for the dead and the past, and perhaps as bearers of legacies of suffering in the present. The manifold quiet of "Korea's Hiroshima"—which has so much to tell us about Korean survivors of the bomb and their experiences—goes unheard and unappreciated. Here, as elsewhere, discourses of silence may themselves become processes of social silencing. And yet Yi Suyong and other survivors responded to each of these repressions by assimilating them to a character, and to an art of life.

CHAPTER 5

Bae Ilmyeong

On July 31, 2015, Bae Ilmyeong, Yi Suyong's senior by one year, sat across from another woman resident of the welfare center in an art therapy workshop. They were coloring a printed-out mandala (Figure 5.1). I asked the artist who led the workshop about the purpose of the session, and she told me that she hoped the mandala exercise would be a source of peace for the residents who participated.

The two women worked together on the same black-and-white printout. They colored quickly, without speaking. Bae Ilmyeong worked on the circumference of the circle, steadily coloring twenty-four little rainbows blue, red, pink, and yellow. At the center was a flower with twelve red petals. The whole thing looked rather like a clock.

8

When they were done, Bae Ilmyeong started another by herself. She worked carefully and uniformly, starting with the flower at the center. She colored the eight stamens yellow and the eight petals red. The last ring consisted of thirty-six triangles; she colored five of these yellow, six black, five purple, five yellow, four green, five purple, one orange, and one pink. That achieved a balance, with yellow triangles at left and right, the purple triangles at top right and bottom left, and black and green offsetting one another at top left and bottom right. The single pink and orange triangles stood out, side by side, disrupting or perhaps relaxing the feeling of balance (see Figure 5.2the color image online).

When Bae Ilmyeong was done, she filled in the blanks at the top of the page. She wrote the date, speaking the words out as she read and wrote,

Quietude. Joshua D. Pilzer, Oxford University Press. © Oxford University Press 2023.
DOI: 10.1093/oso/9780197615089.003.0005

Figure 5.1 Bae Ilmyeong coloring a mandala in an art therapy class at the welfare center, July 2015. Photo by the author.

talking to me and to my video camera. The page asked for a description of the weather—rain, sunshine, that sort of thing. "Awe—some!" (*jo—ta!*), she said as she wrote, and laughed.

A few days later we were in her room talking about clocks. She pointed at the various timepieces at hand. The clock on the wall, she said, was six minutes fast. The clock on her bedside table was two minutes fast. She told me about other clocks throughout the welfare center.

The standard Korean calendar on the wall showed the month of August, but also the names of each day in the Sino-Korean lunisolar calendar. She scanned it and pointed out significant upcoming dates: *ipchu*, August 7, the day which heralds the coming of fall; *malbok*, the last day of summer, in mid-August; *cheoseo*, the day of the last summer heat two weeks later. Bae Ilmyeong was in her late eighties, and like most Koreans of her age she measured time in both the Gregorian and Korean traditional calendrical systems. She always knew the date and what time it was.

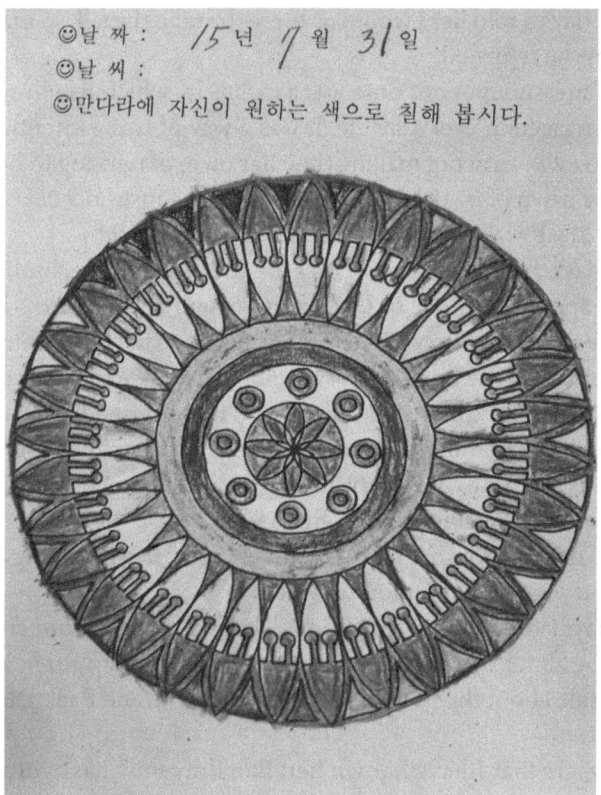

Figure 5.2 One of Bae Ilmyeong's completed mandalas.

Bae Ilmyeong told me about her morning routine: up, morning coffee, medicine, breakfast, prayer at ten. She explained the schedule of regular events at the center that she participated in—the weekly trip to the bathhouse, haircuts, art therapy classes like the one where she had painted the mandalas. She told me what was happening that day. She told me about the schedule of the center's bus, which took regular trips into town to Hapcheon hospital and the post office. It made special trips on market day, every five days (*o-il jang*, five-day market), a remnant of the traditional ten-day week. She told me about her bi-weekly trips to Hapcheon Central Church for Wednesday and Sunday services and Bible study, which she never missed even if she had to walk.

She looked at the calendar again and asked me how long I would be in Hapcheon. Workers were remodeling the center and it was at half-capacity. One half of the residents had gone to stay with family for about twenty days, until August 28. Bae Ilmyeong explained that she was part of the next group, which would disperse to family homes on that day for the same number of days. I told her I would be there through the fall, so that we could meet when she returned.

Careful measurement of time was a means by which Bae Ilmyeong kept alert and engaged in everyday life. It was a way of living intentionally. Her timekeeping was an act of making time her own, of refusing to be an object of time or a pawn of institutional time, and being instead a deliberate practitioner of life. It was, above all, a means of being *present*.

Some days later we sat together in the third-floor common room. A woman approached me and asked me where I was from. I introduced myself; she didn't mention her name. She began to tell me of things she saw in the aftermath of the bombing, assuming that as a foreign researcher I had come to hear about that sort of thing. She told me she had been thirteen at the time of the bombing. She remembered a man with his stomach torn open and his intestines hanging out. She saw dead people in the river. "I see those things with my mind even right now."

"There's no need for that kind of conversation," Bae Ilmyeong interjected shortly. The woman, her junior, subsided.

A few days later we were in her room. Her friend and roommate Baek Du-i was talking about working in a paper factory as a young girl in Hiroshima. "Let's not talk about the past," Bae Ilmyeong put in, and Baek Du-i changed the subject.

In the years that I have known her, Bae Ilmyeong has avoided talking about the most dreadful aspects of her past with me or anyone else to my knowledge. She preferred not to listen to others talk about such things as well, and she told me that she tried not to think about them. She told me that she did not testify for researchers, the media, or other visitors to the welfare center. When I asked her why, she shrugged off the question; her gesture was its own kind of answer. She did say, however, that she felt it was better to leave the past alone and focus on the Christian path, and on the grace which it afforded. Her pastor, she told me, had suggested as much. Her refusal to play the role of the bomb witness was key to her way of living with the past and living for the present and its future.

She told me that one of the benefits of age is that one learns how to forget painful things, to leave the specters of the past behind, and just live. For the most part she seemed to have done it, too. She laughed easily. She maintained a youthful complexion and looked about twenty years younger than she was. Her face lacked even the laugh lines one would expect from someone who smiled so often.

I told Bae Ilmyeong about the basic principles of my project, my intention to focus not on the past but on people in the present, on their wisdom, character, and their arts of survival. She liked the project, which suited her aversion to dredging up the past, and explained it to Baek Du-I when she started talking about the past again: "You see, the professor here is interested in people, in who we are and things we know, not just in stories of the past (*yennal iyagi*)." Over the years we stayed focused on the present together, and I took an interest in her practices of timekeeping, storytelling, reading, and religious devotion, and the part these played in her work of survival and flourishing and in her ongoing work of maintaining a truce with the past.

When I asked Bae Ilmyeong for basic biographic information she gave it willingly, keeping things brief and avoiding the worst bits of her life history. She told me she was born in 1928, one of five women in the welfare center born in that year. She was the oldest of a family of nine siblings, three girls and six boys. All but the last two were born in Japan. Three of her younger brothers had died by the time we met, although she didn't say how or when and I didn't ask.

In Hiroshima she had not lived in a Korean enclave but among Japanese people, in a row of tenement houses. Her family had been given the Japanese name Sugiyama (杉山), and she grew up speaking Japanese at home. She remembered the earthquakes, and how she and her family would escape to a bamboo grove when they came.

She met her husband in Japan, and they came to Korea together. She had three sons and two daughters; her oldest son was already seventy-one, a retired professor in Daegu. Her husband had been fond of alcohol, but she didn't say if any trouble had come of it. He died, anyway, when the kids were all grown.

Bae Ilmyeong spoke more freely of the period of her life after she left Japan in 1946 at eighteen for Korea. She spoke of it colorfully and well, in her rapid, lilting, Southeastern voice. At times in the midst of these recollections she would touch briefly on the wartime past but return quickly to the postwar and the present. She was an enthusiastic storyteller, recalling the past in the interests of the present, in the interest of enlivening the day, of pleasing and educating her audiences, and of tending social relationships. Her intricate and highly aestheticized ways of speaking borrowed the energy of the present to bring the past to life and gave life to the present as a moment of dynamic, social remembering. Her stories led through strife and struggle always inexorably back to the present, its social relations, and its relative contentment, comfort, and grace.

On August 22, 2011, Bae Ilmyeong and her floormate Gu Seon-i, the mother of Han Jeongsun, the president of the second-generation bomb victims' Hapcheon Peacehouse, sat on the sofas in the third-floor common room. I joined them and Bae Ilmyeong started to talk about leaving Japan to begin life in Korea. Over the next thirty minutes or so she told me and

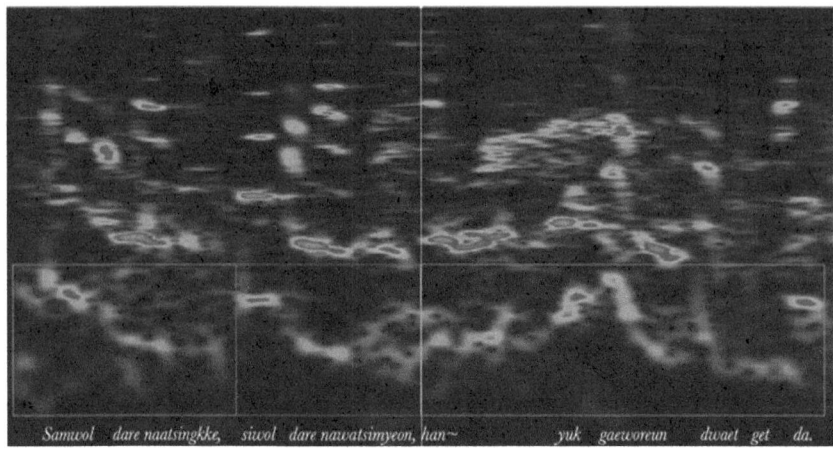

Samwol dare naatsingkke, siwol dare nawatsimyeon, han~ yuk gaeworeun dwaet get da.

Figure 5.3 A melodic range spectrogram of Bae Ilmyeong's "months" sentence. Created with Sonic Visualizer.

Gu Seon-i a story of her life, mostly concerning the time after she came to Korea.

She began with her passage from Japan to Korea. "I came out in February or March [1946] . . . I came out in March, came out in April, it must have been about six months [after the end of the war] . . . It must have been six months."[1] She had a way of repeating herself to underline what she was saying that took on a compelling rhythmic and melodic quality as she did so. It was a sharp contrast from the deliberately unexpressive, quasi-documentarian cadences of Yi Suyong's way of speaking.

Bae Ilmyeong spoke at a characteristically fast tempo, reeling off expressions and alliterations and mimetic speech at a dizzying rate. Throughout the story she averaged about 260 syllables per minute, with each sentence coming out in an articulate rush with short pauses in between. This was a dramatic contrast with the steady 200-syllable per minute march of Yi Suyong's testimony and storytelling, with its protracted silences.

Bae Ilmyeong's was a voice that told much when listened to musically for its prosodic aspects. It was timbrally rich and a bit raspy, owing to the way she tightened her vocal cords and spoke at the back of the throat. In doing so, she placed emphasis on upper harmonics over the fundamental frequency at which she spoke (see the bright spots in Figure 5.3). She slid in and out of definite pitch.

---

1. *Iwol dal samwol dare nasingkkene, samwol dare naatsingkke siwol dare nawatsimyeon han yukgaeworeun dwaetgetda . . . han yukgaeworeun dwaetgetda.*

The overall sense of pitch contour in Bae Ilmyeong's speech was very strong. When she said, "I came out in March, came out in April, it must have been six months,"[2] she spoke these three clauses in three similar descending pitch contours, although not all of her syllables had definite pitch. The similarity of the pitch contour matched the similarity of text that linked the three phrases. The twelve months of the year, in Korea, are not named but numbered. Each clause started as a high-pitched exclamation of a number: three, four, six (*sam, si, yuk*). The first two clauses were of the same length and number of syllables, and after the number, she arced quickly down into her reciting tone area, the pitch area one uses most frequently in melodicized speech or recitation. In the third and longest clause she angled upwards on the word "months" (*gaewol*) and passed downward through the reciting tone area, inflecting down quickly again at the end of the sentence. Such movement downward at the end of a sentence is a standard speech gesture of finishing in Korean and signifies a kind of closure. It is often accompanied by a release of pitch definition, but Bae Ilmyeong landed clearly on a definite pitch, emphasizing the melodic aspects of her speech.

The melodic range spectrogram in Figure 5.3 shows Bae Ilmyeong's first two clauses with the very similar length and contour, marked by two rectangles at bottom left. Looking closely one can see that the starting pitches for each are different. "Three" (*samwol*) started higher that the subsequent "four," so there was not only a descent within each phrase but also a subtle terraced descent between them.[3] She began the final clause, "six months" (*yukgaewol*), seen in the rectangle on the right side of the figure, by rising back up just shy of the starting point of the first clause; after this flourish upward she gradually descended through the reciting area, arriving at a final tonal area lower than any she had reached previously. Bae Ilmyeong thus spoke this sentence by folding descent upon descent, falling and rising and falling lower still several times. She used the same contour to stitch the phrases together but defied the pattern in a closing cadence.

Much of Bae Ilmyeong's speech was marked by these intricacies of rhythmic and pitch expression, which were part of her energetic mode of storytelling. She used the propulsion afforded by such quasi-melodic pitch contours and rhythmic repetitions to expressively enlivened her talk. These devices served to move the narrative forward and underline its contents at the same time.

"It must have been six months," Bae Ilmyeong added, in an almost verbatim textual, rhythmic, and pitched repetition of what she had just said.

---

2. *Samwol dare naatsingkke, siwol dare nawatsimyeon, han yukgaeworeun dwaetgetda.*
3. "Month three" commenced at A3 + 6 cents, "month four" at G3# + 19 cents.

"Yeah, it was six months," she said, repeating "six months" for the third time, "and I came out and got on the boat and *ma ma ma* [an expression of surprise] the food was, *right?*, and my stomach was empty, *right* . . . ." This was another highly melodicized sentence, with more sections of stable pitch: in "*Eumshikdo geureo***jjae**, *baeneun bijap***jjae**" (the food was, *right?*, and my stomach was empty, *right*) she drew out the shorter second phrase to make it as long as the first, dropping below a relatively stable reciting pitch with "jjae" ("*right?*") by way of contrast. Bae Ilmyeong's two descending "rights" started at progressively lower pitches as she went, creating that very subtle terraced descent effect again. She also allowed her vocal cords to rattle together as air passed through them on the syllable, in two brief instances of "vocal fry." This was one among many timbral variations she made use of to add interest and expressive power to her speech.

Bae Ilmyeong spoke so quickly and forcefully that her formidable friend Gu Seon-i only had time for short, staccato replies in which she tried to slip in her own story of leaving Japan. "My god, we came out and took an illegal boat and slept on it for fifteen days," she managed to slip in. Bae Ilmyeong replied without pause, borrowing Gu Seon-i's words: "Right, came out and took an illegal boat, and later I fetched water, sea water and put rice in it and it was salty salty and do you suppose you can eat that, that stuff?" "Right, what, even just one, what, you think there were side dishes [to go with it]?" Gu Seon-i replied. In this brisk, intertextual back-and-forth the two women's stories wove together into an uneasy whole. Bae Ilmyeong listened to Gu Seon-i and took verbal cues from her, borrowing words. But the rush, intensity, and virtuosity of Bae Ilmyeong's talk meant that Gu Seon-i definitely remained in a supporting role for now. Sometimes Bae Ilmyeong poached even that role, answering her own questions.

Bae Ilmyeong continued with the story of her coming to Korea, relating how much she had struggled with the Korean language, having spoken Japanese both at home and at school. "*Okāsan otōsan onīchan onēchan gohan tabeteyo sōyo gakkō ittekita yo*" (mother father big brother big sister please eat yes that's right I've been to school and back), she said, rattling off the daily flow of speech in Japanese in her childhood home. She understood a little Korean at the time, she said, but could not speak it, and so when she came to Hapcheon she had a hard time fitting in and knowing what was going on.

Relocating to Korea she had to adjust to living on *ondol* floors, not the woven straw mats (*tatami*) that she was used to in Japan. She left Japan wearing *geta*, wooden sandals. By the time she got to Hapcheon her feet were in agony; but her father-in-law made her *jipsin* straw sandals, and she put them on and wore them everywhere.

"It was me and my husband, and his brothers, and my husband's younger siblings . . . two older brothers—my husband was a third son—and a fourth, and we all came to Hapcheon. And we bought a house," she said. As there was some money left over, they bought a rice paddy as well.

But Bae Ilmyeong's husband left for Japan again for work, and she was left alone with his family in Korea. She took care of her in-laws and raised her first child, who was born after her husband left. She had to walk down the hill into the village every time they needed water, and she spilled most of it as she staggered back and forth bringing it up the hill. She had to do all the laundry, even when there was no soap. It was just wretched. "Were there any [decent] clothes? Did we have anything? I really suffered a lot . . . I didn't know what to do and didn't do anything well," she said, breaking into a quiet peal of laughter.

Bae Ilmyeong didn't know how to farm, she told us. When she went to the field with her father-in-law she wept as she weeded.

She didn't know how to cook Korean food, either, but she was expected to make it for the family. She told us a story about her bewilderment in the kitchen. She explained that she was standing in the kitchen making *kkongboribap* (barley or barley rice),[4] a common staple among most commoners before rice became more affordable:

> *The bottom of the pot starts to* pul-pul-pul *boil hard, and the top starts to* bugeul bugeul *boil, and a burnt smell comes out from the bottom layer, and I don't know what I'm doing and the lower level's burning, you know, and if it starts to burn oh my gosh and I'm going* nunmul nunmul konmul nunmul konmul *(tears and tears and runny nose and tears and runny nose)! And I blow on it* huuuuk *to put out the fire and* kk! *the smoke comes raging out! Yeah, oh my gosh, I don't know what to do.*[5]

She spoke in the present tense, as if the past were happening now. It was just one of many of her techniques of being in the present: the past became present for the duration of her story, enhancing the drama of the scene. I could smell the smoke from the pot.

---

4. This might have been barley mixed with rice but was probably just plain barley, a more common dish at the time.

5. *Miteneun pulpulpul kkeulko, ueneun bugeulbugeul kkeulko, miteneun hageunnaega naneun gira, hal jureul mollagatgo miteneun hageunnae najana, hageunnae namyeon aigo nunmul nunmul konmul nunmul konmul [useum] bureun kkeojiji! Huk! bureuman ma pak yeongineun cheonbullaje! Geuraega, aigo geunyang ujjalkkino sipeo.*

She used mimetic speech to great effect here, both onomatopoeias and visually mimetic expressions. The Korean language has a massive vocabulary of mimetic words; it has, for instance, the many words that imitate the sound and look of boiling at varying degrees of intensity—"*pul-pul*" and "*bugeul-bugeul*" are only two of these, in decreasing order of intensity.[6] In her description of the boiling pot, Bae Ilmyeong drew from this vast repertoire, using sound effects to create a feeling of liveness—of the events of the past appearing before the mind's eye in the present, and of the present energized by vibrant talk. Her last sentence was accented by two onomatopoeic vocalizations imitating one after another the act of blowing hard (*huk*) and a sound imitating a burst of smoke (*kk!*). The first is a recognized word in dictionaries; the second is not a word but pure sound effect, her departure from conventionalized language forms into pure mimetic sound.

Bae Ilmyeong reached a kind of peak of intensity with her description of her tears and runny nose triggered by smoke and her panicked reaction. Pairing the words *nunmul* (tears, literally "eye water") and *konmul* (a runny nose, literally "nose water"), she accentuated the rhythmic and repetitive aspect of speech, repeating the syllable "*mul*" (water) five times interspersed with "*nun*" (eye) and "*ko*" (nose). She spoke the "*nunmul nunmul konmul nunmul konmul*" expression at a blistering 342 syllables per minute. The sheer speed and repetitiveness brought the story to a climax. It gave a present voice to an hysterical, sobbing body beset by tears and "nose water." But she was half-laughing as she imitated her crying and slowly burst out in unrestrained laughter.

The physiological, psychological, and acoustic features of laughter and crying that link them to one another are useful in the everyday regulation of emotion, and in the expression of emotion in everyday talk (see Lavan et al. 2015 and Erickson et al. 2009).[7] Bae Ilmyeong made use of one potential of this relation here, moving smoothly from a half-laughed mimetic description of herself crying to a paroxysm of laughter. She thus brushed up against sorrow for a moment before objectifying it with the laugh. She laughed through the end of her sentence about "tears and nose water," and for three untexted beats beyond. She continued to laugh through the first half of the next sentence: "I blow on it *huuk* to put out the fire."

Then she stopped laughing quite abruptly and deliberately to finish: "and *kk!* the smoke comes raging out," she said, ending pointedly and with pathos,

---

6. *Bogeul-bogeul*, for instance, is closer to simmering, a notch down from *bugeul-bugeul*.

7. Lavan et al. document how the similarities between laughter and crying force British listeners in their study to identify one or the other by combining speech sounds with facial gestures. Erickson et al. describe the use of the similarities between laughter and crying for emotional regulation.

restoring the balance of mirth and solemnity. The move away from laughter meant that there would be no laughing breakdown of the conversation such as we saw Yi Suyong make use of, no falling into a pause for enjoyment, reflective silence, or a focus on togetherness. Bae Ilmyeong foregrounded the narrative and maintained vigorous control over it.

She went on in a solemn voice. She spoke with pain of the difficulty of raising children, feeding everyone, of the return of her husband from abroad and other things. "I lived on tears," she said, bringing back the laughter briefly before switching it off again. Throughout, Gu Seon-i pitched in with commentary along the lines of "In those days everybody suffered," drawing attention to the fact that Bae Ilmyeong's experiences were not unusual or unusually severe. Bae Ilmyeong quickly conceded the point and went on with her story.

She spoke of the fruits of her struggle: her eldest son had graduated from Seoul National University, her second from Goryeo University, and her third son and daughter graduated from Keimyung University in Daegu. But she switched her tone again, saying, "and it was like that, and gosh, well, well, I don't really know . . . " and laughed. "If I think of all that old stuff it still seems perfectly wretched to me." She broke off. She told me later that they had been financially unable to send their youngest to college.

Gu Seon-i broke in, insisting that Bae had been very lucky. She, herself, had also been lucky, she added quickly. Bae Ilmyeong ceded the conversation to her for a while, and Gu Seon-i went on to describe her own trials— no stable place to live, raising six children. One of her children, the first and the only one born in Japan, had died after a month back in Korea. Gu Seon-i's voice cut sharply, marking the severity of her experiences when compared to Bae Ilmyeong's. But in the end, she returned to her feeling that she had been very lucky, all things considered, and this was something they shared.

The subject turned from luck to long life. "We, I, my life is a long one, I guess . . . " Bae Ilmyeong said. "My husband died, right, my husband's older brother died, right, his other older brother died, right, my contemporaries died, right, my husband's younger brother died, right, and I, aren't I just so unscathed?" And they laughed again. Bae Ilmyeong thus brought this segment of her story to a close, farewelling many of its characters, and returning resolutely to the present and her relative fortune, albeit tinged by the loneliness of the long-lived.

Bae Ilmyeong's stories were almost always like this, preludes to the present. I imagine she would have remained in the present if I had not spoken. But I cast the conversation back into the past, asking her if any of her family members had died in Hiroshima. "No, after coming back here, all of them," she said. She began, however, to talk about life in Japan. She described the

Mitsubishi factory where her husband had worked, which was hastily built towards the end of the war. She didn't say so, but it was utterly destroyed in the bombing. I can only assume her husband hadn't arrived yet when the bomb exploded. "That's right, my husband did that, and I was selling things, and one person, the wife of my cousin, yeah that person also got the atom bomb, at the time of the bomb she was in sales too, is what I mean."[8] She used the Japanese word for sales, *hanbai*.

She said nothing more of the bombing and spoke of her removal to Ninoshima, much as Yi Suyong had done. She told us how she, pregnant, had followed her husband's family back to Korea those six months or so after. They spent ten days on an illegal boat to Masan, and then made their way to Hapcheon. She continued to talk for half a minute or so before passing the conversational torch to Gu Seon-i.

In all my talks with Bae Ilmyeong in private or with others this was the closest she ever came to talking about the bombing. She did so of her own volition, and yet at the same time she circumscribed many silences with her talk. Her talk only glanced off the tragedy of Hiroshima, talking around it and passing over it quickly. Her manner calls to mind cultural theorist Eve Sedgwick's notion of *periperformative* utterance, speech which is adjacent to a subject but marks an inability to approach it directly (2003).[9] Bae Ilmyeong sandwiched her mention of the bomb in between talking about work in Hiroshima, and sandwiched her discussion of her time in Hiroshima between longer segments of talk about her move to Korea after the war. And she ended in the present, where her stories almost always ended, because for the most part she told stories in the interest of the present.

Stories are important as much for what they leave out as for what they tell. Bae Ilmyeong spoke very little and very selectively of her experiences in Hiroshima, and only then under certain specific conditions of her own making. It is tempting, and it would be quite conventional to see a kind of "silence" in this quietude and in her decision not to give testimony at the welfare center. That silence might be attributed to the unspeakability of what she had seen, the depth of her trauma, the personal act of self-repression in the interest of traumatic forgetting that her pastor encouraged, or the social atmosphere of repression that forced Korean survivors to hide their radiation exposure in the postwar.

8. I am not sure whether Bae Ilmyeong was telling us that she worked with her cousin's wife or that they both had the same job.

9. This technique of "talking around" appears again in the last chapter in Han Jeongsun's way of avoiding her own suffering as a subject in testimony.

But it would be a mistake to be sum things up as "silence" here, because Bae Ilmyeong was not silent. She was quiet about the worst aspects of her experience. She was a bit quiet in general, although less so than Yi Suyong. She rarely spoke at such length and when she did, she spoke in a quiet voice, although quickly. She had her own version of the Japanese *otonashī* style of mild, quiet personhood with which she had grown up, compounded by the stiff upper lip spirit of South Korea's long, authoritarian postwar era. That layered quietude was intensified by Bae Ilmyeong's aversion to dwelling on life's unpleasantness. This was the result of a decision she had made about what to do with traumatic memories. She endeavored to forget, which was largely impossible and often undesirable; what remained in memory she kept in a drawer, to take out and look at now and again. In this way she maintained control over the past and its memories, which she willfully set aside and endeavored to forget as a general practice of mastery, and of living mindfully, religiously, and contentedly in the present.

Bae Ilmyeong cultivated a quiet relationship to the past, gracefully brushing up against traumatic memory in disciplined conditions of her own design. You could feel the texture of that quiet relation and feel the firm grip of her control in her brief mention of the bomb. It lay at the center of a larger, symmetrical narrative: she spoke of coming to Korea, then work in Hiroshima, then the bomb, back to work in Hiroshima, and finally returned to her arrival in Korea, bookending her narrative.

I had seen this kind of mirroring symmetry before: when comfort woman survivor Pak Duri sang of her sorrows, her most agonized verses were sandwiched between jokes (Pilzer 2012: 50). It is an everyday means of living with and processing traumatic memory, brushing up against trauma amidst the energy and society of jokes and stories. Bae Ilmyeong, who never in my knowledge rose to Pak Duri's heights of emotionality, nonetheless used this technique, using stories as a way in and a way out, bringing out traumatic memory for a brief glinting display before quickly tucking it away again.

It is tempting to think of such muted or cushioned expression as a midway point between silence and disclosure, between repression and freedom. People speak, but they do not speak *out* for long, if at all. The rise of "broken silence" discourse since the fall of South Korean authoritarianism in the late 1980s might suggest that Bae Ilmyeong's quietude was an imperfect version of breaking the silence that had yet to be fully realized, and perhaps never would be, due to the thorough and persistent effects of social silencing. But Bae Ilmyeong's gentle expression seemed to me altogether too complex and intentional to be a kind of limbo between silence and speech, repression and freedom. Her quiet talk destabilized the binary of "speaking out" and remaining silent, and made me question the terms and their validity—in much the same way that others have questioned the idea that the intimate must be made public to attain true subjectivity (see Sinnott 2013 and O'Brien 2020).[10] As silence can be many things other than repression and death, so can quietude. And in this way Bae Ilmyeong and many others in Hapcheon held the mastery, folding silence into quietude rather than collapsing into it.

As I got to know Bae Ilmyeong over the years, I came to hear her version of the quiet of "Korea's Hiroshima" as part of a general program of gentle presentness. Her quietude about the past, her short answers, her changing the subject, refusals, silent reflection, and prayer added up to something quite different than a patterned repression. Her quietude may have been rooted in her traumatic experiences, but she had transformed it over the years, and now it bore a very different shape, one of her own design.

For the last forty years or so, Bae Ilmyeong had cultivated quietude as a practice of Christian devotion in the present. It was part of a program of living gracefully and believing in better things in the world and better things to come. This was perhaps the most important reason she kept her focus on the here and now: she worked towards an image of an eternal present, where one abides among the timeless—the certainty of God's love, the believer's salvation, peace, and grace.

Bae Ilmyeong was one of many bomb victims who found religion in the postwar period, and used it, in the absence of other forms of social or state support, to intervene in and interrogate fate and to cope with traumatic memory. She told me the story of her conversion. She had been a rather casual and inconsistent Buddhist devotee until her daughter, then in elementary school,

---

10. In her 2013 article on female same-sex intimacy in Thailand, anthropologist Megan Sinnott describes how, in queer studies, the critique of the public "invisibility" of women's intimacy worldwide is underpinned by an equation of publicity, visibility, and sexual emancipation, and a corresponding conflation of privacy, invisibility, and sexual repression. This notion, she argues, turns on essentially Western ideas about the division of space—and life—into public and private spheres, and masculinist, liberal notions which hold that visibility is the measure of an individual's freedom (334). Yet, she demonstrates, intimacy in spaces marked as "private" is no less important to the production of same-sex intimacy and may indeed not be marked by "repression." I feel similarly about the confessional politics of the South Korean public sphere—it marks victims' silence as solely a product of social repression, but that silence may be a choice. There are myriad practices which challenge the whole binarism and opposition of audibility versus silence, just as Sinnott describes forms of intimacy that challenge the duality of public/private and visibility/repression. A related challenge to this duality can be found in Alia O'Brien's 2020 dissertation, which describes the way that LGBTQ + Muslims in Toronto contend simultaneously with the "Silence=Death" discourse and the value of silence in spiritual devotion.

started going to church with a friend. Bae Ilmyeong went along and converted to Christianity some years later, when she was in her forties. When I met her, she had been a practicing Christian for more than four decades. Religious devotion had seen her through thyroid trouble, likely caused by her radiation exposure. It had also seen her through her son's cancer treatment and recovery, and her and her son's collective effort to quit smoking.

She was a devout Methodist and faithfully attended the Hapcheon Central Church (Hapcheon jung-ang gyohoe), the only Methodist church among the many churches scattered around the hills of Hapcheon (see Figure 5.4). She went to church on Sundays at eleven, staying for the morning service, lunch, and the afternoon service. She went to the mid-week prayer on Wednesday evenings and she took part in a Bible study meeting at the welfare center. On days where there was no church service she prayed twice a day, once at ten and once in the mid-afternoon. She spent much of her spare time studying her Bible, in which she had underlined and highlighted key passages she wanted to remember.

Bae Ilmyeong was one of several women from the center who attended Hapcheon Central Church. An Buja, a powerhouse matron of the center's social scene (see Chapter 6), was a frequent attendee, as was resident Ha Malja. But Bae Ilmyeong was by far the most consistent—in all the years of my intermittent visits to Hapcheon, I never saw her miss a service when she was in town. Sometimes a church member would pick her up and take her to church and back, but when no such person was available she would make the twenty-five-to-thirty-minute walk, even in the broiling summer heat. When in Daegu with her family she attended the church she had frequented for many years before moving into the welfare center.

Bae Ilmyeong invited me to go to church with her and I readily accepted. But she was not insistent or overbearing about it, like many more missionary South Korean Christians I have met. We went to church together many times in 2011 and after for the Sunday morning and afternoon sessions.

One Sunday the day after the bomb memorial in 2016 I walked the five minutes from my tiny motel room to Hapcheon Central Church in time for the morning service. Bae Ilmyeong greeted me as I came in and we sat together in a middle pew on the left side of the church, in her usual spot. The church had seats for about eighty or so, but there were perhaps fifteen people there, excluding the staff, musicians, and choir, who made up another twenty or so. Before us on the left the pianist sat at her white baby grand. A drum kit and seats for other musicians were set up before the edge of the stage. On the stage there was a central lectern for the deacon, and a larger lectern that rose above the deacon's place for minister Kim Byeonggi. At the back wall to the left of the minister's podium was a plain wooden cross. In my years of attendance many things have changed, but that cross has always been there.

Figure 5.4 Bae Ilmyeong praying at Hapcheon Central Church, August 14, 2011. Fellow welfare center resident Ha Malja is at right. Photo by the author.

To the right of the podium there was a rolled-up screen for laptop projection, an electric piano, and the choir seated at far right. Printed on the wall to the right of the podium there was a quotation from Matthew 6:33: "But seek first his kingdom and his righteousness and all these things will be given to you." The passage was in Korean, with English words here and there—"his kingdom," "his righteousness," "all these things will be given to you"—in a display of the global reach and the Western roots of Korean Christianity. The name of the church was in brackets in Korean script below that.

A young man operating a laptop computer threw a switch and the projection screen lowered. The screen, which remained down for the rest of the service, displayed lyrics and the melody of the opening praise song above an illustration of a very white Jesus with children gathered around him. The service began with everyone singing the refrain "Let us praise, let us praise," to the accompaniment of the electric piano. The congregation sang five hymns that morning, beginning with number 289 in the hymn book, "Since Jesus Came into My Heart" ("Ju Yesunim nae mame deureowa"), followed a bit later on by hymn 384, "All the Way My Savior Leads Me" ("Naui galgil da gadorok").[11]

11. The Korean titles of hyms differ from the English: the second means "To Follow of My Appointed Road."

Bae Ilmyeong had been quiet at the start of the service, occasionally leaning over to me to whisper about the participants, or to give me pertinent information about the course of the service. Now she sang, in a full voice and quite distinctly. I noticed that she generally sang this way when she knew the hymns well: in a somewhat rigid manner, following the text between the hymnal and the big screen, pronouncing all the words clearly and projecting her voice. When she knew a song less well, she read diligently and omitted some words, singing a bit behind the beat and practicing. Once she had got the hang of it, she sang loudly and forcefully.

Bae Ilmyeong was more concerned with textual accuracy than with melody, and she deviated from the printed melody here and there, mostly in the direction of simplification. She treated rhythm in the same manner, occasionally skipping rests and starting new verses ahead of the group before correcting herself. Throughout, she showed a focus on text over music: her microscopic deviations were little demusicalizations which gestured to the primacy of text. Her concern with text reflected, among other things, a predominant Methodist value: text, and scripture in particular, are typically considered paramount and perfect in Methodism, and the one path to God. The traditions of the church, such as music, are of secondary importance and have no claim to perfection.

▶10

At the end of each song, Bae Ilmyeong skipped the rest that prepared the final "Amen," arriving at this final word noticeably early. She did this at every service we attended together, moving away from song along a continuum that led her towards the written word: from song, to spoken prayer, to half-spoken prayer, and finally to silent reading. Moving along this continuum we find a fair précis of Bae Ilmyeong's hierarchy of religious activity: she was least interested in singing; she anticipated the minister's sermons every week and listened attentively; and she valued reading the Bible above all else, often reading aloud, but not in a way that drew attention to the voice.

On that day, Minister Kim Byeonggi's sermon was entitled "Racing with Faith," and was a meditation on Hebrews 12: 1–3. He began with the passage, in his rich baritone: "Therefore, since we are surrounded by such a great cloud of witnesses, let us throw off everything that hinders and the sin that so easily entangles. And let us run with perseverance the race marked out for us, fixing our eyes on Jesus, the pioneer and perfecter of faith." Behind him he showed a slide with text that encouraged the parishioners to cast off those attachments which weigh down the soul and obstruct its path to salvation, and to be patient, remembering the suffering of Jesus, who endured so much on his path to the throne of God.

Every day Bae Ilmyeong practiced the work of throwing off hindrances and remaining focused on the present and its path toward God. It was one origin of her interest in forgetting trouble and pursuing her present life. She allowed the language of the Bible and of Kim Byeonggi's weekly sermons to transform her daily practice of life.

One way she accomplished this was by folding scripture and the minister's sermons into her everyday talk. One day at the welfare center in August 2011 she was talking with me, Gu Seon-i, and others in the common room of the third floor. The subject came around to the many difficult life experiences of the residents. "Not everything is unconditionally good or bad," she said. "There is a time for keeping and a time for throwing away . . . there is a front and back . . . and there is good and bad. Not everything is unconditionally bad." She was, in part, quoting from the well-known text from Ecclesiastes 3, "a time to keep and a time to throw away." She borrowed the duality expressed there to make her point about the ambivalence of experience: negative experience is a phase which gives on to good, so it forms a necessary part of the dyad of good and bad.

Another woman with us asked her about the atom bomb. What was good about that? Was it not unconditionally bad? "That, too, was fate," Bae Ilmyeong said simply. She repeated it a few more times in between the responses of her friends.

Bae Ilmyeong endeavored, above all things, to be reconciled with fate. She told me, "At first when I became Christian I thought 'God, please give me this, please do well by me,' that sort of thing." But as time went by her requests ceased, as she took on the doctrine of unconditional faith. She prayed for her children, especially those who had not become Christians, to "see the light." She was concerned about one of her daughters, who had become Catholic, which according to Bae Ilmyeong made her salvation uncertain. She took careful note of people in her family and in the church community who were in need or in trouble of one kind or another and prayed for them. She prayed for the young adults of the church when they sat for their college entrance exams, and she prayed for the sick and wounded. She prayed, as many survivors of the atom bomb have done, for divine intervention to stop the handing down of radiation-related illness and disability, like when she prayed for her son during his bout with cancer. Her prayers were full of requests, but, she told me, not for herself. "I'm not worried about much nowadays, or about living a long time," she told me. "If God calls me, I'll just go," she told me. "Now I'm old, and my family mostly believes . . . so it's enough for me to wait for God's call: 'Come on up!'"

Prayer for Bae Ilmyeong was a means of helping others, but it was also a practice of faith and grace. Grace in Christian theology (*eunhye* in Korean), refers to the favor which God bestows upon humanity. There are varying opinions among theologists about whether grace is earned or freely given, but in practice people do a fair amount of work to stay in God's good graces. Prayer is a primary means to grace, one of the two large categories of piety in contemporary Methodist thought together with works of mercy. Reading, studying, and meditating on scripture, faithfully attending services, healthy living, and sharing the faith with others are some other works of piety which help one live in grace.

Bae Ilmyeong spent much of her day on such works of piety. She prayed earnestly, read and studied the Bible and books of religious interest, and attended services and Bible study. I am certain that some portion of her interest in me had to do with a hope that I would become a believer. She led a daily life geared towards staying on the path and the peace that this afforded.

She told me that people falling off that path of righteousness accounted for most of the suffering in the world. A few months after the Fukushima nuclear disaster on March 11, 2011, we were talking about longevity, and countries where people live a long time. Speaking of the many centenarians in Korea and Japan, Bae Ilmyeong said that a hundred years or so wasn't a long time to live. Abraham lived for 900 years, she said, and as people's arrogance and greed led them further and further from God's way, and as they claimed more and more mastery over life, their lives ironically grew shorter and shorter. "For example: electricity. Edison invented electricity, right? But people use it unwisely, and greedily, and many people suffer," she said, referring to the Fukushima disaster. But, she told me, people were starting to realize the mistakes they have made, and so lives are starting to lengthen again.

Bae Ilmyeong took greed to be a cardinal sin and returned to it again and again in her meditations. She told me that one should not greedily desire more than their share of grace. She said that one should not lust for a long life either. "No matter how much you may want to live, you may die; and no matter how much you may want to die, you may live. It's not your choice." I had heard that expression before, again from "comfort woman" survivor Pak Duri (Pilzer 2012: 65), in rather a more Buddhist vein, meditating on the capriciousness of fate and the evanescence of life. But Bae Ilmyeong used the saying as evidence of the powerlessness of human beings in the face of God.

The life of someone waiting for God's call, Bae Ilmyeong told me, should be as simple as possible. She was the most vehement of the many people at the center who chastised me when I brought presents. On several occasions she politely made me take back the small gift of fruit or snacks that I had brought, telling me to eat it when I was back in my motel room. When she accepted the gift, a strident if friendly scolding was a condition of her acceptance. She told me that all her needs were taken care of by the center. Anyway, she added, "What sort of things do I need at this age?"

Bae Ilmyeong thus led a life of carefully constructed simplicity at the welfare center, staying focused on the practice of faith. It was a quiet life by design, a contemplative one of engagement with scripture and text. And as such, she steered clear of many of the more boisterous activities put on by the center, including most musical activities. She did sing alone in her room sometimes. "I don't have a good singing voice, but when I'm alone, I'm Number One," she told me, and laughed.

But she said it wasn't proper for a woman of her age to be cavorting and singing karaoke in front of others. Like so many other adherents of the transcendental religions through history, she felt the earthiness of music keenly, and sought the ideality associated with text, the word of God. At the group karaoke events at the center she never sang, sitting to the side or even leaving, returning to her room to read the Bible. The staff, who often encouraged the residents to sing, had learned not to press her. She also declined to participate in the short-lived choir that Han Jeongsun and the Hapcheon Peacehouse had organized, which practiced in the meeting room on the first floor. Her thyroid trouble earlier in life, which left her unconfident about her voice, may have been one source of reluctance; but it was not the main reason.

Bae Ilmyeong was not averse to some aspects of music, though—she welcomed those that contributed to the quiet and refined atmosphere she had designed. One day I was sitting and chatting with her and fellow resident Jo Gyeongsuk in her room. I had recently arrived from Japan. Bae Ilmyeong went to a dresser in her room and brought out some sheets of old Japanese song lyrics to show to us. One of her sons, knowing that she was fond of the songs, had written them down for her in a rather graceful calligraphic hand. She drew our attention to the lyrics to the Japanese film song "Itoshi ano hoshi" ("Beloved Star"), from 1940. It was a famous song of love and devotion from the film *Song of the White Orchid*, produced by the Japanese colonial film industry in wartime Manchuria.[12]

As she looked through the lyrics, she did not sing, but spoke them. When pressed by Jo Gyeongsuk to sing the song she politely declined, saying that her voice was not good. She went on reading:

Basha ga yuku yuku yūkaze ni   *The horse carriage goes and goes on the evening breeze*

---

12. One of many films by the Japanese colonial Toho Film and Manchurian Film Institute which starred Li Xianglan, an ethnically Japanese film star and singer who impersonated Chinese women in these propagandistic films.

Aoi yanagi ni sasayaite   *And I whisper to the willow*
"Itoshi kono mi wa doko made mo   *"Wherever this beloved body may go*
Kimeta kokoro wa kawarya senu"   *My resolved heart does not change."*

She didn't mention feeling any sort of kinship with this song, despite the wandering that had characterized her own life. Indeed, she didn't offer any commentary about the song. She went on shuffling through the elegant paper in search of songs she liked or remembered, commenting on the fineness of her son's writing, simultaneously proud of this and her own Japanese literacy (Figure 5.5). Like many of the older residents of the center, being bilingual, being literate in both languages, having college-educated children—all of these were sources of pride and distinction. Literacy signaled a culturedness of which she was proud, and her children's education was a marker of both learnedness and success. These songs, rendered as written text by her son the scholar, and therefore made silent, were welcome in Bae Ilmyeong's world, where she could give them a quiet voicing.

There was, then, an element of class consciousness in Bae Ilmyeong's propriety and elevation of text over music, even over the voice. Christianity in Korea has long been associated with eliteness, via its associations with the West, modernity, and progress. Much of the contemporary South Korean elite is Christian and participation in Christian worship is for many a practice of class distinction, though Christianity also thrives among the rural poor. Bae Ilmyeong's religious avoidance of public singing was

Figure 5.5 Bae Ilmyeong shows me her son's calligraphy, August 17, 2017. Photo by the author.

simultaneously part of a discourse of class propriety, whereby she held herself to the station which she had inherited through her children's rise through the social ranks, especially through the status of her son the retired professor. Her fondness for text was a similar practice of distinction, as texts connote literacy, education, and elite social membership, which was compounded by her pride in her own educational history and her ability to read and write in two languages.

Bae Ilmyeong's quietude was therefore a layered and compound sensibility. It was a practice of social class and distinction, compounding education, notions of stylized Japanese mildness (*otonashīsa*), and postwar Korean stolidity; but it was also a Christian practice of peace, contentment, and grace. Her focus on the present, her gentle avoidance of traumatic memory in reminiscence and story, her techniques of quiet reflection and demusicalized prayer, which edged towards the silent ideality of religious text—these were practices by which Bae Ilmyeong maintained the peace she had made with a past of unimaginable violence and loss and found something resembling happiness and contentment in the present.

CHAPTER 6
The Arts of Institutional Life

The arts of living that Yi Suyong, Bae Ilmyeong, and other residents of the welfare center practiced were means of living with the bomb, the nuclear legacy, and South Korean public cultural framings of victims and their suffering. But much of life at the center had little to do with these things, which often receded to the background as survivors crafted their daily lives in their institutional setting. Like Bae Ilmyeong, who practiced the graceful art of sidestepping in an environment that pressed bomb survivors into the service of historical memory, most of the residents of the welfare center had their own ways of pushing back against the social forces that would quarantine them in the past. Residents of the welfare center went to additional efforts to lay claim to the present and its future in the face of daily life at the center, which many spoke of as a generic, eternal present where time stood still, or a smooth passage of days that was beyond their control.

The practice of everyday life was the main forum in which survivors undertook this work of reclaiming the present from the nuclear legacy and the institution. This effort of self-constitution and maintenance took place in the face of what Erving Goffman called the "mortification of the self": the process by which people who live in total institutions are stripped of core features of their identities and social relations in the interest of the smooth running of collective life, or in the name of reform (1962: 14). The center staff had little interest in reforming its residents other than in the interest of health and harmonious group living; but these meant different things to different people, and inevitably required residents to make a range of personal and social sacrifices.

The welfare center was replete with masters of the artful organization of everyday life in the present, and the cultivation of routines to keep mind,

Quietude. Joshua D. Pilzer, Oxford University Press. © Oxford University Press 2023.
DOI: 10.1093/oso/9780197615089.003.0006

body, and the social life together. Some mapped the welfare center with their minds and movements in acts of making it home. Some made elaborate and detailed schedules of their days and weeks. Some studied books, or practiced calligraphy or drawing, in the interest of cultivating mind and spirit. Others played card games or Korean chess (*janggi*) in the common rooms, solidifying friendships and exercising their minds at the same time.

Everyone has origins; some of these are in the past, but others lie in the circumstances of present-day life. The public-cultural framing of bomb and radiation victims in South Korea and beyond rarely takes into account these later origins, and never allows the former to fade from view. During my decade of visits to the welfare center the residents did not deny their pasts; if they wished to do so, they would have chosen to live elsewhere. But they invested most of their time in the art of present life, letting the nuclear legacy fade. If this ethnography of their lives insisted on the constant presence of that legacy, I would risk consigning them, yet again, to the past, and reducing them to essences of traumatic experience. I would also likely miss out on much of the effort and artistry with which people organize their presents and futures, which is so central to the art of survival.

In this chapter I mimic that process of putting memory on the back burner, and I write about that artistry, and the presents and selves that survivors vigorously constructed and defended in the institutional environment of the welfare center. These are some of the most important aspects of the quietude of Hapcheon—the truce with the past sustained by quiet attentiveness to the present, and the quiet modulation of institutional time into a living, breathing present. And yet the sum total of this ongoing practice of selfhood and the struggle for time cannot be encompassed by "quietude," either, and to attempt to do so would be to foist yet another essence on the people in this book, and to refuse to acknowledge the limits of that concept's explanatory power. Because people are not quiet all of the time, and some people are rarely quiet at all.

———

"I count my steps," Pak Heun-il told me. He was seventy-one and the youngest male resident of the welfare center. We were in his room on the third floor, and he was talking about his daily routine. He had figured out that he took about 10,000 steps a day. He started the day every morning at five with a dark walk on the small river which fronts the center, which got him several thousand strides. He counted his movements around the center as he went to functions and meals. He knew by heart the number of steps it took him to get to various locations: forty-four steps from the bottom of the first-floor staircase to his room on the third floor; a round trip of about 200 steps from his room to the cafeteria.

Pak Heun-il shared a room with Yun Sugi, the soft-spoken Japanophile, and Kim Pan-geun, who had aspired to be an engine driver in Hiroshima. He was sitting on his bed, planted fixedly in front of his computer. Without taking his eyes from the screen he was telling me about his life and how he came to the center. He was just a baby when the bomb exploded, he said, and didn't remember Japan. He lived for a long time in Seoul and moved back to Hapcheon and into the welfare center in 2009.

For a year or so, he didn't participate in the activities of the center. But you can't go on forever being a *dokbul janggun*—a loner, literally an "isolated general," he said. You can't live alone—you have to understand others, and work together with them. "This room, living as we do, together—we have to understand one another." Pak Heun-il was thus the last to go in for meals, waiting politely for his seniors to go first. The lineup for meals, roughly, was ladies first, from oldest to youngest, and then again for the men. There was no hard and fast rule that said Pak Heun-il should go in last, but he never neglected this custom out of a daily practice of deference to his elders, a practice of well-manneredness and virtue.

Many people at the center are bored, he said, feeling they have nothing to do. "But if you change your thinking just a little, you have lots to do." Pak volunteered at the district office of the Korean Atomic Bomb Victims Association when Shim Jintae was away. He searched the web for items of interest that he shared with his friends and acquaintances, sometimes as links and sometimes copied into his emails. Some pieces he sent person-to-person, others to a wider group of his own making. He sent his list of correspondents nationalist blog entries, links to music, photography, and YouTube videos mostly of natural scenes. He put me on the list, and over the years I have received a blog entry discussing twenty rare songs of the popular singer Na Hun-a, a guide to azalea viewing on nearby Mt Hwangmae, a photo essay about fall colors at the Seoul-area mountain fortress Namhansanseong, a slide show of key exhibits and buildings at Ho-Am Art Museum, a video of undersea creatures in Bali, photos and a short article on California's Mono Lake and its majestic tufa limestone columns, a list noting South Korea's best qualities and evidence of its global power, and several critiques of left-wing political parties as unpatriotic. He sent me personally a guide to Canada's fall colors and a screed opposing free school lunches for children in Korean schools, among other things. He never added any text of his own to these emails.

Internet browsing and forwarding was, for Pak Heun-il as it is for many of us, a way of passing the time; but it is also about cultivating a sense of the world in which one lives, an act of the imagination that brings a version of that world into being. It is about finding a self to call one's own, enmeshed in a mediated web of relationships with other people and other places. Pak Heun-il engaged with his online friends and acquaintances, with the imagined community of Koreans,[1] with art worlds, worlds of music, and the natural world, often all at once. The nationalist writings he was drawn to were intensely preoccupied with comparing Korea to other places and locating Korea in the global system of nation-states.[2]

He told me that these acts of the imagination and this work of making social and political relationships were particularly important to him now, for he was used to living independently in the megalopolis, but now spent almost all his time in the rural and institutional environment of the welfare center. They were his daily practice of cosmopolitanism and urban sophistication, the continuation of a life that had left and exceeded Hapcheon, and that refused to collapse back into it despite his return.

Pak Heun-il told me that his browsing was a kind of study, a work of self-improvement and cultivation of mind. He learned about different places in the world and natural phenomena, and he encountered new forms of art and music. He rehearsed and inflected his ideological convictions, although they didn't perhaps change that much. Pak Heun-il, like many residents of the welfare center, devoted his daily life to a system of self-improvement and maintenance, based in his online research and his physical regimen. He designed that system within the range of available options at the welfare center and with the support of the staff, who among other things had arranged for him to have wireless internet in his room.

Pak Heun-il spoke to me of his research, of his exercise regime, and of his intricate knowledge of distances at the center with pride—for it was a life of his own making. It was his way of living intentionally and healthily and according to his own compass, a system of care and self-maintenance that blended institutional constraints with his own sense of how to live and how to live with others. It was a kind of twofold "living with care" —living deliberately and carefully in a care facility (Cook et al.: 2015). Life routines like this seem essential to a satisfying life in a residential facility, as the move into such a place is destabilizing for fundamental social life and relationships, as well as for senses of space, self, and control (ibid.; Goffman 1962).

It is no surprise that walking and footsteps are central to systems of "living with care." "Footsteps are the primary means by which walkers take

---

1. I am referring here to Benedict Anderson's classic concept of nations as "imagined communities" (1983).

2. Literary theorist William Egginton calls this work of global and national imagining "theatrical identification" in his work *How the World Became a Stage: Presence, Theatricality, and the Question of Modernity* (2003).

care," writes anthropologist Jo Lee Vergunst in an essay on walking and taking care in Scottish everyday life. "Each footstep produces a distinctive relationship through which the walker comes to know something of his or her textural environment" (2008: 115). Pak Heun-il's and others' walking were ways of knowing the new environment of the welfare center and becoming functioning social beings there—a means of making the welfare center something like "home," and transforming oneself into someone that lives there. Residents often spoke of feeling like guests at the welfare center, like people living in a hotel; and so they strived to make it their own, and to become someone "at home."

In particular, such walking work helped people establish a sense of what particular parts of the center were most like "home" and which were less so. Life in total institutions like the welfare center are characterized by a compression of the former spaces of life: work, play, and home life all take place under the same roof (Goffman 1962: 5-6). The counting of steps was therefore a means by which some residents created a sense of the relative separation of these spaces, and zeroed in on "their place" of semi-privacy.

Pak Heun-il's and others' walking at the center was part of a system of living; but it was also an artful way of being in the world and had any number of aestheticized aspects. Vergunst, speaking with hill-walkers and mountaineers in the Scottish highlands, found a discourse of regularity and "rhythm" in describing the experience of walking that was at odds with the lack of regularity and repetition they experienced walking along slippery and treacherous paths and trails (2008: 116). He found an explanation for this in the way walkers create rhythms of movement and experience which variously overlay and organize the irregularity of the walking. Steps which take varying lengths of time may be conceived of as a rhythmic procession of identical rhythmic values, which vary with respect to duration like quarter notes in music that vary in free rhythm or rubato.[3] Vergunst also found that some walkers experienced each movement—jumping onto the right or left foot, sidestepping, switchbacking, and so on—as a particular qualitative kind of rhythmic strike or duration, which joined together with others in all different sorts of elaborate and prolonged rhythmic patterns. He found that walkers primarily assembled such intricate patterns on the fly, transforming them as walking environments changed.

We can find such rhythmic behaviors in the walking practices at the welfare center, although it was laid out rather differently than a Scottish highland. The center had been constructed to make walking as regular and as easy

---

3. This is roughly the way rhythm is conceived of in East Asian court musics—one hears a tremendous amount of real-time difference between the length of beats, but they are notated as if they were equal. It is also similar to the ebb and flow of tempo in Western classical music.

as possible for residents, many of whom have walking-related disabilities, or who have difficulty walking for long. Those who walked with difficulty in the center had similar experiences to hikers on treacherous paths, taking enormous care not to fall. Kim Imseon was one such person, who aggressively pursued her walking regimen after she became infirm with a cane and then with a walker, until at last she deemed it impossible. She and many others walked very slowly, putting thought into each step. Their methodical footsteps and the sound of canes and walkers striking the floor echoed throughout the tiled building.

There was a long ramp which connected the first floor to the second, convenient for wheelchairs in the event that the elevator was unusable or quick evacuation became necessary. The staff encouraged residents to go to and from their rooms without the elevator, and almost all of the residents who came down for meals walked up and down the ramp. Yi Suyong had swollen legs, which had afflicted her ever since her leg injury in Hiroshima, but she walked vigorously up the ramp many times a day, bent over from years of hard work. Sometimes she used a cane.

The building was designed with smooth floors and without sudden turnings, with long open corridors fronting the residents' rooms, staff offices, and meeting rooms. Thus more mobile residents of the center found no need for a mental practice of regularity to contrast with the irregularity of walking. There was no friction, only smoothness. That smoothness brought with it the threat of a lack of differentiation, the specter of the eternal recurrence of the same. "For there to be rhythm, there must be repetition in a movement, but not just any repetition," wrote Henri Lefebvre in *Rhythmanalysis*. "For there to be rhythm, strong times and weak times, which return in accordance with a rule or law—long and short times, recurring in a recognizable way, stops, silences, blanks, resumptions and intervals in accordance with regularity, must appear in movement. Rhythm therefore brings with it a differentiated time" (1992: 78).

Lefebvre might have been better off using the musical term *meter*, a more precise term than rhythm for the groupings of time units that render time heterogeneous and give it flow. In any case such patterns and their senses of differentiated time felt in short supply to some at the welfare center, like at other total institutions, despite the efforts of the staff to provide variety. People complained of the way that time slipped away without notice. One reason Bae Ilmyeong paid such close attention to time, she told me, was that if you didn't pay attention, a day could go by so smoothly that time hardly seemed to pass at all and vanished without your notice. The lack of differentiation of movement in the confines of the welfare center contributed to this feeling for many. When residents at the welfare center created systems of living, involving ways of moving through the space, they created patterns and progressions that differentiated time and made it feel like it was not standing still.

Residents had various walking practices that helped create variety in the nature of daily movements, promoting the sense of time passing and cementing the reality and continuity of past, present, and future. Walks beyond the center grounds, for instance, were means by which residents staked claims to independence, by which they made their lives non-identical to life in the total institution. Pak Heun-il and Yi Suyong both took early morning walks, and Kim Imseon took two a day, one in the early morning and one at dusk, until she became too infirm. Down by the river there was a herd of goats grazing, and in the summer one could hear the drone of insects and the croaking of frogs and see the sudden luminescent flash of the common kingfisher (*mulchongsae*) as it streaked by fishing.

Many residents chose to walk to town, despite the fact that the district bus and the center's bus were both available to take them numerous times during the day. Some heeded the electronic bell which sounded to announce the imminent departure of the bus, like Bae Ilmyeong, for whom it was another signpost in her measurement of time. Others ignored it. Many walked to the market, although they mostly caught the bus back with their shopping. Many went for walks on scheduled center outings—trips to nearby Haeinsa temple and other scenic spots (See Figure 6.1). About half of the residents traveled periodically to stay with family.

Yun Sugi and Gu Gyeong-won took daily trips to the pool at the Hapcheon Sports Center, driving after lunch in Gu Gyeong-won's car or catching a ride with another resident who swam. We met there on occasion. One sweltering day in August 2015, Gu Gyeong-won and I were resting at the end of the pool by its red digital clock and he was telling me about the complicated social life of the welfare center. People can be so self-interested, he said. "I keep out of it." He gestured to Yun Sugi: "That guy and me, we put our hearts together and take care of each other. Aside from that I stay away from others."

A moment later Yun Sugi returned from his lap. They swam off together, moving at the same speed slowly down the lane. Yun Sugi swam with a pool noodle curved under his arms. Gu Gyeong-won swam with two, one under his arms and one between his legs. He swam the length of the pool without touching the bottom. Yun Sugi swam the breaststroke, with his lower body angled downwards towards the bottom of the pool. It took them about two or three minutes to get the end of the pool. Then they rested, without talking. They split up for the next lap; I can't remember who left the wall first.

Yun Sugi spoke fondly of swimming freestyle, backstroke, and other strokes when he was a boy in Japan. When he came to Korea, he told me, he had no chance to swim for years and years, and had just started again

Figure 6.1 An outing for flower viewing organized by the welfare center, November 10, 2011. Kim Doshik (at left) and Yun Sugi (third from the right) are facing forward; Kim Pan-geun stands to the right of Kim Doshik. Photo by the author.

recently while living at the center. It reminded him of being young, and of the life he had lost. These daily trips, then, were a moment not just outside of the center, but outside of its present as well.

Swimming is a radically different form of movement that breaks the feel and the routine of everyday walking and talking life. One's perception of sound alters dramatically (see Helmreich 2007: 624).[4] One's whole body is in contact with the water and the world, and yet floating as well. Yun Sugi and Gu Gyeong-won's swimming seemed to me a practice of both separation and connectedness, a moment of stepping outside the ordinary while retaining and enhancing the intimacy of friendship.[5] Also, the ability to swim, like the ability to read and write, was rare among their generation in Korea. Yun Sugi and Gu Gyeong-won took pride in the exercise as a marker of distinction and modern education, and a gateway to health not open to everyone.

4. Helmreich describes at length how underwater sound is either imperceptible to human beings or registered via the bones in the skull, and the typical left–right stereo image of hearing is confounded.
5. When Albert Camus described swimming he focused on this connectedness, the unity of things joined by water and immersion, and the bonds between friends (Martin 2010: 46–7).

After their trips to the pool, the two men often stopped in town for coffee, or even went out to dinner. They preferred to dine in *reseutorang*, a Koreanization of "restaurant," which served Korean versions of Western food, which were often Koreanized versions of Japanese versions of Western food inherited during the colonial period. Thus the meals briefly ameliorated Yun Sugi's nostalgia for Japan. But that day when we got out of the pool they had to rush, because their ride was waiting for them outside. Gu Gyeong-won complained about not being able to take their time. Yun Sugi expressed regret that they couldn't stop to have a cup of coffee and a chat before returning to the welfare center. "It's better when you can do things at your own pace," he rued.

They offered me a ride back to the center with them. In the car, in the back seat, Yun Sugi told me in Korean that next time they should just go together in Gu Gyeong-won's car, as the driver's schedule and their own didn't match. The driver made no reply. Gu Gyeong-won, thinking of his feelings, joked that he and the driver's schedules and temperaments matched quite nicely, and suggested that Yun Sugi should go alone to the pool. We got out of the car at the welfare center. Yun Sugi invited me to join them for coffee or dinner next time, sustaining the struggle to make time his own despite this temporary setback.

We got back to the welfare center around four, which was early for them. Yun Sugi and Gu Gyeong-won retired to their rooms. After checking in with the staff in the main office I went to Yun Sugi's room, which he shared with Pak Heun-il and Kim Pan-geun. Pak Heun-il was not there. Kim Pan-geun and Yun Sugi were drinking homemade plum liquor (*maesilju*), made by soaking green plums in white liquor. Someone in Kim Pan-geun's family had made it and snuck it into the center, despite the official prohibition on drinking there. For many residents, that prohibition meant abandoning a ritual behavior which was key to social life and their senses of self. The staff therefore turned a blind eye to moderate drinking done in private.

Nonetheless, the ritual was an act of quiet defiance of the rule. Yun Sugi reached into Kim Pan-geun's closet for his secret stash and poured some into a paper cup for me. He brought out a bag of Hershey's Kisses for drinking snacks (*anju*). He smiled and proclaimed in English "Made in America!!!"

The plum liquor was about thirty percent alcohol, I'd guess, much stronger than store-bought plum wine. Yun Sugi told me that the men had one or two leisurely cups a day in the late afternoon before dinner, in defiance of the rules, making the space and time their own. The social order of the welfare center and its rules loosened in this ritual of defiant drinking. A different, displaced social order and its social time rose to the fore.

In his study of Xhosa beer-drinking rituals, anthropologist Patrick McAllister describes the importance of alcohol consumption in the construction of social relations: "in drinking beer people are making and re-making reciprocal social connections with each other, connections which are of extreme social and economic significance in the context of everyday life" (2006: 17). The secret drink we shared at the welfare center was one of many moments of assertion among men who lived there, a moment in which they quietly asserted the masculinity and sociability of their genera-tion in the face of a younger social welfare system that balanced controlling elders' lives with deferring to them out of respect.

As we drank in the room on the third floor, the codes of this social order were on display. Yun Sugi and Kim Pan-geun were the same age, both born in 1930, and that made drinking together comfortable, removing many of the protocols which would have to be observed otherwise. That said, the drink was not without ceremony. Yun Sugi acted as host, pouring the drinks; he was pouring from Kim Pan-geun's stash, and the work of doling out the drink was a way of thanking Kim Pan-geun while he sat at his ease. He saw to Kim Pan-geun's drink first, then mine. He served me with the paternalistic warmth that older men show to their juniors and urged me to seconds with the pleasure that many older people take in watching others consume more than their own daily ration of alcohol. He poured for Kim Pan-geun with both hands, in a gesture of utmost respect, and for me with one, in a gesture of seniority and familiarity. I offered to pour for him, but he declined, saying he had had a cupful already, and he always stopped at one drink. Yun Sugi did not keep filling Kim Pan-geun's cup up to the top— the Japanese custom—but waited Korean-style until it was empty before asking if he would like another. Kim accepted the offer silently, with a smile and a nod.

They drank quietly. Many Korean people of middle-age, especially men, make a harsh fricative exclamation after taking a sip of the clear liquor *soju*, expressive of the strength of the alcohol and/or their own fortitude (Harkness 2011).[6] Many younger people make a slightly less harsh sound after drinking, indicative of the softening of the liquor and the language in recent years (see Harkness 2013).[7] Kim and Yun made no such sound, though the white liquor mellowed by the soaked plums was almost three times as strong as today's *soju*. This was surreptitious drinking, although they drank with the door open. The efforts they made to conceal what they were doing were largely symbolic, part of an unspoken accommodation

---

6. Harkness describes these sounds as Fricative Vocal Gestures (2011).

7. Harkness gives reasons why the sound, with its rich associations with Korean masculinity, has softened over time: the alcohol content of *soju* has declined as more women have become *soju* drinkers, and new models of gentility in public culture have gradually taken hold, discour-aging roughness, which has been reframed as a symbol of uncouth and backward Koreanness.

between institutional rules and semi-private life. To make the rasping exclamation would be to push the limits of that unspoken agreement too far. But in any case, they showed no sign that they wished to make such exclamations. They would have made facial gestures in lieu of the fricative gesture if they had wanted to react in this way without drawing attention to themselves, but they did not. These were quiet men, who prided themselves on a quiet masculine gentility associated with a modern, urban upbringing in Japan, the stiff upper lip spirit of postwar South Korea, and a strong, silent masculinity. They smiled, silently. They watched my face, prepared to laugh if I reacted to the strong drink. Time mellowed and stretched out and the room filled with a warm sociability. The institutional quiet was replaced with a quietude redolent of strength, friendship, and broken rules.

After about a half an hour of plum wine and conversation Yun Sugi asked me if I could play table tennis. He was thinking of playing a match in the third-floor common room. I said I could return the ball if my opponent was being nice. We drifted out and started to play. It was a few minutes to 5:00 p.m., the dinner hour. The ping-pong table was right behind the treadmills, which face out the wraparound windows towards the river. Yun Sugi served gently, and so I was able to stay in the game. After a while Bae Ilmyeong's youngest brother, Bae Cheongnam, who was in his early seventies and one of the youngest residents, asked to swap in. I stepped aside and started shooting video, listening to the rhythmic plonking of the plastic ball and watching the smooth, practiced movements of the two men.

They played in a friendly fashion, neither making difficult serves or returns, both aiming to keep the ball in play rather than score. They did not rush, and the volleys proceeded evenly, about eight volleys in six seconds, about eighty per minute counting serves and returns. This was punctuated by the sound of the ball hitting the table and interrupted by long pauses while one player or both retrieved the ball. They didn't speak.

▶11

The quiet atmosphere was suddenly broken by a strident female voice in the distance: "Let's go for dinner!!!" A few seconds later, a member of the staff entered. She was moving quickly through the third floor, reminding stragglers that dinner was at five. Now entering the common room, she walked briskly towards Bae Cheongnam. She clapped as she walked, in the manner one might clap to startle a child into activity. She smiled all the while, ironizing the performance of power. She walked and clapped evenly, performing the smooth and efficient rhythm of welfare center time with a laugh, with a suggestion that those who get in step are bound for wonderful things. It reminded me of those children's clap songs—"If You're

Happy and You Know It," or the Japanese "Let's Clap our Hands" ("Te wo tatakimashō")—that promise happiness in exchange for collective behavior that relies on a shared sense of time.

She turned around and walked towards Yun Sugi with her hands apart, as if she was about to clap again. She turned to me as she walked: "Hey, professor! Take a picture of me hitting this guy!" She reached Yun Sugi, tall and towering over her, and faked slapping him across the face. Then she quickly clapped her hands again. They both laughed, Yun Sugi smiling brightly. "Hurry up and finish!" she said, and went off muttering about the stubbornness of old men.

The slap was her ironic performance of Korean "tough love," the rough *jeong* (affection) tinged with power that underlies much social interaction and that rationalizes much domestic and institutional violence. She clearly thought it was harmless, going out of her way to ask me to record the event, and Yun Sugi laughed it off. But the parody of violence did nothing to destabilize the unbalanced relations of power that it referenced.

The two men resumed playing table tennis without hurrying (Figure 6.2). In the next volley their pace was noticeably slower. The ball bounced higher, leaving a beat before each shot that hadn't been there before. Each serve and volley took about a second to make, slowing the pace to about

Figure 6.2 Yun Sugi (right) and Bae Cheongnam playing table tennis, August 5, 2015. Photo by the author.

sixty per minute. But soon things settled back to their former tempo, about eight in six seconds. They continued like this for some minutes, as if nothing had happened. Still neither spoke. "Let's go have dinner," Yun Sugi finally said. The two men put down their racquets and headed to the elevator, having made their point.

Through such means people make the time of life their own in the face of institutional time. In so doing they resist the institution's mortifications of the self.

Small acts of defiance were parts of many residents' means of keeping their identities and their social lives together in the face of institutional power and routine. That resistance was everyday and rarely came to a head. It was not aimed at revolution but at making life possible at the center despite the inevitable losses of identity, control, and society which life there entailed.

———

Next door to the third-floor common room and the ping-pong table was another common area, lined on one wall by a bookshelf. It was the area where Yun Sugi played *go* online, and where other men gathered to play *janggi* ("Korean chess," closely related to *xiangqi*, "Chinese chess"). The bookshelf was filled with donated books. Many were related to the history of the atomic bombing of Hiroshima or its Korean victims and were rarely read by residents. Most were in Korean: inspirational books, novels, scholarly books with their blend of Sino-Korean characters and the Korean alphabet, novels, a well-thumbed translation of Sun Tsu's *The Art of War*. About a third of the books were in Japanese, and these were similar in content, with a tendency towards novels, classical Japanese literature, and legends. There was an anthology of Japanese translations of famous stories and novels from around the world. There were a few books in English, mostly related to Hiroshima and the atomic experience.

Walking around the center, Korean visitors were often surprised to see so many elderly people reading, given the low literacy rates of rural Koreans born in the 1920s and 30s. But many of the residents had learned to read in Japan as children, and had later applied that literacy to the task of learning to read Korean. There were a few female residents who only read Japanese, as they had not been sent to Korean schools or had not been able to learn some other way. The center staff were always on the lookout for Japanese-language book donations, and I organized donations now and then.

Residents had their own stashes of books and passed them around to one another—especially the Japanese ones, which made the circuit and were often read multiple times until other Japanese-language materials could be found. People also studied Bibles, Buddhist sutras, and books about religion. Throughout the day many residents also went down to read the newspaper at the rack in the lobby out front of the cafeteria, and newspapers and magazines circulated throughout the upper floors as well.

At the center, reading was a rich and meaningful practice. The quiet of religious reading was a work of seeking contentment, of seeking to understand fate via religious philosophy, to intervene in fate via prayer, and to visualize the future, as we saw Bae Il-myeong do. Reading in Japanese was a means of maintaining connections to Japan and a means of keeping one's own past alive, like Kim Pan-geun's perusal of train literature and Bae Il-myeong's readings from her son's calligraphy. At the same time, reading in Japanese, like all reading at the center, was about passing the time and about self-improvement. Then again, like other kinds of reading there, it was about rehearsing and performing literacy, a claim to a kind of class distinction which was inseparable from the effort of self-improvement. The quietude of the reader was an elite quiet, akin to the staid, traditional, aristocratic quiet of the painter or calligrapher.

Residents at the center were subject to a system of social welfare that administered to their health and well-being, one for which they were generally grateful. They were surrounded by medical and social welfare professionals. They spent a great deal of time being told what to do. They lived in a regime of health knowledge of which they could only partially partake. In the midst of this atmosphere everyday reading, and writing as well, were practices and performances of exclusive knowledge, practices of belonging to other sorts of knowledge communities than the ones to which they were subject, yet partially excluded from, in daily life.

———

Gu Gyeong-won, Yun Sugi's friend, swimming partner, and interlocutor, was the only current resident of the welfare center who had been to college, a fact of which he was tremendously proud. He had gone on to a career in the civil service, and then to business, and finished his career as a schoolteacher. He was generally happy at the welfare center and spoke highly of the staff and the quality of the rice; but he missed family, independence, and the love that one finds in the taste of home-cooked food. "This is someone else's house, you know? And I'm just living here," he told me.

Gu Gyeong-won kept up an impressive schedule at the welfare center. On top of his swimming, lunch, and coffee with Yun Sugi, and his participation in center activities, he was an avid calligrapher. He described himself as a hobbyist, which was a gesture of humility, but also an honorable label

Figure 6.3 Gu Gyeong-won practicing calligraphy at the welfare center, July 30, 2015. Photo by the author.

to bestow upon oneself in East Asian literate circles—one who practices high-cultural literacy for self-improvement and not for personal financial gain, like the literati of old.

In July 2015 I stood looking over his shoulder in the activity room across from the staff office on the first floor, where they had set up a small desk for him. He was seated, with a book on a stand before him, and was copying from it onto white *hanji*, traditional handmade Korean paper, with a long calligraphy brush. To the left of the book was his calligraphy box (*pilmukam*), in which he kept his brushes, calligraphy knife, inkstone (*byeoru*) and inkstick (*meok*). He had already ground the inkstick on the stone, and now he mixed the ink dust with water until a small pool of ink sat in the well of the stone. The paper was weighted down with two round bronze paperweights from Gyeongsang National University, his alma mater (Figure 6.3).

The book he had before him was a Korean translation and annotated guide to the *Caigentan*, the "Vegetable Roots Discourse" of the enigmatic Ming Dynasty scholar and philosopher Hong Zicheng (Hong 2013). The book is an eccentric collection of aphorisms that combines Confucian, Daoist, and Buddhist teachings. The title refers to the simple life of poverty the author led, with its steady diet of root vegetables; it also compares the cultivation of wisdom to the tending of plants.[8] In its eclectic pages Hong Zicheng advocates for moderation in life, work, and old age. The book has become a classic of Chinese philosophy, and literati have used for centuries in China, Korea, Japan, and elsewhere as a manual for right living.

The cover of Gu Gyeong-won's annotated copy of the book, published by the well-known educational publisher Gyohaksa, proclaims, "Let's learn from the wisdom of the virtuous and live today!" The book presents each of the aphorisms in turn, explaining rare Chinese characters and particular terms resulting from their combination. This is followed by a short Korean-language interpretation.

Gu Gyeong-won applied himself diligently to copying the aphorisms from the *Vegetable Roots Discourse*. The page in front of him was covered with his calligraphy. He was writing from left to right in even columns. At the top of the page was aphorism 102, a maxim for the practice of calligraphy: "To make an excellent piece of writing one does not need special skills. The best character is written without any fancy adornment." And then aphorism 118: "Novelty wears off soon. Austerity does not last long. He who likes novelty does not have a long-term perspective; those who live in abnormal austerity do not last long." And 169: "Be unique but not weird. Be clean but not extreme." And 242: "One who views wealth and power as passing clouds does not have to live in a remote area [like a monk]. Mountains and streams may provide great pleasure to an enlightened person, but poetry and wine will do the same."

Gu Gyeong-won worked by moving through the book in order, choosing aphorisms sometimes because of their Chinese characters, sometimes because of their content. At the end of the page he broke from this pattern and doubled back, working on aphorism 224: "Magnificent plum and pear blossoms wither soon, while plain cedars and pines persist. The fragrances of sweet pears and apricots are less stimulating than the scent of oranges and tangerines. It is true that the plain outlives the lavish, and late success is greater than early accomplishment." The passage was one of the book's many arguments for the durability of simplicity, as well as a reminder that things of great value take a long time to achieve.

Gu Gyeong-won skipped the Korean grammatical bits which were interpellated for clarity's sake into the Chinese text in the book. He didn't copy all of each aphorism, only selections, the parts he wanted to practice. He was not, then, copying out texts by rote, but selecting from them. Sometimes he reversed the orders of characters, like in the middle line

---

8. Translations of the title reflect this double meaning: Isobe Yaichiro's 1926 translation is *Thoughts of a Chinese Vegetarian*; Paul White's more recent translation is titled *Tending the Roots of Wisdom* (2003).

of the last aphorism, writing 何如 (how does it even compare) as 如何 (how?). He was focused not on the textual content as such, but the practice of writing. The textual content created a refined and learned environment, but it did not need to be reproduced exactly. It was an atmosphere. Writing the complex Chinese characters, on the other hand, was a practice of self-hood, self-improvement and maintenance, and social power. Gu Gyeong-won was one of the few residents of the center who could do it.

Until the twentieth century in Korea calligraphy was reserved for men of the elite. In the neo-Confucian Joseon Dynasty (1392–1910) the male royalty were taught to read and write so that they could study the Confucian classics and use them to govern wisely. Aristocratic men and members of the traditional middle class (*jungin*) learned reading and writing and studied the Confucian classics for reasons of self-improvement, or so they could pass the Confucian examinations that were the necessary gateway to careers in Joseon Dynasty bureaucracy. Scholars spent their entire lives copying Confucian classics. Writing was the means of passing the knowledge of the all-important ancestors into the future, and it is still valued by older generations of Koreans for this reason.

"Calligraphy derives its social power from the idea that writing is an integral part to becoming a person," writes Yuehping Yen in her compelling study of calligraphy and social power in contemporary China (Yen 2005: 32). Among the elderly in contemporary South Korea, it is a marker of a cultured person, and of that person's membership in a contemporary version of the scholarly class. As such, it continues to this day to be vested with notions of tremendous power and virtue.

Calligraphy is itself a kind of exercise, a kind of controlled application of strength. Proper calligraphic technique proscribes a relaxed, upright posture, and a relaxed grip on the brush. Philosophers of calligraphy through the centuries conceived of the brush stroke as a gesture of power; and yet the calligrapher must meticulously control that power to make the writing look effortless and graceful (Yen 2005: 85). Many enthusiasts treat calligraphy as part of their daily exercise regimen, part of the daily practice of disciplining and maintaining body and mind (ibid.: 107). Here as elsewhere, if one can make one's use of power seem natural and effortless, that power appears to be a legitimate, natural inheritance. Thus calligraphy, as a practice of literacy as power, also naturalizes that power as social.

Gu Gyeong-won rested his brush on his forefinger, with the other three fingers steadying the brush from behind. This is a non-standard grip: one typically holds the brush with thumb, first, and middle fingers, supporting with the other two from the back. He rested his right hand on top of his left hand and put his palm down on the paper to steady his writing. When he was done with a character—typically one character, but occasionally two simpler ones—he passed the brush to his left hand, dipped it, dabbed off extra ink if necessary, and passed it back to his writing hand. He then scrutinized the book for a moment or two, poised the brush above the paper, and continued.

⏵12

As he studied, Gu Gyeong-won attended carefully to his posture and proceeded slowly, stopping and taking care as he went. I watched him copy the second line of aphorism 224 from the *Vegetable Roots Discourse*, the one about the beautiful scent of the rather plain citrus flowers. He dipped and dabbed the brush, estimating how much ink he would need. At first, he worked quickly, taking about four seconds to ready the brush. But midway through the line he came on a string of complex characters and began to take more time. After readying the brush to write a complex or rare character, he paused, studying the book. Then he poised the brush over the paper, considering the character and his first stroke. On several occasions his writing hand fluttered up and down twice, wafting down in stages before allowing the brush to touch the page. Even his hesitation was graceful.

Such was Gu Gyeong-won's work of care and deliberation. There was no empty time and very little rest, but instead a measured progression of events. It was a free rhythm but nonetheless had rhythmic structure. These events—passing the brush, dipping and dabbing, and so on—were unequal in length, like the hill-walking that Vergunst (2008) wrote about, where people produce a sense of regularity by focusing on sequence rather than duration, and by the steady flow of continuous movement. Gu Gyeong-won's actions were well-articulated and transitioned seamlessly into one another. It was reminiscent of ceremonial behavior, in which ideas of hierarchy and order are prioritized over uniformity of duration or repetition, and the focus is shifted to sequence and flow. I was reminded of the loose time-feel of many East Asian court musics, which stress ordered events over measured durations. It felt lyrical, which was not surprising since it was an art of writing words. It was also a harmony of mind and body that produced single actions at precise moments. Gu Gyeong-won's calligraphy was a kind of exercise that brought together parts of his person into an ensemble idea of selfhood—a self that writes, makes meaning on a page, and interprets, remaking that meaning in contemplation. It was a self that subordinates emotion to action and contemplation, in the tradition of the Korean literati. Gu Gyeong-won's self and its practice were also profoundly imitative—imitating both the author of the *Vegetable Roots Discourse* and the scholarly tradition of copying—and the kind of selfhood he aspired to was on display.

One might expect calligraphy, as a practice of strength or energy, to abhor frailty. But age is welcome and prized, as it is in Hong Zicheng's aphorisms. The accumulated knowledge of age, the hard-won understandings, and the calm hand of a settled nature are all celebrated. Aphorism 224, which Gu Gyeong-won was working on, rehearsed the value of longevity. The quick may make a strong impression, like the intricate flowers of pear and apricot trees; but the enduring scent of tangerines and oranges—which do not have such brilliant flowers—lasts much longer. The quickly achieved is less valuable and interesting than that which takes its time in maturation. One should strive for simplicity and longevity in life and in scholarship.

Gu Gyeong-won practiced and reaffirmed this philosophical outlook and his scholarly identity at the calligraphy table, and also throughout everyday life. He did so when he stayed aloof from the complicated society of the welfare center, and when he sought out the healthfulness and simplicity of swimming. He did so when he drove Yun Sugi around Hapcheon County, taking in the sights—mountains, rivers, and lakes. He did so sitting at the computer on the third floor and watching nature videos on YouTube, many of which he showed to me, presenting them with no comment, a tableau of the quiet scholar contemplating the wonders of the natural world.

―――

In November 2011 I was sitting with An Buja in her room on the second floor in the West wing of the welfare center. She had asked me in for an instant coffee, which she took out from a drawer and put in a cup before taking these out into the common room to fill with hot water from the filtered water dispenser, all with great ceremony.

An Buja was eighty years old and shared the small room with her younger sister, An Palja. Their given names were plays on the words for "rich person" and "fortune," respectively.

An Buja, rich in spirit anyway, passed the time vigorously. She was one of the most public figures at the center, always in motion and at the center of social events. She lived on the second floor near the common room where most of the big events took place, and where group visitors were brought to socialize with survivors. She took part in most lectures, conferences, art sessions, teas, and karaoke sessions (Figure 6.4). As we sat together in her room, she pointed to the many photographs of herself taking part in center expeditions, and pictures of family and friends—many of whom she had met at the center. One photograph showed her on horseback, a wide-brimmed hat on her head, her left hand on the reins, her right arm rakishly bent with her hand on her waist.

Figure 6.4 An Buja sings *noraebang* (karaoke) at an event at the welfare center, October 22, 2011. Photo by the author.

An Buja had moved into the center in 2001 and after ten years felt a proprietary interest in the place. She took it upon herself to act as hostess and bustled around making coffee or tea for guests, serving snacks, and making outsiders feel welcome with casual conversation. She always had a cup of something—instant coffee, green tea, magnolia berry tea (*omijacha*)—for regular visitors like Shim Jintae or myself, or for special guests. As An Buja hosted she laid claim to the center as her home. And she made her life more interesting, meeting new people and consolidating and transforming her relationships with others.

On another day in 2011 I arrived at the center at midday, just in time to have lunch with the staff. An Buja greeted me, speaking with her characteristic blend of deference and familiarity. "*Osyeoseoyo?*" (So you've come?), she asked me formally, attaching an honorific to the verb and using a medium-polite *yo* sentence ending. "*Siksa hasyeoseoyo?*" (Have you eaten?), she asked, repeating the honorific pattern. I told her that I had been invited to have lunch with my friend Suhan and the other senior staff. "*Cha hanjan julkkayo?*" "Can I give you a cup of tea?" This was a familiar yet polite expression, a level down in terms of politeness from the former two statements, retaining the medium-polite *yo* ending but using the familiar verb for "to give" (*juda*) that elders use when speaking to their juniors.

As she navigated these inflections of hierarchy and intimacy she used standard Korean throughout, toning down her rich Southeastern dialect, although she didn't slow her quick way of talking, which is also characteristic of the region. She used standard Korean in a gesture of formality. Also, she was used to talking to people from elsewhere in the country and spoke standard Korean to make things easier for me to understand. She gauged these things to a nicety.

It was just before lunch, so there wasn't time for the cup of tea. But after lunch I found An Buja in the common area and she spirited me away to her room. She served me a cup of green tea with snacks, simply but elegantly prepared. She had found a small branch to use in place of a toothpick for skewering apple slices (Figure 6.5). "*Meositjiyo?*"—"Stylish, right?" she asked me. It was a stylish device indeed, expressive of an aesthetics which valued nature and naturalness, the kind of thing you read about in books on Korean traditional aesthetics and folk culture.

Figure 6.5 An Buja prepares a tray of apples, August 18, 2011. Photo by the author.

An Buja often pointed to her possessions that she felt had style (*meot*), and she also complemented herself on particularly stylish traits and behavior. Her pursuit of style was one part of a larger campaign for living that she had designed.

As I had tea, she told me stories: a folk tale about why there is no Year of the Cat, a story about the original meaning of the ubiquitous Korean new folk song (*sinminyo*) "Arirang," which is a kind of unofficial second national anthem. Whenever there was a pause, she would bring forth another anecdote, song, or question. Like Yi Suyong, she expressed concern that I was living in a rented room in a downtown Hapcheon motel with no one to spend time with or look out for me. She often sent me home with a heavy load of fruit and cartons of milk, which she told me to enjoy in the evenings when I was bored. She instructed me to stuff this plunder into my small camera bag, which looked about to explode when I left.

An Buja was an enthusiastic singer. She attended every center *noraebang* (karaoke) session in the common rooms from beginning to end. She took part in the multi-generational choir of radiation victims, organized by the Han Jeongsun and the Hapcheon Peacehouse, which rehearsed at the center once a week during its brief duration.

An Buja told me that singing was her favorite way of passing the time and that she often sang in her room. In contrast to many of the book-minded residents at the welfare center, she had only two items in her personal library, and they were both song books. One was a book of folk songs that she had gotten as part of a class she attended at the Hapcheon Social Welfare Center downtown, which we attended once together. The other was a binder of her favorite popular song lyrics that she had slowly accumulated, periodically asking the office staff to find and print lyrics for her.

As An Buja leafed through her binder she stopped on songs that she particularly liked. When I or others were there, her singing became part of her hosting, and she paused on songs that she felt would create opportunities for conversation or cultivate a pleasant atmosphere.

An Buja took out the binder filled with lyrics and began to leaf through it, showing her collection to me. She stopped on one of her current favorite songs, "The Broken Wall-Clock" ("Gojang nan byeoksigye"), crooner Na Hun-a's 2005 hit ballad in the *teuroteu* genre, a favorite pop genre of her generation. The genre evolved out of Japanese-influenced colonial popular song in the latter half of the twentieth century; its name is a Koreanization of the "trot" in "foxtrot." "'The Broken Wall-Clock' is a song that we grandmothers sing," An Buja told me. "Although that broken wall-clock has stopped, time and tide never break," she sang.

"This is a grandmothers' song because my life has up and passed," she told me. The broken clock tells you that time doesn't move, and yet you feel it slipping away. An Buja told me that she regretted the passage of time. But that regret also served to remind her of her past, and to remind her that time was yet still in motion. In the administered life of the welfare center, that bittersweet reminder was useful and important—it was an injunction to live intentionally. "I sing that song a lot, because I've become a grandma. *Meositjiyo?*" (stylish, right?), she said, and laughed.

An Buja's repertoire was mostly made up of late twentieth-century pop songs in the *teuroteu* genre and dominated by the genre's common themes of love, loss, nostalgia, and the passing of time and life. She was particularly fond of Na Hun-a and sang hits from the long span of his stardom from the 1960s to the present. She sang "Crying? Why Cry" ("Ulgin wae ureo," 1982) and "Please Send Back (my) Youth" ("Cheongchun-eul dollyeodayo," 1985). She also sang a few quite older popular songs— several songs from the early twentieth-century "new folk song" genre such as "Nodeul Riverbank" ("Nodeul Gangbyeon") and the ubiquitous new folk song "Arirang."

An Buja had the lyrics to Son Mogin's 1934 composition "Living Abroad" ("Tahyang sali"), that classic of expatriate life, and she sang it for me as I ate the apple slices. "Living Abroad" is a wistful recollection of one's hometown from the perspective of someone who has lived abroad for many years. "The willow tree in front of my home blossoms again this year; but it has been a long time since I plucked a reed and played the reed pipe there," An Buja concluded, singing the final verse while thumbing through the book. "I've been singing 'Living in a Foreign Land' for more than fifty years," she told me. "I didn't sing it when I was young," she said. She had started singing it on leaving Japan for Korea when she was fourteen. Now, since moving into the welfare center, she sang it thinking of her former life in her own home, with her three children and her husband, of whom she said she had been quite fond. "Life here is life abroad, and so that song comes into my thoughts," she told me.

As she reminisced about her family she showed me a picture she had drawn of herself and her husband as a young couple. It was one of many drawings she had done with the encouragement of an art therapy teacher and the staff. The drawing showed her looking elegant to a degree, in a gold necklace, purple earrings, and a spectacular red cloche hat with purple ribbon (Figure 6.6).

An Buja continued to reminisce of the past and began to sing some old Japanese songs which she remembered from her childhood—the 1940 film song duet "Niizuma kagami" (A New Wife's Mirror), among others. She also sang these when asked by visitors to sing songs from her childhood in Japan. And she sang them when she conversed with Japanese visitors. She

Figure 6.6 One of An Buja's drawings of herself and her husband.

told me she remembered singing in first and second grade at elementary school in Hiroshima.

An Buja had a singularly free way of singing. Many devotees of her favorite genre *teuroteu* are rather strict about adherence to original melodies and texts in their own renditions. They do so in the interest of participating in a collective knowledge of a song, in deference to and respect for professional singers and canonical versions, in the interest of claiming virtuosity, or in order to do things properly, a practice of propriety. In contrast, An Buja made little attempt to recall and match original tempos, melody, and sometimes even lyrics. She sang most of the time in a kind of recitative, halfway between speech and music, wavering between definite and indefinite pitch.

At iconic places in a melody, however, such as the culminating line about the clock in "The Broken Wall-Clock," her articulation of pitch became more focused and the canonical melody became clearly discernable. Her melodic freedom was not due to an inability to match pitch. Pitch-matching and precision were just not priorities for her. Her singing, poised between speech and song, never ventured far from the registers of conversation, which was her focus.

She followed this same pattern with respect to rhythm as well: she sang choruses closely adhering to the time signature, but otherwise sang more freely, without fixed meter. She didn't sing songs at the same tempo across versions but adjusted each song to the tenor and pace of the conversations upon which her songs entered. Chatting animatedly with several other women and myself in the second-floor common room, she sang her verse of "Broken Wall-Clock" in forty-one seconds, in the cut and thrust of energetic conversation. When we were at leisure alone together in her room, the same verse had taken almost a minute.

⏵13

An Buja stuck closely to the lyrics when singing through her song books. But in social settings she made some minor changes to lyrics, fusing verses together and modifying the order of words. She fused elements of the second verse of "The Broken Wall-Clock" into the first, perhaps by way of distilling the song's essence, or perhaps because she had forgotten the lyrics. In any case the combination she created was a minute-long unit that could be neatly inserted into conversation:

> Time and tide, why do you never even look back?
> You are crueler than the person who threw me away.
> I cried once because of love,
> That much time and tide has already passed . . .
> Although that broken clock on the wall has stopped,
> Time and tide never break.[9]

An Buja may have taken liberties with lyrics, but she was nonetheless remarkably true to the content of original versions. While she made changes, she did not, as others in my experience of her generation have done (see

9. *Sewora neoneun eojji dorado boji anneunya*
   Nareul beorin saramboda niga deouk mujeonghadeora
   Sarang ttae hanbeon ulgo natdeoni
   Jeomankeum gabeorin sewol
   Gojangnan byeoksigyeneun meomchueonneunde
   Seworeun gojangdo eomne.

Pilzer 2012: 67–104), alter meanings in the interest of assimilating the songs to her own life and making them speak to her experiences. This was perhaps the only realm where An Buja demonstrated such rule-abiding behaviors as a singer. Nonetheless, it showed that she balanced an appreciation for composed song texts with an otherwise general freedom to change things as she adjusted songs for herself and for use in her social life.

An Buja was, above all, interested in bringing the content of song to bear on the present moment. Singing was one way she deepened, energized, and personalized that present. When in a group, her songs always arose from conversation. She adjusted everything about the song but its meaning to the social environment, event, or conversation that the song arose from. She ribbed me warmly and incessantly with Nam Jin's 2009 hit "I Like You" ("Dangsini joa"), in ways that made other women at the center squeal with laughter and even embarrassment. She brought out the "The Broken Wall-Clock" when the conversation turned to the topic of aging or the passage of time, and she sang Japanese songs when the subject turned to her childhood there. Her singing was an aspect of her general socializing, of her hosting, of her dynamic social role at the welfare center, and of her energetic approach to life and the present. It was part of the way that she stayed in the game: she made the place her own, she made friends, she made the self that sat at the helm, and she made the time of life her own.

———

Walking, swimming, drinking, exercise, calligraphy, singing: many of the practices we have encountered so far in this chapter were in part practices of passing time. These pastimes were accompanied by a rich discourse of passing the time in both Korean and Japanese—in Korean *shiganeul bonaeda*, literally "to send time," and in Japanese *jikan o sugosu*, quite close to the English "passing time."

When most residents at the center spoke of passing or sending time, they did so in an offhand, dismissive way that suggested that whatever they were doing was rather unimportant—just a means of spending days when there is nothing else to do, passing time in retirement, which Yun Sugi referred to in Japanese as the "season of twilight" (*tasogare no jiki*). This dismissal was important for the way that it contrasted the present with more youthful and elevated pasts.

And yet the melancholy of such statements was a clue that the work of passing the time in the present was rather important as well. This elderly community had an overwhelming sense of not having that much time left, even as the days seemed long. Time was, for many, precious and preciously spent. Residents were shadowed by a sense of lack—of the society and the purpose which had formerly animated and guided life, and of the relative autonomy of that life. Residents were far from their former homes and families. They were retired and lived on pensions and subsidies, including the stipend from the Japanese government for bomb victims, and of course the support of the welfare center. The future can feel far away when the past is far away; days stretch on like one another into an eternal present, which nonetheless slips inexorably and finally away, whether or not the clocks are on time, fast, late, or broken.

Passing time at the center was, in part, an artful response to these concerns. It was variously about maintaining a sense of self, struggling to control one's own fate in the midst of an administered life, making the impersonal welfare center into a home, keeping up one's health, and sustaining social positions and relations, many of which predated life at the center.

People strive to remain themselves through the struggle for time. The struggle to jumpstart the broken wall-clock, to maintain the sense that time is passing under some degree of one's own governance, is crucial to this. The moving hands of the clock enable one to sense the past, to fight for ownership of the present, and to imagine a future to look forward to.

Residents thus developed elaborate awarenesses of the center's weekly schedules, the intersections of Gregorian and Korean lunisolar calendars, and their own meticulous daily routines, punctuated by meals, medicine, prayer, events, and many personal routines, as we saw with Yi Suyong and even more so with Bae Ilmyeong. To be aware of time is to frame it in terms of qualities and quantities, and to design one's own consciousness of life in its passing. Being aware of time and exercising some measure of control over it are interwoven processes, because marking time is also a work of making time, or at least wresting partial governance of it from the institution and the world beyond. And marking and making time are acts of making and sustaining the self in the face of its mortification by institutional life and as a part of aging.

Yi Suyong's speaking style, her prayer and her pottery; Bae Ilmyeong's conversation, clocks, and calendars; Pak Heun-il's walking; Yun Sugi and Gu Gyeong-won's swimming; Yun Sugi's table tennis; men's ceremonialized drinking; Gu Gyeong-won's calligraphy; An Buja's hosting and singing— these acts allowed these people not just to measure and mark the passing of time, but also to stamp their daily lives, to stamp their experience of time's passing with a pattern of their own choosing, and to solidify the sense of past, present, and future necessary to sustain the self. And we find within these casual activities by which elderly people pass the time a rich work of social life and selfhood: in short, an energized present and an art of life. Korean bomb victims who live at the welfare center may sometimes find the quality of life and continuity of self in extraordinary moments of walking the halls of memory and expressing those experiences. But in the day-to-day lives of residents such memories are only occasionally welcome, and we find the quality of life and the continuity of self upon more mundane, everyday terrain.

CHAPTER 7
Han Jeongsun

Though I cross mountain pass after mountain pass, one more yet remains.
Though I cross and cross, this endless road of mountain passes . . . [1]

—Han Jeongsun, *"Hot Pepper"*

In that long talk that Bae Ilmyeong had begun about life in Japan and the postwar period, her conversational partner Gu Seon-i had eventually taken the reins and told her own story, the tale of her long struggle to raise her children and her travels from Hiroshima to Hapcheon and elsewhere in South Korea. She spoke about her eldest son, who was a high-ranking officer in the Hapcheon police department, and about moving to Jinju with her daughter-in-law so that one of her grandsons could get a better education. She had two sons and four daughters. She didn't speak about any of her daughters or granddaughters.

One evening in July 2011 I sat in a private room of one of Hapcheon's several *noraebang* (karaoke) bars with Gu Seon-i's youngest daughter (*mangnaettal*), Han Jeongsun, President of the second-generation-focused community center Hapcheon Peacehouse and the affiliated Second Generation Atomic Bomb Sufferers Association (see Figure 7.1). The secretary of the Peacehouse was with us as well. Han Jeongsun was singing Yi Hyojeong's 2002 pop hit "Our Mother," which told the story of a long-suffering mother of six children who develops Alzheimer's disease in her old age. She ended the song:

1. *Gogae gogae neomeogado tto han gogae namanne*
   Neomeogado neomeogado kkeuchi eomneun gogaetgil

Quietude. Joshua D. Pilzer, Oxford University Press. © Oxford University Press 2023.
DOI: 10.1093/oso/9780197615089.003.0007

Our mother
You couldn't sleep at night
For worrying about your six children
You've had a thorny road for seventy lifetimes
I thought you'd live forever
But now the day you will leave us isn't so far off
Your youngest daughter cried
Your youngest daughter cried.[2]

Han Jeongsun noted the amazing similarities between the song and her family. She was the youngest daughter of six. Her mother had developed Alzheimer's dementia in recent years and she sensed that her life was nearing its end, and it was a constant source of sorrow for her. But in this song's ruminations on a village mother and her youngest daughter, Han Jeongsun, the child of a bomb victim and a radiation sufferer herself, found comfort; she found her way from banishment on the periphery of Korean public consciousness into the very heart and soul of Korean popular culture and society.

———

Han Jeongsun's parents were both from Hapcheon and had gone to Hiroshima when they were young. Both of them were there on the day of the bombing—Gu Seon-i was nineteen years old and her husband was in his late twenties. Gu Seon-i had gone to Japan with her own mother following her older brother, who had gone there for work. Han Jeongsun's father was the oldest of eight brothers and had gone to Japan with his whole family. He brought them back to Korea after the war ended. He struggled with heart disease for decades and died in 1979. Gu Seon-i's Alzheimer's advanced dramatically in the years after we met; she passed away in 2017 at ninety-one years of age, when Han Jeongsun was fifty-seven.

I got to know Han Jeongsun starting in 2011, when I spent several months living at the Hapcheon Peacehouse, the little center of community, social welfare support, and political activism for Korean

2. *Urieomeoni . . .*
   Yeoseonnammae jasikgeokjeong bamjameul mosirugo
   Chilsippyeongsaeng gasibatgil saraosyeonne
   Cheonmannyeon sasineunjul arasseonneunde
   Tteonasillal geudajido meolji anaseo
   Mangnaettaleun ureotdamnida
   Mangnaettaleun ureotdamnida

Figure 7.1 Han Jeongsun (right) walking in Hapcheon Market with Jin Gyeongsuk, November 8, 2011. Photo by the author.

second-generation radiation sufferers.[3] As President of the Sufferers Association and the Peacehouse, she split her time between Daegu, where she had a small apartment, and Hapcheon, where she ran the Peacehouse, gave presentations for students and Japanese visitors, took part in annual and seasonal events for bomb survivors and radiation sufferers, and traveled around the district visiting second-generation bomb victims in need of welfare support.

Han Jeongsun had physical difficulties, which she linked to her parents' radiation exposure. She began to suspect something was wrong with her legs at age fifteen, when she was in middle school. But since the age of thirty, she suffered from osteonecrosis (literally "bone death") of the femoral head, a condition in which interrupted blood flow causes cellular death of bone components in the tops of both femurs. This caused her hips to collapse. She spent years in her early thirties in such pain that she was unable to stand, and she got around by pushing herself around on her palms.

3. This was not our first meeting. I first met Han Jeongsun at the House of Sharing, a rest home and center of activism for survivors of the "comfort women" system, sometime in the mid-2000s, when we both were visiting. We also met in the summer of 2010, on my first trip to Hapcheon.

Soon after this, Han Jeongsun had hip replacement surgery; but the process of bone death was ongoing and soon after she needed another replacement. She has had four thus far. She told me that the pain of recovery from these surgeries lasts for months. She spoke of the agony of standing, and of the agony of sitting after she had stood, and of the fear to do either. She said the most terrifying thing was the idea of getting stuck—immobilized by pain—while crossing the broad streets of Daegu, hostile to even ordinary pedestrians.

Han Jeongsun raised two sons with great difficulty during the onset and the progression of her condition. Her eldest son has cerebral palsy; she considered both her and his conditions to be inherited results of her parents' radiation exposure. She felt this way about the heart problems suffered by two of her older brothers as well. Her family was rife with disabilities and illnesses that are prevalent among the children and grandchildren of bomb survivors and victims of nuclear radiation.

Han Jeongsun told me guardedly of her divorce, and of losing custody of her two children to their father, which is typical in divorce cases in South Korea. She told me of the debilitating depression that she struggled with, which combined with her physical difficulties to cause total collapse. She lived off and on with her big sister, unable to afford her own apartment. She tried to drink *soju*, Korean liquor, to self-medicate, but ended up in the hospital with an extreme allergic reaction to alcohol.

"There was no one to offer me a helping hand," Han Jeongsun told me. After some months, she decided she couldn't go on living without making a change. She resolved to go out in the world and help others with similar struggles, to take them by the hand when they needed one.

The importance of the hand—both literal and metaphorical—played through her story of herself and her vision of the world. Han Jeongsun was in considerable physical pain, and at times she struggled to walk at all. But she knew herself to be capable of reaching out to others and giving them a helping hand, and she was reborn in the pursuit of her new purpose. Around this time, she was interviewed for a book of testimonies of second-generation radiation sufferers put together by Solidarity for Peace and Human Rights of Asia. She told the interviewer "I have no interest in receiving some sort of benefit and just sitting down to eat and play around. The fact that I am able to move . . . if there is work that I can do, I don't want to sit down and just let life pass me by . . . if there is something I can do, I want to do it" (Solidarity for Peace and Human Rights of Asia 2006: 151). At the end of her testimony, she lamented her financial difficulties, which kept her busy at work and without time to volunteer.

But Han Jeongsun gradually became active in the Korean Second Generation Atomic Bomb Sufferers Association, joining local events, protests, and gatherings throughout the country. Several years after the death of founder and president Kim Hyeongryul, whose voice opens the preface of this book, she became president of the Sufferers Association and the newly established Hapcheon Peacehouse, a brainchild of Hyeongryul's that he did not live to see realized.

Until 2013 Han Jeongsun supported herself by working one seventy-two-hour shift a week at a hospital in Daegu, about an hour away from Hapcheon, to supplement her small disability stipend. The government stipend was from the state's general disability fund, and not related to her status as a second-generation radiation sufferer—there was and remains no governmental support for the second generation.

Han Jeongsun slept at her spare apartment in west Daegu only one or two nights a week and spent the rest of her nights either at the hospital or in Hapcheon, visiting second-generation sufferers, whom she said "have more difficulty living than I do" (see Figure 7.2). She paid regular visits to check on victims and see to the welfare of the aging parents who cared for them. I went with her on many of these visits: to meet a man who had suddenly and mysteriously gone blind and the octogenarian mother who cared for him; to visit a pair of brothers with Down syndrome who lived alone in the countryside; to visit the Jeon family, who had two daughters with

Figure 7.2 Han Jeongsun (at left) visiting the Jeon family residence, August 12, 2016. Photo by the author.

mental disabilities, one severe, whose mother and brother supported them through farm work. She attempted to prevent the villagers among whom they lived from exploiting their disabilities, such as the farmer who had used a young man with Down syndrome for unpaid labor in the fields to "give him something to do." She picked up people to take to the Peacehouse for activities, many of which she programmed and oversaw. When she retired from nursing work at the Daegu hospital she devoted herself to her activism and social welfare work in Hapcheon and took up fulltime residence there. In 2016, when the Peacehouse opened a residential facility, she was in the middle of its efforts to bring people there to live. The residence closed down the next year, due to the reluctance of radiation sufferers and their parents to live separately.

After becoming President of the Sufferers Association, Han Jeongsun became one of the most prominent and outspoken activists in the movement on behalf of the second generation. After finishing her term as President, she remained active in second-generation activism in Hapcheon and beyond, and was eventually made Honorary President for an indefinite term due to her centrality in the movement.

Han Jeongsun was a kind of spokesperson and ambassador for second-generation Korean radiation victims, in much the same way that Shim Jintae was for first-generation Korean bomb survivors. In the course of their ambassadorial duties, they met many of the same press people, activists, and other visitors in Hapcheon. They traveled together to give testimony and to protest. They traveled around South Korea and Japan together raising awareness about Korean atom bomb and radiation victims. Han Jeongsun was with Shim Jintae and I that day in Hiroshima outside the gates of the Peace Memorial Park, calling on President Obama to apologize for the bombings (see Figure 2.3).

Like Shim Jintae, Han Jeongsun had been appointed to her position because of her energy and her eloquence. She was a skilled and often ebullient master of ceremonies, entertaining people with song and story in her high, musical voice through the bus PA on the biannual sightseeing trips for radiation victims and their parents that the Peacehouse sponsored. She peppered her speeches with the thematic content and expressive devices of *teuroteu*, the Korean sentimental pop ballad genre of which An Buja was also a devotee. Han Jeongsun's testimonies were both personal and philosophical, combining discussion of her own background with her observations of the life situations of other members of the second generation and with her political views. She spoke movingly about the need for Japan and the United States to take responsibility for the far-reaching consequences of nuclear war, and for Korean society to take care of its own. She spoke the language of the international discourse about nuclear victims, as she folded Korean victims into that identity. She also spoke fluently in the post-authoritarian South Korean discourse of victimization—that lynchpin of post-colonial South Korean national identity—by which she staked a claim for members of the second generation to membership in Korea's tragic panoply of victims of colonialism, war, and authoritarian repression. Making these forceful and effective claims to membership in these moral communities, Han Jeongsun was thus enabled to demand consideration from both Korean and Japanese governments similar to those afforded to other victims, and to make similar demands towards the United States.

On a hot August evening in 2011 Han Jeongsun and I sat in a small room in the Hapcheon Nature School. Pak Jinpil and Hwang Se-gyeong, the couple that ran the school, had invited Shim Jintae and Han Jeongsun out to the repurposed elementary school in the countryside to speak to campers enrolled in the school's week-long Peace Camp.

Shim Jintae had just spoken to the group about the experiences of the first generation, ending by asking them not to forget about Korea's atomic history and its atomic bomb victims and radiation sufferers. Now Principal Hwang introduced Han Jeongsun, who began by greeting the campers, mentioning that they must be tired after such a long day. She quizzed them about the request Shim Jintae had made of them, guessing that they had forgotten. A young girl answered that he had asked them to remember "Korea's Hiroshima."

Han Jeongsun's voice rose and fell in a loud, definite-pitched arc of delight. "O~h! Applause!" she said, exhorting the other students to clap. It was a near-musical exclamation, well above her usual speaking range; she made it now, but also when people finished singing at social events, and even at the end of her own songs in half-mocking self-appreciation. It was a simple moment, but by creating this excuse to praise the student like a proud teacher or parent, she brought them that much closer together. The other campers broke into applause, shouting the girls name in appreciation.

Han Jeongsun began to speak, ruminating on the nature of the "peace" in the moniker "Peace Camp." "This thing called, peace," she said, "what is it?" It is a state of mind, she said, which the world either makes possible or does not. The atomic bomb, she said, began a war which did not end. That is because, she said, the effect of radiation is to make peace of mind impossible for those who live with its effects, regardless of whether or not nations are "at war."

The intergenerational transference of victimhood, she said, made the bomb very unusual, and hence it was little understood and easily overlooked. Because of that legacy, she said, the bomb was not something which happened back then, but something that keeps happening every day to those living with its effects, down the generations. Her war, she said, "began the day I was born." At other times, also, she told me and others that the war would end for radiation sufferers on the day they died; but she refrained from mentioning this now. She spoke of the importance of Korean government support and of Japanese apology and reparations. She told of the difficulties the second generation faces living with the genetic inheritance of the bomb with no special medical attention.

Han Jeongsun spoke about the relatively new arrangement made with Hapcheon Hospital and Hapcheon Goryeo Clinic to treat second-generation victims for free, just like first-generation survivors, and the tremendous warmth and caring that motivated that decision. The warmth of that kindness is so precious, she said: you can feel that warmth, as well, in the hands of victims. "If they offer you their hand, please take it . . . Try and give them the peace in your mind," she said. And so she came back to her opening rumination on the nature of peace, tying it together with the gestures of hand-holding of which she spoke so often, and which formed such an important part of her own self-narration and sense of purpose. She borrowed themes and expressive devices from her self-narration for her activist speech, and vice-versa. And as she returned to the theme of peace, she showed another aspect of her rhetorical brilliance: she gave a bookended, symmetrical form to the entire speech, something we shall see her do again.

Han Jeongsun's vast expressive abilities arose from a facility and creativity with language, but also from her remarkable facility with her voice. At the Nature School, Han Jeongsun spoke for the most part in a low, sing-song voice, punctuating her speech with exclamations, sighs, and other instances of definite pitch vocalization. Her sentences generally followed two pitch contours, one which rose and fell in an arch, and another which settled along a descending contour. Her arching sentences reached up to two relatively distinct plateaus of high and mid-range pitch, before settling down to sentence endings in the relatively indefinite lower register from which she had departed, which served as the baseline of her speech. Her "settling" sentences began with a high outburst and settled back down to earth.

Even at her most oratorical, Han Jeongsun did not rise to peaks of emphatic speech, in the manner of many Western orators. She descended from emphatic speech to a kind of home base, a kind of tonal center, with its intimations of naturalness, rest, and finality, in the manner of the most crucial moments in Korean folk song and *teuroteu*, her favorite genre of popular song.

Han Jeongsun added expressivity to her voice by varying the pitch register at which she spoke. At Hapcheon Nature School she spoke in a notably lower register and narrower range than when speaking to me casually or when singing. She spoke this way to make her voice comparatively unornamented, in a stylistic gesture of humility found throughout the atom bomb victims movement: she wished to speak on behalf of others and not draw attention to herself. She also spoke in this low register for purposes of intimacy: she spoke to the campers like a kindly, confiding aunt speaking of intimate and difficult things. Her voice emphasized not itself but its message and the social relation between the students and herself. She referred to herself several times as "auntie" (*ajumma*), a word used to refer to middle-aged women, invoking the auntie figure of the fictive kinship that is such an important part of Korean social relations.

Han Jeongsun spoke of herself as an "ill-formed Auntie" (*meonnan ajumma*), a phrase by which she offered herself as evidence of the plight of second-generation radiation sufferers. But this was the only time when she spoke about herself. In general, she steered clear of discussing her own story when speaking publicly, only giving details when pressed. When people asked her for the details of her medical condition, or when she was called upon to speak as an individual victim, she spoke fluently and well about her condition and her experiences, but returned the conversation quickly to speaking about others, or to discussing her advocacy work. When speaking of herself, she preferred not to dwell on her own status as a victim but to speak of her activism. She told me she found speaking about those things in a formal setting to be rather trying, because she had become accustomed to grinning and bearing them. Even in private, in casual talk, she told me, it was very rare for her to speak of her own struggles with any specificity and at any great length.

Han Jeongsun's speech about her social and political activity was part of a process of empowerment—her voice was a source of her power, and here it also projected her many other abilities, rooted for them, and encouraged her to action—her ability to get up, to walk, to speak on behalf of others. But her aversion to speaking of her own troubles bore the stamp of the stiff-upper-lip spirit of the authoritarian era and its repression of suffering in the name of national progress, the period in which she had come of age. In this way, Han Jeongsun, like many of the first generation we have encountered, partook of a kind of quietude about herself in speech, her own version of the quiet of "Korea's Hiroshima," despite being such a vocal and verbal person.

I have heard moments when the membrane of Han Jeongsun's restraint gave way, although even then she was quiet about herself. A television crew interviewed her in 2016 a few days after Independence Day, the annual season of South Korean public cultural interest in the colonial past. She began by discussing the general situation of the second generation and the demands that the Sufferers Association had made of the Korean state, Japan, and the United States. Her voice was strong, and higher than it had been at the Nature School. She spoke of the community of second-generation radiation sufferers as "us," and advocated for its needs and wishes in impassioned political oratory, avoiding speaking the first person. This was a voice of complaint made resolutely public, vastly different from the voice of intimacy and selflessness I heard her use at the Nature School. It was a voice of a resolutely political solidarity, of people united in injury, set against those who had victimized, marginalized, and neglected them. Speaking as the voice of the community was yet another way to balance her wish to speak out with the necessity of doing so without appearing selfishly motivated.

As the interview progressed, however, Han Jeongsun touched a more personal note. She was speaking of the extreme difficulties that some second- and third-generation radiation sufferers face in life. She passed over her own struggles and began to speak of her son, and his quite debilitating form of cerebral palsy. "He spends all day laying down," she said. What sort of life could he have in a vigorous, frenzied South Korean "competition society" hostile to disabilities? Her voice dropped to a lower register, and she spoke quietly. "Imagine how that must feel," she said.

She went on to speak of her mother, Gu Seon-i, Bae Ilmyeong's conversation partner. She said that her progressed Alzheimer's had given her back her happiness, because for the first time she had been able to forget the bomb and its aftermath.

Han Jeongsun began to cry. Whereas she had emphasized the collective before, she spoke of family here. The forcefulness went out of her voice and the voice of familial intimacy returned as she spoke of the suffering of her family.

But she refrained from speaking of her own struggles even here, despite being given every opportunity. She spoke *around* herself; she was a gravitational center that rarely came into focus. Her mode of speech was, like Bae Ilmyeong's, reminiscent of Eve Sedgwick's notion of periperformative expression. It was not so much that she was unable to speak of her own suffering as that she preferred not to, and that there was much to gain from deemphasizing it. As she raised her voice in empathy with others' suffering, she performed the role of the caregiver, and she found confidence and a measure of power in that role.

But Han Jeongsun said that she lacked sufficient power to actually help others. Her voice faltered as she said this, expressing appeal in the face of this helplessness. She spoke not so much to the television crew as to their imagined audience and appealed to the public to help. She asked people in South Korea's active civil society to demand justice and care for second-generation radiation sufferers. She spoke to the South Korean state, which was still a year out from enacting the "Special Act for Supporting Korean Atomic Bomb Victims," in the hope that the special act would include support for subsequent generations of radiation sufferers. She also mentioned the Japanese government, whom she felt should treat second-generation radiation sufferers the same as first-generation bomb victims.

The combined power of people and the state would still be insufficient, she went on to say. Radiation suffering cannot be cured or expunged: it is with you from the day of your birth until you die, whether you know it or not. And it endures beyond the term of a single generation, and you never know when it will strike. The interview ended in tears.

In another interview that same Independence Day season, Han Jeongsun spoke with Sungkonghoe University history professor Han Hongkoo on his internet television program. Speaking about the second generation, she told him that "In order for radiation sufferers to have *our* Independence Day, we have to die." This was another appeal for the care and consideration—*baeryeo*—of the public and the state, by demonstrating the extremity of radiation sufferers' position. But it was also a kind of terminus of thought, a place that social action could not touch. Speech, too, could only trace—in its cessation—the outline of that space of resignation. Thus another reason Han Jeongsun's voice grew softer and faltered was that she was on her way to silence.

Han Jeongsun's headshot for the advertisement of that program shows her against a black background (Figure 7.3). Her shoulders are swathed in a black shawl, which fades into the black back drop. Her face and hands stand out, however, just as Yi Suyong's face had stood out in the "Hapcheon's Tears" article. In the program, Han Jeongsun's quiet voice and its finality resonate with that same South Korean post-colonial culture of injury

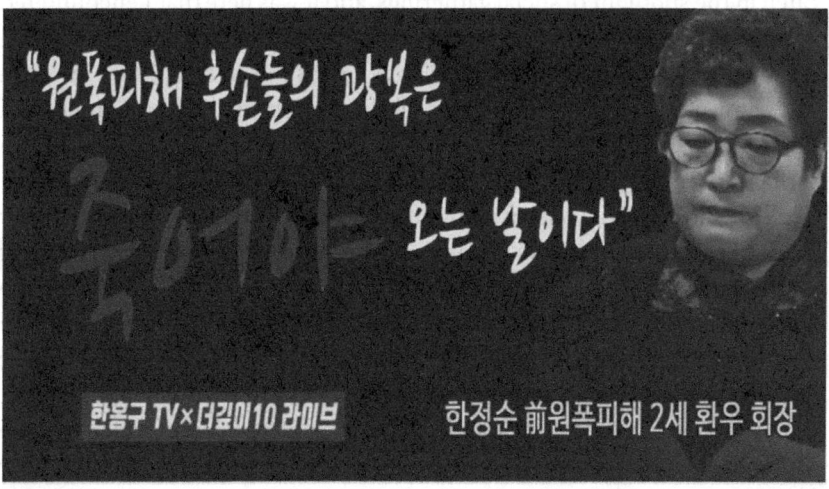

Figure 7.3 The advertisement and title page of the episode of Han Hongkoo's interview with Han Jeongsun.

and its discourses of silence which Yi Suyong navigated so adroitly. Han Jeongsun knew what she had to do to make people listen to her voice. And yet her voice was not silence, or something that merely drew outlines around silences. It was a species of the quiet of "Korea's Hiroshima," which spoke clearly if quietly.

Han Jeongsun was a tremendously vocal person, despite avoiding subjects about which she preferred not to speak. She spoke eloquently of the suffering of the second generation, and of her family. She spoke of how important it was that people in society care for one another, and that governments care for their most precarious charges. The things that she refrained from speaking about were a source of power and voice for her— refraining from discussing her own suffering, she emphasized her abilities. And the suffering that she circumscribed with her silence fueled her outrage and amplified her voice.

———

Han Jeongsun loved singing and told me that songs had been there for her when no one else had. She had always loved to sing, she said, and she had sung to herself and gone to *noraebang* (karaoke) rooms since she was young. She, like An Buja, was devoted to *teuroteu*, the sentimental pop ballad genre, although much of her repertoire was a shade younger. Singing for me over the years, and weaving song and speech together in personal narrative, she showed me a great reservoir of expressive ability and power that motivated her everyday and activist speech.

In her central position in the second-generation movement, she was often in the spotlight of social gatherings, and it was here that I encountered Han Jeongsun the singer and weaver of song into story for the first time. In the manner of other members of her generation, she sang often in social and semi-official settings by way of self-introduction and in the interest of entertaining herself and others. She sang forcefully in her high, reedy, glittering voice, relating the generic laments of popular song as if they were her own; in this way she used popular songs to probe the nature of her own sufferings and sorrows and to connect these experiences with those of others. When she sang, she cast off the traces of deference that often made their way into her activist speaking voice. Shielded by the fact that these popular songs were written by others, she sang them rather obviously about her own suffering, and even occasionally admitted that to me in speech. And she looked to the power and expressivity of her singing voice and the structures and dynamism of music to energize other parts of her life—her activist speech, her daily struggle to walk. And that voice, which lived at the center of the Hapcheon Peacehouse and the movement on behalf of

Korean radiation sufferers, echoed far and wide in Hapcheon and left its imprint on the movement.

Han Jeongsun wove pop songs throughout her everyday life. She continually updated her cell phone ringtone to her new favorite *teuroteu* songs and discoursed happily and earnestly about them all. She quoted from across the landscape of the genre and burst into snippets of song when something in conversation reminded her of one. In contrast to Yi Suyong and Bae Ilmyeong, who demusicalized speech and prayer, Han Jeongsun spent her days endeavoring to fill her life with song.

The *teuroteu* genre, which reached its heyday in the seventies and eighties, is largely concerned with loss, struggle, and woundedness. Like Japanese *enka*, it is a genre which binds its listening public together in a mutual sharing of the tribulations and tragedies of the modern world, fostering a "communally broken heart" (Yano 2002: 3). This heart is a damaged yet resilient core of modern Korean identity. Han Jeongsun used the tropes and forms of broken-heartedness, woundedness, and loss in the genre to bind herself, her fellow radiation sufferers, and their marginalized experiences to this core of national identity. And in this world of song, she cultivated the voice which she used in political speech, which was itself quite musical.

I sat many evenings at the Hapcheon Peacehouse listening to Han Jeongsun sing. She folded songs and speech together in long narratives of impressive length and intricate construction, which were tapestries of identity. She wove the texts and tropes of *teuroteu* into her spoken narratives, and she moved fluidly between speech and song, her speaking voice shading towards music, song erupting out of speech.

Song was a special expressive space to which Han Jeongsun was greatly attached, and in the midst of her long narratives she showed a reluctance to return to the register of mundane speech. She resented interruptions: one night at Hapcheon Peacehouse in 2014 as she sang and spoke, Secretary Jin Gyeongsuk asked her for a phone number she needed. Han Jeongsun sighed, found the number on her cell phone, and sang it out rather than coming down from that exalted place in which music and speech are conjoined.

On an evening of socializing in October 2011, we were sitting in the main room of the Peacehouse with Secretary Jin Gyeongsuk and Mr. Okada, a Japanese activist and language teacher who was visiting from Daegu, who had facilitated the interview with Yi Suyong discussed at the end of Chapter 4. Mr. Okada taught free Japanese language classes at night in Daegu, and both Han Jeongsun and the secretary were attending. They called him Okada *sensei*, using the Japanese word for teacher. Okada *sensei* had brought his guitar, and so we sat together singing Japanese protest songs and Korean folk and popular songs, and talking (see Figure 7.4).

Figure 7.4 Han Jeongsun (Centre) and Jin Gyeongsuk look through a song book while Okada *sensei* tunes up, October 19, 2011. Photo by the author.

Before us was a generous spread of snacks and drinks—grapes, Japanese *kakiage* (fritters) we had bought earlier at a local festival, Korean mugwort pancakes (*ssukjeon*), an assortment of dried snacks, beer, *soju*, and *makgeolli*, Korean unfiltered rice wine. Han Jeongsun drank orange juice. "I would like to be able to drink alcohol and let go of my pains and troubles," she lamented.

We spent an hour or so singing and talking, while Okada *sensei* strummed the guitar. He led us through "Aoi sora wa" ("The Blue Sky"), a 1971 peace movement song about the bombing of Hiroshima. We looked through a book of popular Korean folk songs, many of which Han Jeongsun knew, and I pointed out the song "Haebangga" ("Liberation Song"), a modern variant of a famous folk song[4] that narrates the end of the colonial period and the outbreak of the Korean War. It is the only canonical folk song I know that makes reference to the atomic bombing of Japan: "Everybody else's husbands lived and came back, so why couldn't mine? Was he struck by the atomic bomb? Why do I have no news?"

4. "Changbu taryeong" ("Ballad of the Traveling Entertainer"), a folk song from Gyeonggi Province popular throughout the peninsula.

As time passed, I noticed that Han Jeongsun was eating a kind of puffed corn snack (*oksusu ppeongtwigi*) with the onomatopoetic brand name "*ppeongsori*" ("*ppeong* sound"). This "*ppeong*" refers to the sound that is made when the grains, heated in a sealed container, are suddenly released, expanding rapidly all at once.

Han Jeongsun was eating the snacks with chopsticks, choosing each one with methodical precision. When I pointed this out, she laughed, and thought for a heartbeat about how to answer. Instead of speaking, she burst out in song, seemingly apropos of nothing:

▶14

> In this world full of han, cold-hearted lover,
> You depart, leaving your heart to me, and I cry . . .
> Of course it is so, surely it is so . . .
> I say "let's live 500 years," and why do you fuss?
> A devastating love trampled by youth—
> It's so heartless that I don't think I can live.[5]

The song was "Han obaengnyeon" ("About 500 Years"), a Gangwon province folk song popularized by Seoul-area singers in the early twentieth century, and again by late-twentieth-century pop stars. The song's title plays on the complex emotional cluster concept *han*. Often translated along the lines of "resentful sorrow," *han* rose to prominence as a discourse of emotion in the struggle against authoritarianism in post-colonial South Korea (see Sasse 1991) and is now a keyword of a South Korean national identity rooted in colonial and post-colonial suffering (see Chi Kim 2017). The song is performed by many pop singers nowadays; Han Jeongsun's was based on a 1979 version made famous by the *teuroteu*-inflected rocker Jo Yongpil. Yu Ji-na, one of Han Jeongsun's favorite singers, sang it as well.

Han Jeongsun sang the last line and burst out laughing without a pause. As our applause faded away Okada *sensei* spoke:

▶15

5. *Han maneun isesang yasokan nima*
   Jeongeul dugo momman gani nunmuri nane
   Amuryeom geureochi geureoku malgo
   Han obaengnyeon saljaneunde wen seonghwayo
   Cheongchune jitbaphin aekkeulleun sarang
   Dongjeongsim eopseoseo naneun motsalgenne

OKADA *sensei*:	"About 500 Years."
JOSH:	Why did you suddenly sing "About 500 Years?"
HAN JEONGSUN:	Eh?
JOSH:	I asked why you suddenly sang "About 500 Years."
JIN GYEONGSUK:	*Ppeongsori* with chopsticks . . . she got fed up with life—

HAN JEONGSUN: *Ppeongsori* . . . I've been sitting here coooonstantly picking up and eating *ppeongsori* one by one, and so [Josh: That's how you've passed five hundred years of *han*.] . . . this world full of *han*, if I want to live in it . . . I mean that (fate) tells me to grab the *ppeongsori* [that way], and so I eat them, passing the time of life that way . . . (general laughter)

HAN JEONGSUN: Dipping them in my tears. (laughs)[6]

At these words everyone fell silent, crunching *ppeongsori*.

After a short pause, Han Jeongsun went on to speak of the importance of "Han obaengnyeon" for people who have lots of *han* in their lives. Jin Gyeongsuk chimed in, wondering why she didn't much care for the song. "Perhaps because I have no *han*?" she joked. Han Jeongsun began to talk about young mothers in traditional Korea, raising children alone, singing a song like this and finding solace in it as an opportunity for the expression of accumulated despair. She modulated to the present and described the difficulties a woman faces living alone—of survival, of unresolved sorrows. She didn't identify that woman as herself; but she had spoken of her *han*. In this hedged way, Han Jeongsun used the song to connect experiences like hers to forms of suffering thought to be a rather universal part of Korean life, old and new. At the outset of the evening both Okada *sensei* and I had brought up songs specific to the atomic bomb; and yet Han Jeongsun went straight to the most general and non-specific level of culture and sought to make connections between the experiences of those on the margins like herself and essentialized Korean experience. It was part of her ongoing work of seeking, as a radiation sufferer, admission to Korean society, and to the forms of belonging and citizenship that such status conferred.

Han Jeongsun continued her narrative. "If you try to cross that mountain pass it's so very difficult," she sighed, then laughed, and paused. I was a bit confused, appreciating the metaphor, but not sure why she was laughing. Then she began to sing with exaggerated emotionality:

▶16

6. Grabbing something with chopsticks, dipping it in a sauce, and eating it is a common way of seasoning and eating food in Korea and throughout East Asia.

Mountain pass after mountain pass I cro—(laughs)

Though I cross, though I cross, this endless road of mountain passes . . .

Life in this world, living this life, it's spicier than a hot pepper.[7]

Han Jeongsun was quoting this song, Yu Ji-na's 2009 "Gochu" (Hot Pepper), when she spoke of mountain passes, preliminary to singing it.

Yu Ji-na, one of Han Jeongsun's favorite female singers, went through primary and secondary schooling as a traditional music voice major before becoming a pop star. Her voice therefore had the raspy timbre expected of *pansori* (traditional epic storysinging) singers and her songs often had folk themes. This song, her latest hit, was only two years old, and quite popular on radio and television.

The song focuses on the trope of repetitive walking, a metaphor for struggle that permeates Korean folklore and popular culture. Walking over mountain passes is one of several tropes of walking-as-struggle that appear throughout Korean folk and pop culture. It is a central theme of many versions of the ubiquitous folk song "Arirang" and many others, perhaps because the majority of the Korean peninsula is mountainous—as I had found out on climbing up top of Hapcheon, when one gets a view of the far distance in Korea, what one often sees is a seemingly endless chain of mountain passes.

The story of struggle which "Hot Pepper" relates contrasts dramatically with the dynamism and the rhythmic and melodic propulsion of the song. The song, which Han Jeongsun sang at seventy-six beats per minute, is in 4/4, and characterized by a repeating dotted quarter/eighth note/quarter note motif (see Figure 7.5, top). Just like the lyrics are a reference to the folkloric trope of the mountain pass, this rhythmic motif is a reference to the metric patterns of Korean folk music and dance. These patterns often involve the division of the basic pulse into three— so-called "compound meter"—in contrast to the duple division of the beat in most Western and Korean popular music, influenced as it has been by Japan and the West. In "Hot Pepper," squarely set in 4/4, the most common meter in *teuroteu*, the reference to threes is striking, referring quite explicitly to such compound meters as the one shown at the bottom of Figure 7.5.

The "threeness" in Korean folk music is accompanied by movement by singers, percussionists, dancers, and often listeners as well, and in live

7. *Gogae gogae neo . . . tto han gogae namanne*
   Neomeogado neomeogado kkeuchi eomneun gogaetgil
   Sesangsariga insaengsariga gochuboda maepda maewo

neo meo ga do - neo meo ga do   kkeu - chieom-neun - gogaet gil

Figure 7.5 A comparison of the second line of "Hot Pepper" (top) with the Korean traditional rhythmic pattern *gutgeori*. The two notes after the dotted quarter notes in "Hot Pepper" are loose imitations of the grace note/eighth note figure below, a common feature of Korean traditional meter.

performance Yu Ji-na and her entourage often accompany the rhythmic motif of "Hot Pepper" with traditional dance gestures. The movement involves settling downward on the downbeat and just beyond, and then a long rising, through the second beat, culminating with a grace note and an emphatic upward movement on the third beat, the pinnacle of the motion. As Korean percussion master and educator Kim Dongwon explained to me, it is a kind of movement that emphasizes elasticity, dynamism and a comfortable flow, with basically two gestures stretched comfortably over three beats. The movement and the rhythm are quite well-suited to walking, and such patterns are common in farmers' band music (*pungmul*) for processions and parades. There is no one-two-one-two drive to suggest mechanical left-right-left-right stepping; instead, one takes the whole three beats for a single revolution of the walking cycle—stepping and striding with plenty of time for the various recoveries.

The struggle to walk was not only a metaphor for social struggle for Han Jeongsun; it was also a literal, daily concern. But while she sang of the difficulties of walking, she moved in sound and body with an easy flow. As she sang "Hot Pepper," she was seated, but she gesture-danced with her arms and shoulders, which rose and fell as she sang. She emphasized the dotted aspect of rhythm, dancing along the endless mountain road, stretching the dotted quarter note, giving the song that sense of sticky time so common in Korean folk music and dance. Many songs of suffering the world over often have these devices of rhythmic propulsion in them, schemes for organizing and fortifying the self and the body in the face of struggle, techniques that allow for the expression of sorrow without collapse. The insistent backbeat and fast tempos of some positively miserable North American bluegrass and old-time songs; the rhythmic drive of many mournful Yiddish songs of the Holocaust period (Gilbert 2005); and groove in the blues, soul, and other African American genres: all of these devices allow us to plumb the depths of human emotion without going altogether to pieces.[8] The *teuroteu* genre to which "Hot Pepper" belongs and the Korean folk music to which the song alludes are both replete with such contrasts of form and content, and so both genres are major cultural resources for coping with suffering.[9]

Han Jeongsun's song of endless mountain passes resonated with her slow, laborious, ongoing enjoyment of the *ppeongsori*, suggesting an association of suffering and play. This was just one of the many formal homologies that she wove through her narrative to give it and herself energy, efficacy, and coherence. She ended the song with one of her arcing sighs of half serious, half-mocking approval, and then laughed.

Then she talked us through the song. She described how long one anticipates finally summitting a mountain pass, only to reach the pass and see the next one waiting on the other side of the valley. Soon after that evening I would make my own climb up a nearby mountain to look out over the layered ranges of small mountains and their foreboding passes.

Han Jeongsun proceeded with her narrative, now delving into completely unveiled reflections on her own life as struggle, interwoven with songs. She described the difficulty of raising her children, her separation from her husband, her life alone once he had left, taking the children with him, and her struggles with loneliness, depression, and disability. She spoke of the sinking feeling that she had every time she came back to her solitary home, the realization she had no one to share food with, no one to cook for. This was how she had lived up until the present, which found her living alone in a small one-room apartment in west Daegu.

8. "Ain't Nobody Going to Miss Me When I'm Gone" and "I am a Man of Constant Sorrow" are just a few of the legion of up-tempo songs of misery in North American bluegrass and old-time music. In African American musics and elsewhere groove is often a means of rhythmical propulsion through sorrow—Nina Simone's "Mississippi Goddam," with its driving piano and traumatized lyrics, is a quintessential example of this (thanks to Melvin Butler for the suggestion). Marvin Gaye's album *What's Going On* stands out as well: in the title track the groove, based on the syncopations and micro-rhythmic displacements of the guitars, drumkit, and box drum (played by Gaye himself) propels the listener through misery in the face of social violence towards awareness and solidarity. Smokey Robinson's upbeat "Tears of a Clown" is another particularly poignant example. For examples of Holocaust-era Yiddish songs that contrast mournful lyrics with rhythmically driven dance music, see Gilbert's *Music in the Holocaust* (2005). The Nepali *dohori* genre combines up-tempo dance music with sorrowful songs of loss and longing: see Anna Stirr's *Singing across Divides* (2017: 64 and elsewhere throughout the book).

9. The many different up-tempo Northwest Korean "Song of Decadence" (*Nanbongga*) songs are excellent examples of this contrast of form and content in traditional Korean music. In *teuroteu*, one canonical example is Song Daegwan's "Nebakja" (4/4), in which a bright disco drum track contrasts with lyrics like "Within these (measures of) four beats there is love, there is parting, and there are tears."

Not able to drink, or to run outside and scream, as she said, "I had to deal with my troubles in my heart, on my own." One way she had done this was to sing. "I'd go to *noraebang* (karaoke), or . . . " she said, trailing off.

Han Jeongsun spoke about how she had long used songs to find release for pent-up emotions, to make light of her troubles, and to find expression, structure, and energy for life. Some songs had acquired such power over the years that she couldn't sing them any more. "These days," she said, "I don't sing "A Woman's Life" ("Yeojaui ilsaeng") or that kind of song." She laughed ruefully. "A Woman's Life" was debuted in 1968 by the great diva of *teuroteu* Yi Mija, known as Korea's "Queen of Elegy" after her song of the same name. The song begins with this famous line: "Though my breast hurts so much I can't contain it, I cannot say a word, because I am a woman." She explained the lyrics to us—the lonely, arduous path that a woman must walk down "life's road" (*insaenggil*), and of the "unmeasurable sorrow" (*hearilsu eomneun seorum*) she deals with by crying.

"How you must have cried," commented Jin Gyeongsuk, who had been listening closely to Han Jeongsun's narrative. "I really cried a lot," Han Jeongsun answered. "Alone, this way, if I started to sing . . . I've never been able to sing that song all the way through." "Exhausted from crying" (*ulda jijeoseo*), she sang, and repeated, speaking: "I really was exhausted from crying."

I thought this might be a quote from "A Woman's Life," but when I checked later, I found out I was wrong. Han Jeongsun was quoting from another Yi Mija song, "Camellia Girl" ("Dongbaek Agassi"):

> How much did you cry, Camellia Girl?
> Exhausted from longing, exhausted from crying
> My petals are bruised red.

Han Jeongsun had heard Jin Gyeongsuk say "How you must have cried," and noted its similarity to the "How much did you cry" of "Camellia Girl." She had then replied, moving through the lyrics in her mind, with the next line that made sense in the course of conversation. This was the extent of her virtuosity at harmonizing her story to the tropes of popular culture—she did it in prepared ways, but also on the fly in the moment-to-moment give and take of conversation, like this and the *ppeongsori* episode.

"That [other] Yi Mija song, 'Cry, Storm Wind' ('Uleora yeolpung-a')—that kind of song—I can't sing that all the way through either," Han Jeongsun went on, moving down the list of the diva's most affecting songs. "Cry, Storm Wind," like "A Woman's Life," made her start crying midway through, she said, and then sang the first verse:

Though it torments me beyond endurance, I cannot cry.
Who will understand how I felt as I saw my beloved off with a
  smile—
Who will understand my wretched situation?
Cry, storm wind, through the night till morning.[10]

She stressed the line "who is going to understand my wretched situation?" The original line had been "who is going to understand my wretched love?," and she had substituted the word *sayeon* (situation or circumstances) for "love" (*sarang*). In so doing she transformed a broken-hearted love song into a song about a lonesome struggle, like her other favorites. I marveled at the dexterity with which she modified the text of popular song to suit her story, weaving Yi Mija's and her fates together. In these ways—through quoting songs and melodies and modifying song lyrics—she laced her narrative with the language and the sounds of popular song.

Han Jeongsun now smoothly returned to the theme of the road. "Anyway, there's only one road, and I've got to take it and walk it by myself. Will someone come along and take me by the hand? Things aren't like that. So I walk along, and if someone needs my help I give them a hand . . . " she said, returning to the persistent theme of absent and proffered hands. She was referring to her work as an activist, which she described as an effort to ensure that others wouldn't have to "walk life's path" (*sesanggil*) alone. Han Jeongsun probably was thinking about songs when she spoke of "life's path": she had just used a variant of this expression, *insaenggil*, which literally means "life path," from the lyrics of "A Woman's Life." The related trope of the "path through this world" shows up in several of her favorite *teuroteu* pieces, including "Sleeping Princess" ("Jam janeun gongju"), male *teuroteu* singer Shin Yu's 2008 ballad about walking, a song to which she was much addicted at the time. Popular tropes of walking and the life road crossed and fused in the story of her troubles.

She paused for a moment and then continued. "And so I'm just sitting here grabbing and eating these *ppeongsori* one by one . . . hahahaha . . . as I pick up these *ppeongsori* and eat them one by one my heart keeps beating." With this she stopped talking.

We all laughed, surprised by the return of the joke after the odyssey she had just taken us on. She had been talking and singing for twenty-eight

10. *Mot gyeondige goerowodo ulji motago*
   Ganeun imeul useumeuro bonaeneun maeum
   Geu nuguga arajuna gimakin nae sayeoneul
   Ureora yeolpunga bami saedorok

minutes, telling the devastating story of her life with unflinching pathos and humor. It was an improvised narrative of magnificent construction. It had an extended symmetrical composition, bookended by the *ppeongsori* motif. The whole story, which she revealed to be a complete unit only in this last moment, hung together through many different kinds of formal devices and affective sensibilities. There were formal coherences such as the *ppeongsori* motif, and the themes of the road and mountain passes that appeared in both speech and song. There was the continuum of suffering and play in the permeable relationship between the struggle to walk and the dynamic motion of music and dance. There was a continuum as well that linked the self that is incapacitated to the self that walks and works and helps others.

Perhaps most importantly, her narrative brought together her story in its particularity with the stories of others, through the medium of pop cultural tales that bind people together in arrangements of cultural intimacy. On occasions like this Han Jeongsun selected and assembled songs and stories into coherences of identity, and in this way, she built bridges to different sorts of social memberships—the transhistorical club of Korean womanhood, Korean civil society and its fickle concern for the social welfare of others, and the mass of victims of modernity whose suffering lay at the heart of post-colonial South Korean identity.

Most people in South Korea either do not know about the second-generation of radiation suffers or only find out about them around Independence Day, when grievances against Japan and other foreign countries emerge in a tide of nationalist fervor. For this reason, Han Jeongsun's struggle to gain admission to the very heart of Korean intimacy based in notions of suffering and struggle was a perpetual and embattled one. Yet in activist speech and in tapestries of song and story such as this she created kinds of resonance and connectivity between herself, other radiation sufferers, and the social whole; and these led to a feeling of belonging that served as a foundation for everyday life and political action.

———

Han Jeongsun's narratives like the *ppeongsori* one were part of the process by which she forged and maintained senses of belonging. But they were also a means by which she found the energy and cultivated the skills she needed for everyday life. Her songs of walking linked tropes of walking as struggle with her actual practices of walking in a formal, affective chain. That connection energized her daily walking, borrowing the propulsion and the formal structures of musical movement. This was one reason she wove songs of walking into her everyday life, bringing them into contact with everyday movement. She peppered her talk with references to songs of walking and quotations from them. She hummed to herself as she went about daily tasks like cleaning and cooking. Every time her phone rang, it rang out with walking songs: "Hot Pepper," with its mountain passes, had been her cell phone's ring tone in late summer of 2011, and in the fall she changed it to "Sleeping Princess," the song which meditated on the toil involved in walking one's path in this world.

One day in November of that year we sat in the backseat of Shim Jintae's car as he drove us through the Hapcheon countryside on the way to Haeinsa (Haein Temple). Shim Jintae chatted with a Korean American visitor in the passenger seat. Her family was originally from Hapcheon, and she had donated generously to the Korean bomb and radiation victims community. The trip had been arranged to show her the temple, the most famous landmark in the Hapcheon area and the repository of the Tripitaka Koreana, one of the oldest complete sets of woodblock Buddhist scripture in the world.

Han Jeongsun and I were chatting, and I was half-waiting for her phone to ring, as it often did, curious to hear if it was still set to "Sleeping Princess." After a half an hour or so, I asked her about the song, and the refrain which played when her phone rang:

> I kiss you gently
> On your fine pink cheek
> Will you wake up
> And give me your pearly smile?[11]

A rather straightforward love song, I thought. I wondered why Han Jeongsun liked it so much. I asked her why she had chosen it for her ringtone, and she walked me line by line through the first two verses.

> Have you grown to hate the world?
> Is there someone you must forget?
> Do you fall down, day after day, and get up again
> But nothing changes?

11. *Aengdubit geu goun du ppore*
    Salmyeosi kiseureul haejumyeo
    Geudaeneun jameseo kkaeeona
    Naege hayan miso jieulkka

If you walk down your path in the world and look,
You find there is a path that goes around.
If you spend one day crying, you have to spend the next laughing.
Only then will you be able to stand it . . .[12]

Han Jeongsun repeated the lines about walking life's path, falling down, getting up, and finding a way around several times, alternately speaking and singing the lines. She told me this was her favorite part of the song. She thought the part about falling down every day and getting up to find that nothing has changed expressed things perfectly. She had mentioned it to me before, comparing the repeated action of falling down to the repeated occurrence of disease and disability among generation after generation of radiation victims—herself, her eldest son, hopefully not her two granddaughters.

Like "Hot Pepper," with its interminable road lined with mountain passes, "Sleeping Princess" addresses the feeling that life is an endless path of difficulties. But the song differs in its counsel that there is a "path that goes around" (*ppingdora ganeun gil*). When Han Jeongsun repeated this part of the song as we drove, she ended on this line each time, even though it left her at a rather unresolved place about halfway through the melody. She told me that she took heart and found the will to carry on in these words.

Han Jeongsun also found inspiration in the song's musical surfaces. Like "Hot Pepper," "Sleeping Princess" has a rhythmic propulsion which is akin to movement, embodying the act of walking which it describes. The verses of "Sleeping Princess" are characterized by a 4/4 rhythmic motif of seven or eight consecutive eighth notes. This shows up rather emphatically when the text is about walking, as in the crucial couplet "*se-sang-gil geot-da-ga bom-yeon, pping do-ra-ga-neun gil-do is-seo*" (If you walk down your path in the world and look, you find there is a path that goes around). This sounds like a sonic characterization of persistence. It begins on the upbeat after beat one and crosses the bar line into the next measure, thereby deemphasizing heavy downbeats and giving the song a relaxed and flowing feeling. When

12. *Sesangi miwojyeonnayo*
   Nugunga ijeoyaman hana
   Nalmada sseureojigo ttodasi ireoseojiman
   Dallajingeon eomneungayo
   Sesanggil geotdaga bomyeon
   Ppingdora ganeun gil do isseo
   Harureul ureosseumyeon haruneun useoya haeyo
   Geuraeyaman gyeondilsu isseo

its singer, Shin Yu, sang of walking the world road in concert, he used his right hand to trace life's path in a lilting rhythmic gesture.[13] Han Jeongsun also moved rhythmically as she sang this line. "Sleeping Princess" was another instance of how walking appeared in her songs not just as a textual trope, but as embodied movement in the rhythmic features of music.

Over several years of working with Han Jeongsun it slowly dawned on me that movement and walking were present in her singing as both theme and embodied rhythm. In both her singing and her speech, I had seen her use these generic tropes of walking from popular song to connect her quite particular experiences as a radiation sufferer to Korean suffering in general. She had told me that she found inspiration in them that helped her in her daily life. But I wanted to find out more in detail about what that translated to in practice. Did song and its embodied movement have particular influence on her actual walking practices, and vice versa, and what sort of affective and formal resonances existed between the two practices? Did she borrow particular features of the rhythmic life of music and its movement to help her cope with the pain and difficulties she experienced walking? If everyday walking is a practice and an expression of "embodied skills of footwork" (Ingold 2004: 315), I wondered in her case if music and dance were part of what was embodied. And I wanted to find out which of the patterns of movement that her singing embodied were her own and originated in her own movement practices.

After several years of rather slowly awakening to the importance of walking in Han Jeongsun's expressive life, I began to pay attention to her actual walking practices. We had always walked together; now I made notes and videos, and we talked more about her particular walking feats and challenges. We walked in big cities and small villages. We walked barefoot on the acupressure course in the park on the banks of the Hwang River in Hapcheon town. Han Jeongsun put me to shame by walking the entire course without complaint, while I oo'ed and ow'ed the whole way through. She told me that the small pointy stones were nothing compared to the pain she had experienced in her life.

As we rode in Shim Jintae's car to Haein Temple I looked forward to a walk together. We left the car in the main parking lot and walked along the long, gradually rising valley which led to the temple and its woodblock collection, stopping to rest as we went. Our two companions sped ahead to the temple; Han Jeongsun told me that it was too far and too steep a hike for her.

13. See, for instance, this performance on the TBC television program "Gayo syo" (Pop song show): https://www.youtube.com/watch?v=Ej4wTQW3wqA.

As we walked, listening to the flowing stream that ran through the valley, she told me a Korean parable: *the frog cannot remember its time as a tadpole*. Old age should not scold youth, she said, for it does not remember the worries of that time. Likewise, those in power, politicians especially, cannot remember their time as commoners, and the everyday sufferings they endured. She spoke with dismay of the lack of concern which South Korean society showed for the plight of bomb and radiation victims. "If we speak [of our troubles], they just walk on by," she said. She said that some politicians who had suffered had spoken words of encouragement to her in their meetings—"Please have strength, have the courage to live"—but nothing more.

We came across a bench near a coffee kiosk on the way up the mountain. Han Jeongsun had walked as far as she could, and we sat down to wait for the others to come back. When she stopped walking her speech became faster, unregulated by the slow and steady pace of walking. Pilgrims and laughing tourists walked on by as she continued her narrative. "I could yell, as people passed, about my fifty years of suffering, but would anyone listen? And I don't want to live that way. I never wanted to be a victim. My parents didn't want to be victims either." And they didn't want to pass on anything but the best of themselves to their children.

Han Jeongsun walked slowly and for short distances also on the way back to the car. She stopped to rest in between to ease the pain. That pain, she told me, ebbed and flowed with the progression of her chronic necrosis. And yet when she walked, she did so with great decisiveness and constancy, setting a speed and only varying it if the terrain changed. She set her pace slower or faster to accommodate others but did not fall into lock step with them, keeping her regular gait and elongating her strides to keep up. She, like most people, walked at different speeds depending on what she was doing, whom she was walking with, and what sort of mood she was in.

As I became more familiar with the details of Han Jeongsun's walking life, particularly with her pace of walking, I also began to pay more attention to tempo in her singing. I noticed that whenever she sang a particular song she set the tempo in exactly the same place. She sang multiple versions of "Hot Pepper" for me over the years, and all clocked in at seventy-six beats per minute. She did not speed up as she sang, which is so common among singers, even professionals.

I began to wonder if there was an affective resonance between the steadiness of her singing and the even pace of the way she walked. There was certainly a resonance between the relative slowness of her walking and singing. Han Jeongsun's versions of songs were uniformly slower than the canonical recordings from which she had learned them via radio, cassette, television, and karaoke. Yu Jina typically sang "Hot Pepper" at eighty-eight beats per minute, making Han Jeongsun's version twelve beats per minute slower. Han Jeongsun sang "Sleeping Princess" at about eighty-four beats per minute compared to the original's ninety-three. And she sang another of her favorites, Yi Tae-ho's "The Time of Living" ("Saneun dongan"), at around 135 beats per minute, as compared to the original 156.

On our walk to the temple and at other times Han Jeongsun spoke slowly as she walked, coordinating the pace of speech and walking, and then spoke more quickly when seated. Thus her speech did not always resonate affectively with her slow and methodical walking. By contrast, the relative slowness of her singing was not temporary or dependent upon what she was doing. Whenever she sang, her singing retained its relative slowness. It seemed to be a harmonization of the body and the song, a slowing down that enabled her to sing more comfortably.

My guess is that for Han Jeongsun, speech was an arena which transcended the limitations of her walking practices, while music was an arena that supported them, that traded power and sensibility with her walking body. It was not only that music inspired and enabled her walking; that very music was deeply imprinted by her struggle to walk. A long chain of affect and technique connected Han Jeongsun's songs with her walking life. Affective resonances and formal features crossed from walking practice to song to walking again. The tropes of walking made their way into her speech and song, and this solidified a long chain connecting the three activities. That interwovenness of expressive practices served as a tenuous coherence of identity, an engine of possibility, and a program of action.

Importantly, this affective and formal chain that connected walking with speech and song was a means by which Han Jeongsun energized her activism, and a way in which she left her imprint on her political movement and its surrounding discourse. Han Jeongsun's walking was itself a kind of activism: as she walked about Hapcheon on her visits to radiation sufferers, and as she met the press and other activists, her acts of walking were performances of disability, suffering, and membership in different communities—radiation sufferers, the disabled community in South Korea, and post-colonial South Korean society in general. She put her steady, effortful way of walking on unaffected display and it struck a chord in South Korean media and public culture. It was taken as a kind of evidence of the history of suffering that Han Jeongsun was supposed to represent, a metonym that represented the second generation at large.

The 2013 Munhwa Broadcasting Corporation news documentary "The Atom Bomb's Cruel Inheritance," about the children of bomb victims, focuses notably on Han Jeongsun's walking. In the film we see her moving about her small apartment, making tea, and taking a stroll with her mother at the Hapcheon Atomic Bomb Victims Welfare Center. Another television documentary from 2015 shows Han Jeongsun walking beside Secretary Jin Gyeongsuk and radiation sufferer Jeon Ongnam, who are holding hands as the two Peacehouse workers walk to their car after a visit at the Jeon household. It was a path Han Jeongsun and I had walked many times together. The narrator asks, rhetorically: "In the midst of this exhausting life, how nice must it be to have a friend to walk together with you this way?" Gradually, as Han Jeongsun walked, and as she spoke and sang of her struggle to walk and her desire to take people by the hand as they walk down life's road, others took up these themes; and walking became a frequent trope in the media and the movement surrounding the second generation of radiation sufferers.

Early in 2013 the social media fundraising website We Generation ran a campaign ad, put together by young visitors to the Peacehouse to raise money for social welfare services for second-generation radiation sufferers. The landing page featured an image of Han Jeongsun with three other women from the second-generation Korean radiation sufferers community (Figure 7.6). The caption read "Though awkward, our steps go forward in search of hope . . . please walk with us!" The photograph is from one of the Peacehouse's periodic bus trips for survivors and radiation sufferers and shows the women standing beside a mountain temple. Several of the creators of the fundraising campaign had gone on that outing and had

Figure 7.6 The image on the home page of the We Generation funding campaign. Han Jeongsun (left) with Jin Gyeongsuk at far right, Jeon Ongnam and her mother at center.

walked together with Han Jeongsun and other members of the second generation. The impression her walking left on them, perhaps coupled with her talk or songs about walking, inspired the poster's slogan. This was but one instance of the political output of the chain of affect and form that linked Han Jeongsun's song, speech, walking, and activism. It was an example of how this continuity affected the larger political arena in which she moved.

This was an instance of Han Jeongsun's agency and power and the power of her expressive life in the movement. But in order to achieve this power and impact she had to adhere to the terms of South Korean state and public-cultural discourse about suffering. Her disability was taken as an instance of post-colonial injury and articulated to the meta-trope of woundedness as national identity. She had traction in the movement not just because of her eloquence, but because her eloquent performance of disability resonated with these terms and tropes. She was one of many Korean victims of the twentieth century whom are recognized for their displays of "competent brokenness" (Pilzer 2012: 64), and conditionally granted a hedged agency on the basis of it, an agency inextricably tied to being disabled.

But Han Jeongsun, like so many other victims in South Korean society, was willing to make this trade, because of the audience and the social membership which it won her and other second-generation radiation sufferers. She put the discourse of suffering to work on behalf of herself and others, transforming it ever so slightly in the process. Woundedness in South Korean culture, as a trope of national identity, often appropriates disability as a metaphor for the wounds of the communally broken heart, while paying little attention to actual disabled people (see Kim Eunjung 2017). But just as Han Jeongsun appropriated pop songs that use walking as a metaphor for struggle to address her actual walking difficulties, she converted disability from metaphor to reality in her activism. This opened up avenues for social membership and rights claims for radiation sufferers; although like other victims of the colonial era and war, they faced the continual threat of casual banishment back to the black hole of metaphor, and the agony of only being attended to when symbols of victimization were required.

Han Jeongsun found inspiration and techniques for daily movement in songs of walking, and the long affective chain she constructed that connected walking, speech, and song became an important part of her activism. Her modulations of the voice in her activism—and her use of a sing-song voice in particular—were another means by which she connected song to other aspects of her life, borrowing its energy and formal structures for spoken expression.

Much of this was veiled by different sorts of restraint, Han Jeongsun's version of the quiet of "Korea's Hiroshima." It was rare to get such a relatively full rendering of her expressive universe as that *ppeongsori* episode, that magnificent artwork of self-narration. As we listened back to the recording over the following year, she told me it had been an exception to her general rule of restraint and self-effacement. She spoke of the special time that it had been, and the particular conditions which had inspired it. The sympathetic ear of the Peacehouse secretary, Jin Gyeongsuk, had made it possible, as had my enthusiasm for singing and my desire to hear about Han Jeongsun's favorite songs. But Jin Gyeongsuk had left in late 2015; and with her lost friend went much of Han Jeongsun's enjoyment of life in Hapcheon and many of her opportunities for song.

The *ppeongsori* narrative may have been unusual, but nonetheless in the cracks of life, in the day-in and day-out artwork of survival, Han Jeongsun had cultivated the expressive abilities, the voice, and the rhetorical brilliance to make it happen. That work of cultivation was part of the cultivation and maintenance of the self. She did it while singing, dancing, entertaining, speech-making, and walking. She took up residence on popular song and popular culture's generalized, shareable plane of suffering, which was at least in the neighborhood of her own difficulties. She had done this on the margins throughout the authoritarian era, struggling with the discrimination and erasure that people with disabilities and radiation sufferers faced, and with the generally repressive atmosphere. And in the 2000s, when the time was ripe, she leapt straight into the heart of the South Korean conversation about the colonial and wartime pasts and their legacies of victimization.

Five years after the first *ppeongsori* episode, Han Jeongsun and I sat together at the Peacehouse. We had found another bag of the snacks and we were eating them for old times' sake. She was telling me about the deeper story of *ppeongsori*: "*ppeong*" refers to the sound that corn kernels, heated under pressure, make when the puffed corn snack device is opened and they suddenly expand. Such machines can still be found throughout Korea, she said, typically at public markets. They are of Japanese origin. I replied that I had seen a few of them, and was familiar with that always surprising, almost painfully loud sound. She spoke of how when she was young she had waited excitedly for the "*ppeong*" explosion, not knowing when it would come, and of the way the machine drew the attention of passersby. As they waited for the sound, people drew together, and then the sound reached out and grabbed them, putting the seal on their togetherness. She spoke in a philosophical vein of the gift of affection that the person who had bought those *ppeongsori* in 2011 had given the party. We couldn't remember who had bought them.

I mentioned how she had described eating *ppeongsori* with chopsticks as similar to the struggle to endure life's trials and tribulations. "Actually, you know, eating *ppeongsori* with chopsticks is quite comfortable. It's a good way to do it," she replied, laughing, as if she was delivering a punchline she had waited five years to deliver.

I sat amazed, wondering if Han Jeongsun was retracting her statement about the act as a metaphor for her lifetime of trouble and struggle. But in the end, I took it as evidence that all along, as she struggled, she coped with her troubles with cleverness, skill, grace, and humor. She used all the expressive resources at her disposal to seek comfort as she walked her long path through this world. And so the *ppeongsori* narrative, which I had considered closed with formal elegance, was ongoing, as was the struggle it described.

CHAPTER 8
Epilogue

S him Jintae, Han Jeongsun, the Peacehouse secretary, and I sat around a
table grilling meat at Daeshik's Famous House of Korean Beef (Daeshik
hanu myeongga), up by Hapcheon Dam. It was a dinner scene of plenty: one
of us, I don't remember who, was treating the others.

Director Shim ordered a bottle of *soju*, and we toasted to health and pros-
perity out of little shot glasses. Each of us strained to click our glass below
the level of our companions in a gesture of deference. Shim Jintae, Han
Jeongsun, and I squared off for the toast, he trying to defer to the PhD, I determined to bow to their seniority and wisdom, and Han Jeongsun aiming
to undercut us both. Han Jeongsun drank ice-cold water out of her shot
glass. She downed it in one shot and let out a harsh fricative "cccchhhhhh"
sound, marking the strength of the liquor and demonstrating her own fortitude. We all laughed.

We were talking about food as we cooked on the table, and Shim
Jintae began to speak of the contrast between the bounty of the present and the privations of the past. Like so many others in the immediate aftermath of the move from Hiroshima to Korea his family
couldn't afford rice. He recounted the story of how he, like countless
other Koreans in the immediate post-colonial period and the years surrounding the Korean Civil War (1950–53), had gone to the mountain
and cut the inner bark of pine trees to eat as a substitute for rice. He
said it was pretty good, actually. But his sister, who was born in 1951
and is only seven years younger than he is, grew up not knowing what
hunger was.

Above the sound of the barbecue, Han Jeongsun began to sing. The song
was "Girl Farmer" ("Cheonyeo nonggun"), a 60s pop hit by songstress

Quietude. Joshua D. Pilzer, Oxford University Press. © Oxford University Press 2023.
DOI: 10.1093/oso/9780197615089.003.0008

Choe Jeongja, which had recently become part of the repertoire of Yu Jina, who sang Han Jeongsun's beloved "Hot Pepper." Shim Jintae joined in.

> This body of mine is a girl . . .
> But you think I can't do man's work?
> Let's drive the cow to the rice paddy . . .
> come on, let's go, to that field where the sun is rising,
> let's go plow![1]

Shim Jintae laughed; Han Jeongsun followed a split second later with one of her arcing exclamations of appreciation: "Aaaaaaaaaaaaaah!" She continued, speaking: "The most important part of farming—plowing fields and rice paddies—can't be done without a cow." It was a song about a hard-working young woman, but Han Jeongsun modestly deflected suspicions that she identified with that figure, and made the song about the cow, whom she thought of as we grilled the beef. The secretary pointed out that it was a bit hypocritical to praise the cow while eating its meat, and Han Jeongsun replied that this was precisely why it was so important, laughing again.

⏵17

Han Jeongsun was a bit surprised that Shim Jintae knew the song. But while she had memorized it for its encouraging message to working women, he had memorized it because it had to do with farming, his early morning work before heading to the Korean Atomic Bomb Victims Association office. Shim Jintae and Han Jeongsun found a point of contact here, based in a lifetime of hard work and struggle. Blood, sweat, tears, war, and radiation linked them together; the struggle went on for each of them, and beyond down the generations.

The legacy of the bombs has no end in sight, and the art of survival has no end either. In 2020 Yi Suyong continued to give interviews in her even, unemotional voice. She got up early for a walk and answered her cell phone when I called. "I'm still alive, you know," she laughed, in her steady way, letting a hint of incredulity creep into her voice. Bae Ilmyeong walked the path of God.

1. *I momi cheonyeorago*
   Namja ireul mot hanayo
   So molgo non bateuro irya eoseogaja
   Hae tteuneun jeo deulpane irya eoseogaja
   Batgari gaja

She kept to her routine, stayed focused on the time and the events of the day, and read her Bible to herself, half quietly, half silently. Pak Heun-il counted his steps around the welfare center. Shim Jintae got up early, did his farming chores, and went to work to meet the world on behalf of his community. Yun Sugi and Kim Pan-geun drank from the secret stash. Han Jeongsun struggled with exhaustion but kept up a feverish pace of activism and social welfare work in Hapcheon. The quiet of "Korea's Hiroshima" resounded in its many forms, enfolding many silences but not succumbing to them.

One might quite reasonably wish that the conditions that brought forth Hapcheon's quietude never arise again. Or one might hope that the quiet could be overcome by its bearers. But there is something in that quietude that, for all its fragility, is as strong as anything I have ever encountered. Even Kim Hyeongryul, who died, had that power in his fragile voice, more powerful than all the forces of greed, evil, and ignorance joined in hideous compact against the wretched and their earth. That quietude is a wellspring of life and selfhood, and at times a precarious peace. It floats like gravity and is durable beyond our lives.

In March 2020 I called Han Jeongsun, who was stuck in her Daegu apartment in coronavirus lockdown. "You know that song, 'The Broken Wall-Clock?'" she said, as we passed the time of day. An Buja had sung this song for me while we looked through her folder of song lyrics, and reflected on its chorus, which expresses a wish that time could stop like a broken clock on the wall. "It's not that anybody really wants time to stop. What would happen to all the women giving birth at the moment that time stopped? Horrible, right?" Han Jeongsun said, and laughed. "If time stopped," she continued, "healing would be impossible." She had said before that her total liberation would only come with death. But healing the self and society were ongoing and unfinished parts of the art of survival. The arts of keeping it together and going on as human beings and as social groups that Han Jeongsun, Yi Suyong, Bae Ilmyeong, Shim Jintae, and others have been teaching us about in this book are part of this effort. "That business about wanting time to stop, that's just a feeling," Han Jeongsun said, smiling— the wistful feeling that one's life and energy are flowing away, and a fleeting wish that it didn't have to be that way. But time doesn't stop, nor do the art of life and the work of survival, not yet.

Resources for Support and Activism on Behalf of Atomic Bomb and Radiation Victims

RESOURCES FOR OFFERING DIRECT SUPPORT TO THE VICTIMS IN THIS BOOK

- Hapcheon Atomic Bomb Victims Welfare Center (Korean): http://www.krchcwc.or.kr/

  On this website you will find information about activities at the center, a gallery of photographs of recent events, and information for prospective donors, volunteers, and visitors.

- Hapcheon Peacehouse for second-generation victims of the atomic bombs (Korean): https://cafe.daum.net/peacehousehapcheon

  Descriptions and announcements of current events, atomic bomb victims in the news, and information for prospective donors.

- Korean Atomic Bomb Victims Association (Korean): http://www.won pok.or.kr/

  Basic information about Korean victims of the atomic bombings of Japan and information about becoming a supporter. As of 2022 the website is still under construction.

RESOURCES FOR SUPPORTING AND PARTICIPATING IN THE GLOBAL ANTI-NUCLEAR MOVEMENT

- Japanese Confederation of A- and H-Bomb Sufferers Organization (Japanese and English): http://www.ne.jp/asahi/hidankyo/nihon/english/index.html

Japan's only national organization of bomb victims. The group organizes speaking tours in Japan and internationally, issues statements, and pursues other anti-nuclear activism. The website surveys these activities and hosts an archive of statements and testimonies.

- The Japan Council against Atomic and Hydrogen Bombs (Japanese and English): https://www.antiatom.org/english/

  Political and cultural activism to end the global production and use of nuclear weapons. The group hosts an annual conference, the World Conference against A and H Bombs, which is free. The website provides resources for getting involved, and for learning about the global reach of nuclear bomb and radiation victimization.

- International Campaign to Abolish Nuclear Weapons (ICAN) (English): https://www.icanw.org/

  Headquartered in Switzerland, ICAN describes itself as "a coalition of non-governmental organizations promoting adherence to and implementation of the United Nations nuclear weapon ban treaty." There are numerous options on the website to donate and participate, especially by organizing to put pressure on your home country to join the Treaty on the Prohibition of Nuclear Weapons. Most countries, including the United States, Canada, most of Europe, and most of Asia, have yet to sign.

- Nuclear Age Peace Foundation (English): https://www.wagingpeace.org/

  A partner of ICAN, the US-based Nuclear Age Peace Foundation offers resources for education, volunteering, internship, and organizing. Its "Action Alert Network" makes it easy for US citizens to write their congressional representatives to encourage them to support nuclear disarmament.

- Peace Action (English): https://www.peaceaction.org/

  US organization dedicated to nuclear non-proliferation and disarmament, and advocating for diplomacy over military solutions to problems of international relations. The website suggests ways one can become involved in this grassroots movement, including portals to its different campaigns: for a world without nuclear weapons, for promoting US diplomacy with North Korea and Iran, for ending war in the Middle East, and for reclaiming US tax dollars spent on war for domestic social welfare.

- Campaign for Nuclear Disarmament (English): https://cnduk.org

  British organization dedicated to nuclear disarmament and the banning of nuclear weapons domestically and worldwide, especially focused on opposing the British government's plans to expand its nuclear arsenal. The website offers a calendar of events throughout the UK and quick links for signing petitions against the UK's reinvigoration of its nuclear program.

- International Physicians for the Prevention of Nuclear War (English): https://www.ippnw.org/

  Organization campaigning for nuclear abolition, as well as conducting extensive research on and documentation of the effects of the production, testing and use of nuclear weapons. The website offers educational resources, a donation page, and a campaign kit with educational materials.

- *The Bulletin of the Atomic Scientists (English):* https://thebulletin.org/

  Founded in 1945, The Bulletin is a media organization dedicated to equipping "the public, policy makers, and scientists with the information needed to reduce man-made threats to our existence." The organization also sets and maintains the Doomsday Clock, which was set to 100 seconds to midnight in 2020, the closest it has been to midnight since its creation in 1947.

REFERENCES

Abe, Marié. 2016. "Sounding against Nuclear Power in Post-3.11 Japan: Resonances of Silence and Chindon-ya." *Ethnomusicology* 60/2: 233–62.

Agawu, Kofi. 1992. "Representing African Music." *Critical Inquiry* 18/2 (Winter): 245–66.

Agawu, Kofi. 2003. *Representing African Music: Postcolonial Notes, Queries, Positions.* New York: Routledge.

Anderson, Benedict. 1983. *Imagined Communities: Reflections on the Origin and Spread of Nationalism.* New York and London: Verso.

Atkinson, Meera, and Michael Richardson. 2013. *Traumatic Affect.* Newcastle upon Tyne, UK: Cambridge Scholars Publishing.

Busby, Christopher. 2016. "Letter to the Editor on 'The Hiroshima/Nagasaki Survivor Studies: Discrepancies between Results and General Perception' by Bertrand R. Jordan." *Genetics* 204 (December): 1627–29.

Caruth, Cathy, ed. 1995. *Trauma: Explorations in Memory.* Baltimore, MD and London: Johns Hopkins University Press.

Chang, Yunshik. 1975. "Growth of Education in Korea 1910–1945." *Journal of Asian Sociology* 4: 40–53.

Chi Kim, Sandra So Hee. 2017. "Korean 'Han' and the Postcolonial Afterlives of 'The Beauty of Sorrow.'" *Korean Studies* 41: 253–79.

Chung, Jung Myung, and Ha Jin Choe. 1987. "A Clinical and Chromosomal Study on Those Exposed to the Atomic Bomb and their Offspring." *The Korean Journal of Internal Medicine* 2/2: 227–33.

Clifford, James. 1983. "On Ethnographic Authority." *Representations* 2 (Spring): 118–46.

Cook, Glenda, Juliana Thompson, and Jan Reed. 2015. "Re-conceptualizing the Status of Residents in a Care Home: Older People Wanting to 'Live with Care.'" *Aging and Society* 35: 1587–1613.

Certeau, Michel de. 1984. *The Practice of Everyday Life.* Berkeley and Los Angeles: University of California Press.

Daughtry, J. Martin. 2015. *Listening to War: Sound, Music, Trauma, and Survival in Wartime Iraq.* New York: Oxford University Press.

Demick, Barbara. 2009. *Nothing to Envy: Ordinary Lives in North Korea.* New York: Spiegel and Grau.

Egginton, William. 2003. *How the World Became a Stage: Presence, Theatricality, and the Question of Modernity.* Albany, NY: SUNY Press.

Erickson, Donna, Caroline Menezes, and Ken-ichi Sakakibara. 2009. "About Phonetic and Perceptual Similarities in Laughing, Smiling, and Crying Speech." *Journal of the Acoustical Society of America* 126/4: 2210.

Feld, Stephen. 1988. "Aesthetics as Iconicity of Style, or 'Lift-up-over Sounding': Getting into the Kaluli Groove." *Yearbook for Traditional Music* 20: 74–113.

Fiumara, Gemma Corradi. 1990. *The Other Side of Language: A Philosophy of Listening.* New York: Routledge.

Fox, Aaron. 2004. *Real Country: Music and Language in Working-Class Culture.* Durham, NC: Duke University Press.

Gilbert, Shirli. 2005. *Music in the Holocaust: Confronting Life in the Nazi Ghettos and Camps.* New York: Oxford University Press.

Goffman, Erving. 1962. *Asylums: Essays on the Social Situation of Mental Patients and Other Inmates.* Chicago: Aldine Publishing Company.

Goffman, Erving. 1963. *Behavior in Public Places: Notes on the Social Organization of Gatherings.* New York: The Free Press.

Hanguk wonpok pihaeja hyeophoe. 2020. *Wonpok pihaeja ran?* [Atomic Bomb Victims?]. Available at http://www.wonpok.or.kr/doc/abomb1.html.

Harkness, Nicholas. 2011. "Culture and Interdiscursivity in Korean Fricative Vocal Gestures." *Journal of Linguistic Anthropology* 21/1: 99–123.

Harkness, Nicholas. 2013. "Softer Soju in South Korea." *Anthropological Theory* 13/1–2: 12–30.

Harkness, Nicholas. 2014. *Songs of Seoul: An Ethnography of Voice and Voicing in Christian South Korea.* Berkeley and Los Angeles: University of California Press.

Hedges, Elaine, and Shelley Fisher Fishkin, eds. 1994. *Listening to Silences: New Essays in Feminist Criticism.* New York: Oxford University Press.

Helmreich, Stefan. 2007. "An Anthropologist Underwater: Immersive Soundscapes, Submarine Cyborgs, and Transductive Ethnography." *American Ethnologist* 34/4: 621–41.

Herman, Judith. 1992. *Trauma and Recovery: The Aftermath of Violence—From Domestic Abuse to Political Terror.* New York: Basic Books.

Hersey, John. 1946. *Hiroshima.* New York: A.A. Knopf.

Hill, Jane. 1995. "The Voices of Don Gabriel: Responsibility and Self in a Modern Mexicano Narrative." In *The Dialogic Emergence of Culture,* edited by Dennis Tedlock and Bruce Mannheim, 97–147. Urbana: University of Illinois Press.

Hong, Zicheng. 1926. *Musings of a Chinese Vegetarian.* Translated by Yaichiro Isobe. Tokyo: Yuhodo.

Hong, Zicheng. 2003. *Tending the Roots of Wisdom.* Translated by Paul White. Beijing: New World Press.

Hong, Zicheng. 2013. *Chaegeundam* [Vegetable Roots Discourse]. Translated by Gweon Gyeong-yeol. Seoul: Gyohaksa.

Hur, Kwang-moo. 2011. "Jeonsigi Joseon'in nomuja gangjedongwon gwa wonpok pihe— Hiroshima, Nagasakiui jiyeokjeok teukjingeul jungsimeuro" [Forced Mobilization of Korean Workers during World War II and Atomic Bomb Victimization—Focused on the Characteristics of the Hiroshima and Nagasaki Areas]. *Han-il minjok munje yeon'gu* 20: 5–55.

Ichiba Junko. 1999. "Samjung-go gyeokkgeo'on Hangug'in wonpokpihaejadeul" [The Triple Distress of Korean Atomic Bomb Victims]. *Yeoksa bipyeong* 11: 153–218.

Ichiba Junko. 2003. *Han'gugui Hiroshima: 20-segi baengnyeonui bunno Han'gugin wonpok pihaejadeuleun nugu in'ga* [Korea's Hiroshima: A 20th-century Hundred-year Rage . . . Who are the Korean Atomic Bomb Victims?]. Seoul: Yeoksa bipyeonga.

Ichiba Junko. 2005. *Hiroshima o mochikaetta hitobito: "Kankoku no Hiroshima" wa naze umaretanoka* [People Who Brought Hiroshima Home: What Gave Rise to "Korea's Hiroshima?"]. Tokyo: Gaifūsha.

Ingold, Tim. 2004. "Culture on the Ground: The World Perceived through the Feet." *Journal of Material Culture* 9/3: 315–40.

Jaworski, Adam. 2016. "Visual Silence and Non-Normative Sexualities: Art, Transduction, and Performance." *Gender and Language* 10/3: 433–54.

Jo Mina. 2020. "Yi Yongsu seonsaengui bareon gwa jeongguiyeon: neomeoseoya hal geotgwa georireul dueoya hal geot" [Yi Yongsu's Remarks and the Alliance for Justice and Memory: What Should be Overcome, and What Should be Distanced]. *Newsnjoy*, May 26, http://www.newsnjoy.or.kr/news/articleView.html?idxno=300726.

Jordan, Bertrand R. 2016. "The Hiroshima/Nagasaki Survivor Studies: Discrepancies between Results and General Perception." *Genetics* 203 (August): 1505–12.

Ju, Young-su, Hyung-Joon Jhun, Jung-Bum Kim, and Jin-Kook Kim. 2006. "Non-cancer Diseases of Korean Atomic Bomb Survivors in Residence at Hapcheon, Republic of Korea." *Journal of Korean Medical Sciences* 21: 385–90.

Kang Su-han. 2011. "Jehan wonpok pihaeja jiwonjeongchaegui gaeseonbangan yeongu" [Improving Support Policies for South Korean Victims of the Atom Bomb]. Master's thesis, Gaya University.

Killick, Andrew. 1995. "The Penetrating Intellect: on Being White, Straight, and Male in Korea." In *Taboo: Sex, Identity, and Erotic Subjectivity in Anthropological Fieldwork*, edited by Don Kulick and Margaret Wilson, 58–80. New York: Routledge.

Killick, Andrew. 2001. "Ch'anggŭk Opera and the Category of the 'Traditionesque.'" *Korean Studies* 25/1: 51–71.

Kim Eunjung. 2017. *Curative Violence: Rehabilitating Disability, Gender, and Sexuality in Modern Korea*. Durham, NC and London: Duke University Press.

Kim Hyeongryul. 2015. *Naneun panhaek in-gwon-e moksumeul georeotda* [I Gave My Life for Anti-nuclear Human Rights]. Seoul: Haengbokhan chaek ilkgi.

Kim Seong-nae. 2007. "Mourning Korean Modernity in the Memory of the Cheju April Third Incident." In *The Inter-Asia Cultural Studies Reader*, edited by Kuan-Hsing Chen and Chua Beng Huat, 191–206. New York: Routledge.

Kim Seung-eun. 2012. "Jehan wonpok pihaeja munje e daehan han-il yang-gugui insik gwa gyoseoptaedo (1965–80)" [Korean and Japanese Awareness of and Negotiation of Attitudes toward Korean Atomic Bomb Victims, 1965–1980]. *Asia yeongu* 55/2: 104–35.

Kleinman, Arthur, Veena Das, and Margaret M. Lock, eds. 1997. *Social Suffering*. Berkeley and Los Angeles: University of California Press.

Korean Ministry of Foreign Affairs. 1972–3. *Hangug'in wonpok pihaeja guho* (Relief for Korean Atomic Bomb Victims) http://opendata.mofa.go.kr/mofadocu/resource/Document/5090.page.

LaCapra, Dominick. 1999. "Trauma, Absence, Loss." *Critical Inquiry* 25: 696–727.

Lavan, Nadine, César F. Lima, Hannah Harvey, Sophie K. Scott, and Carolyn McGettigan. 2015. "I Thought I Heard You Laughing: Contextual Facial Expressions Modulate the Perception of Authentic Laughter and Crying." *Cognition and Emotion* 29/5: 935–44.

Lee Haeng-seon. 2018. "Hangug'in wonpok pihaejawa jeung-eonui seosa, wonpok munhak: Kim Oksuk, *Hyungteoui ggot (2017)*" [Korean A-bomb Victims and the Narrative of Testimony, Atomic Bomb Literature: Kim Oksuk, *Flower of Scar* (2017)]. *Gi-eokgwa jeonmang* 39: 148–90.

Lee Hwajun. 2014. "Hangukgwa ilbonui seontaekdoen gieokgwa pihaejauisik: yanggugui ginyeomgwaneul jungsimeuro" [Selective Memory and Victim Consciousness in Korea and Japan: Focusing on the Memorials in Both Nations]. *Sahoe gwahak nonjip* 45/1: 1–24.

Lefebvre, Henri. 1992. *Éléments de rhythmanalyse* [Elements of Rhythmanalysis]. Paris: Éditions Syllepse.

Linner, Rachel. 1995. *City of Silence: Listening to Hiroshima*. Maryknoll, NY: Orbis Books.

Lomax, Alan, with Roswell Rudd, Victor Grauer, Norman Berkowitz, Bess Lomax Hawes, and Carol Kulig. 1976. *Cantometrics: A Method in Musical Anthropology*. Berkeley: University of California Extension Media Center.

Martin, Andy. 2010. "Swimming and Skiing: Two Modes of Existential Consciousness." *Sport, Ethics and Philosophy* 4/1: 42–51.

Massumi, Brian. 2002. *Parables for the Virtual: Movement, Affect, Sensation*. Durham, NC: Duke University Press.

McAllister, Patrick. 2006. *Xhosa Beer Drinking Rituals: Power, Practice and Performance in the South African Rural Periphery*. Durham, NC: Carolina Academic Press.

Meintjes, Louise. 2017. *Dust of the Zulu: Ngoma Aesthetics after Apartheid*. Durham, NC: Duke University Press.

Morris, David B. 1997. "About Suffering: Voice, Genre, and Moral Community." In *Social Suffering*, edited by Arthur Kleinman, Veena Das, and Margaret Lock, 25–46. Berkeley and Los Angeles: University of California Press.

Morton, Timothy. 2007. *Ecology without Nature: Rethinking Environmental Aesthetics*. Cambridge, MA: Harvard University Press.

Naono Akiko. 2010. "Hiroshima no kioku fūkei: kokumin no sōsaku to bukimina toki kūkan" [Hiroshima's Memoryscape: Citizens' Creation and Uncanny Space-time]. *Shakai-gaku hyōron* 60/4: 500–16.

Ndaliko, Chérie Rivers. 2016. *Necessary Noise: Art, Music, and Charitable Imperialism in the East of Congo*. New York: Oxford University Press.

O'Brien, Alia. 2020. "Faithful Listening: On Sound, Survival, and Becoming in Muslim Toronto." PhD dissertation, University of Toronto.

Ochoa Gautier, Ana María. 2014. *Aurality: Listening and Knowledge in Nineteenth-Century Colombia*. Durham, NC: Duke University Press.

Ochoa Gautier, Ana María. 2016. "Silence." In *Keywords in Sound*, edited by David Novak and Matt Sakakeeny, 183–92. Durham, NC: Duke University Press.

Oh Eunjeong. 2017. "Nationalism and Reflexive Cosmopolitanism in Korean A-Bomb Victims' War Memory and Transnational Solidarity." *Journal of Asian Sociology* 46/2 (September): 303–16.

Ohnuki-Tierney, Emiko. 2002. *Kamikaze, Cherry Blossoms, and Nationalisms: The Militarization of Aesthetics in Japanese History*. Chicago: University of Chicago Press.

Olsen, Tillie. 1978. *Silences*. New York: Delacorte Press/Seymour Lawrence.

Pak Subok. 1975. *Sorido eopda ireumdo eopda: Han'guk wonpok pihaeja 30nyeon eiu girok* [Without Sound or Name: A Record of Korean Atomic Bomb Victims' Thirty Years]. Seoul: Changwonsa.

Pilzer, Joshua D. 2012. *Hearts of Pine: Songs in the Lives of Three Korean Survivors of the "Comfort Women."* New York: Oxford University Press.

Pinguet, Catherine. 2006. "'Littrature de la bombe': Silences et dénis—Hiroshima-Nagasaki" ["Literature of the Bomb": Silences and Denials—Hiroshima-Nagasaki]. *Chimères* 62/3: 89–118.

Quintero, Michael Birenbaum. 2019. "Loudness, Excess, Power: A Political Liminology of a Global City of the South." In *Remapping Sound Studies*, edited by Gavin Steingo and Jim Sykes, 135–55. Durham, NC: Duke University Press.

Rice, Tom. 2016. "Listening." In *Keywords in Sound*, edited by David Novak and Matt Sakakeeny, 99–111. Durham, NC: Duke University Press.

Ryang, Sonia. 2003. "The Great Kanto Earthquake and the Massacre of Koreans in 1923: Notes on Japan's Modern National Sovereignty." *Anthropological Quarterly* 76/4 (Autumn): 731–48.

Sandhal, Carrie, and Philip Auslander. 2005. *Bodies in Commotion: Disability and Performance.* Ann Arbor: University of Michigan Press.

Sasse, Werner. 1991. "Minjung Theology and Culture." *BAKS* 1: 29–43.

Schmid, Ulrich. 2015. "Nation and Emotion: The Competition for Victimhood in Europe." In *Melodrama without Tears: New Perspectives on the Politics of Victimhood*, edited by Scott Loren and Jorg Mertelmann, 281–93. Amsterdam: Amsterdam University Press.

Schmitz-Feuerhake, Inge, Chris Busby, and Sebastian Pflugbeil. 2016. "Genetic Radiation Risks: A Neglected Topic in the Low Dose Debate." *Environmental Health and Toxicology* 31: 1–13.

Sedgwick, Eve. 2003. *Affect, Pedagogy, Performativity.* Durham, NC: Duke University Press.

Seeger, Anthony. 1987. *Why Suyá Sing: A Musical Anthropology of an Amazonian People.* New York: Cambridge University Press.

Sheriff, Robin. 2001. *Dreaming Equality: Color, Race, and Racism in Urban Brazil.* New Brunswick, NJ: Rutgers University Press.

Silverstein, Michael. 1976. "Shifters, Linguistic Categories, and Cultural Description." In *Meaning in Anthropology*, edited by Keith H. Basso and Henry A. Selby, 11–55. Albuquerque: University of New Mexico Press.

Sinnott, Megan. 2013. "Dormitories and Other Queer Spaces: An Anthropology of Space, Gender, and the Visibility of Female Homoeroticism in Thailand." *Feminist Studies* 39/ 2: 333–56.

Solidarity for Peace and Human Rights of Asia. 2006. *Salmeun gyesok doe-eoya handa: Han'guk wonpok2se hwan-u jeung-eonnok* [Life Must Go On: Collection of Second-generation Korean Atomic Bomb Sufferers' Testimonies]. Seoul: Solidarity for Peace and Human Rights of Asia.

Spivak, Gayatri Chakravorty. 1988. "Can the Subaltern Speak?" In *Marxism and the Interpretation of Culture*, edited by Cary Nelson and Lawrence Grossberg, 271–313. Urbana: University of Illinois Press.

Sprengel, Darci. 2020. "Reframing the 'Arab Winter': The Importance of Sleep and a Quiet Atmosphere after 'Defeated' Revolutions." *Culture, Theory and Critique* 61/2– 3: 246–266.

Stirr, Anna. 2017. *Singing across Divides: Music and Intimate Politics in Nepal.* New York: Oxford University Press.

Stokes, Martin. 2010. *The Republic of Love: Cultural Intimacy in Turkish Popular Music.* Chicago: University of Chicago Press.

Taussig, Ben. 2019. *Bangkok is Rising: Sound, Space, and Media at Thailand's Red Shirt Protests.* New York: Oxford University Press.

Vergunst, Jo Lee. 2008. "Taking a Trip and Taking Care in Everyday Life." In *Ways of Walking: Ethnography and Practice on Foot*, edited by Tim Ingold and Jo Lee Vergunst, 105–21. Aldershot, UK: Ashgate.

Wang, Yun Emily. 2018. "Sonic Poetics of Home and the Art of Making Do in Sinophone Toronto." PhD dissertation, University of Toronto.

Weidman, Amanda. 2014. "Anthropology and Voice." *Annual Review of Anthropology* 43: 37–51.

Willoughby, Heather. 2000. "The Sound of Han: P'ansori, Timbre, and a Korean Ethos of Pain and Suffering." *Yearbook for Traditional Music* 32: 17–30.

Yano, Christine Reiko. 2002. *Tears of Longing: Nostalgia and the Nation in Japanese Popular Song.* Cambridge, MA: Harvard University Press.

Yen Yuehping. 2005. *Calligraphy and Power in Contemporary Chinese Society.* London: RoutledgeCurzon.

Yi Imha. 2010. *Jeonjaeng mimangin, hanguk hyeondaesaui chimmugeul kkaeda* [War Widows Break the Silence of Modern Korean History]. Seoul: Chaekgwa hamkke.

Yoneyama, Lisa. 1995. "Memory Matters: Hiroshima's Korean Atomic Bomb Memorial and the Politics of Ethnicity." *Public Culture* 7/3: 499–527.

Yoneyama, Lisa. 1999. *Hiroshima Traces: Time, Space, and the Dialects of Memory*. Berkeley and Los Angeles: University of California Press.

Zubek, Izadora Ení. 2016. "Atomic Silence: Contrasting Narratives of Hiroshima and Nagasaki." PhD dissertation, Pontifícia Universidade Católica do Rio de Janeiro.

INDEX

For the benefit of digital users, indexed terms that span two pages (e.g., 52–53) may, on occasion, appear on only one of those pages.

Figures are indicated by *f* following the page number

Agawu, Kofi, 15–16
An Buja, 107, 133–40, 134*f*, 135*f*, 138*f*, 148–49, 154, 176
An Wolseon, 58–59, 76, 87
Atomic Bomb Victims Memorial Ceremony, 23, 39, 43–50, 69, 88, 89

Bae Cheongnam, 125–26, 126*f*
Bae Ilmyeong, 9, 10–11, 14, 39, 53, 55, 57–58, 60, 61, 77–78, 88, 93–114, 94*f*, 95*f*, 98*f*, 108*f*, 113*f*, 115, 120–21, 125, 141, 143, 152, 155, 175–76

Caigentan (*Vegetable Roots Discourse*), 129–30, 132–33
calligraphy, 10, 40, 60, 113*f*, 115–16, 128, 129–33, 129*f*
"comfort women"
    social movement for, viii
    survivors, vii, 8–9, 13, 48, 79, 105, 111
    system, vii, 5, 34–35
cooking, 4, 101–3, 161, 164–65, 174
copresence, x–xi, 84, 85, 91
culture concept, re-evaluation of, 16–18

disability, xi–xii, 7–8, 9, 19–20, 36–38, 65–66, 110, 119–20, 146, 147–48, 152, 161, 166, 169, 171, 172
    performance of as "competent brokenness," 171
drinking, 11, 123–25, 146, 156, 162, 174, 175–76

eating and food, 4, 22, 23*f*, 28, 61, 74, 101–3, 107, 123, 128–29, 156–58, 161, 163, 172–73, 174–75
    colonial extraction of food products, 28
    dietary restrictions, 4, 146, 156
    doenjang mat (the taste of soybean paste), 4
    eating pine bark, 32, 174
    poetics and, 156–58, 163, 172–73, 174–75
    starvation, 28–29, 31–32
ethnomusicology
    without music, xv, 15
    as "studying culture musically," 15–18
exercise, 20, 43, 52, 67, 76, 116–17, 118, 119–20, 121–22, 131–32

farming, 22, 23*f*, 25–26, 28, 74, 101, 147–48, 174–76
forced labor, viii, 5, 13, 28–29, 34–35
forced military conscription, viii, 5, 13, 34–35
fortune telling, 54, 58

gaman, 10, 69, 78–80
games, 51–52, 53–54, 64, 115–16, 127
Goffman, Erving, x–xi, 85, 115, 118, 119
Gu Gyeong-won, 64, 65*f*, 121–23, 128–33, 129*f*, 141–42
Gu Seon-i, 97–98, 100, 103, 104, 110, 143–44, 152

Han Jeongsun, 3–5, 4*f*, 19, 20, 25, 29, 39,
    40–41, 97–98, 104n.9, 112, 136,
    143–73, 145*f*, 147*f*, 153*f*, 156*f*,
    170*f*, 174–76
Hapcheon Atomic Bomb Victims Welfare
    Center, 1–3, 7–8, 9, 11, 20, 23–24,
    35–36, 35*f*, 37, 39, 40, 43–50, 45*f*,
    46*f*, 51–68, 56*f*, 69–71, 72, 75–78,
    79, 82, 88, 89, 90*f*, 93–94, 94*f*, 95–
    96, 97, 104, 107, 110, 111–13, 115–
    42, 169–70, 175–76, 177
Hapcheon Nature School, 40–41, 41*f*,
    48, 149–52
Hapcheon Peacehouse, 3–4, 7–8, 37, 39,
    43–44, 97–98, 112, 136, 143, 144–
    45, 146–49, 154–55, 156*f*, 169–71,
    172, 177
Harkness, Nicholas, 18
Hill, Jane, 18, 124n.6, 124n.7
Hiroshima Children's Song Preservation
    Society, 55–58, 56*f*, 76, 87
Hiroshima Koreans
    Cenotaph for Korean bomb
        victims, 26–27
    illness and disability, xi–xii, 6–7n.2, 9, 32,
        53–54, 65–66, 106–7, 112, 119–20
    neighborhoods and proximity to
        explosion, 29, 72
    number of survivors in contemporary
        South Korea, 7
    population size, casualties and survivors,
        vii, 5–6, 28–30
    post-war discrimination against, 6–7n.2, 9,
        17, 32–33, 37, 172
    recruitment, vii, 1, 5, 28–29, 72
    (re)patriation to South Korea, 21–22, 31–
        32, 74, 82, 97, 98, 104
    school in Japan, 1, 10–11, 29–30, 66,
        67, 72–73, 75, 76, 80, 87, 88,
        100, 137–38
    work in Japan
        munitions factory, vii, 1, 5, 29–30, 66,
            72, 103–4
        other, 61, 72–73, 87, 89–91, 103–4
The Hiroshima Panels (paintings), 34
Hiroshima Peace Memorial Park, 4*f*, 11–12,
    26–27, 26*f*, 48, 57, 59, 79, 148
    Cenotaph for Korean bomb
        victims, 26–27
    Peace Bell, 11–12, 48
House of Sharing, 145n.3

Jeong Hoyeon, 9, 53–54
Jeong Ilbun, 53–54
Jin Gyeongsuk, 145*f*, 155, 156*f*, 158, 162,
    169–70, 170*f*, 172, 174
jishuku, 79
Jo Gyeongsuk, 112
Jo Yongpil, 157

Kim Doshik, 76, 122*f*
Kim Hyeongryul, vii–x, ix*f*, 36, 37, 146–
    47, 176
Kim Iljo, 10, 19, 53, 54–55, 58–59, 60, 63,
    76, 79, 87
Kim Imseon, 10–11, 63, 66–68, 67*f*, 119–
    20, 121
Kim Pan-geun, 61, 62*f*, 64, 117, 122*f*, 123–
    25, 128, 175–76
Korean Atomic Bomb Victims Association,
    7, 21–22, 29–30, 33, 34–35, 39–40,
    117, 175, 177
Korean Second Generation Atomic Bomb
    Sufferers Association, viii, 37, 43–44,
    143, 144–45, 146–47, 148, 151–52

laughter, 2, 66, 82, 84–86, 89, 91, 96, 101,
    102–3, 125–26, 157, 158–59, 161,
    162, 163–64, 166, 173, 174–76
Lefebvre, Henri, 120–21
Li Xianglan, 112n.12
linguistic anthropology, 18–19
listening, x–xi, xii, 18, 77–86, 89, 91–92, 98–
    106, 125–27, 155–64, 172

Mun Pilgi, 32n.7

Na Hun-a, 117, 136, 137
Nagasaki Korean laborers, vii, 5–6, 6–7n.2,
    28–29, 30n.3
Nam Jin, 140
noraebang (song rooms/karaoke), 112, 133,
    134*f*, 136, 154, 162

Okada Takashi (Okada *sensei*), 89, 155–58, 156*f*
omission, 8, 80–81, 104
otonashī, 9–10, 78–79, 105, 114

Pak Duri, 105, 111
Pak Heun-il, 116–19, 121, 123, 175–76
pansori (traditional epic story-singing), 42–
    43, 159
    Chunyangga (*Story of Chunhyang*), 42–43

periperformative utterance, 104, 152
pitch
    contour, 54, 83–84, 99, 149, 150
    definite and indefinite, 78, 83–85, 86,
        98, 138–39
    harmony, 53–54
    manipulation in speech, 78, 83–85, 98–
        100, 150–51
    monotony, 78, 79, 90–91
prayer and devotion, 2–3, 10–12, 32, 69, 70f,
        76, 95, 106–12, 108f

quietude, xvi, 9–14, 70, 71, 77, 80, 81, 86,
        88, 91–92, 104–6, 114, 116, 124–25,
        128, 151–52, 153–54, 172, 175–76
    vis-à-vis silence, 8, 13–14, 80, 86, 105–
        6, 153–54

radiation sufferers
    and disability movement, 37
    medical conditions, vii, 6–7n.2, 19–20, 36,
        37, 110, 146, 147–48, 152, 161, 166,
        169, 172
reading, 10, 25, 109, 112, 127–28, 131
refusal, 14, 104
rhythm
    of breathing, 84
    in daily life, 2–3, 78–79
    fetishization of, 15–16
    in handicrafts and visual arts, 2–3, 132
    meter, 120–21, 139, 159–60
    and repetition, 99–100, 119, 120
    in song and music
        clapping along, 58
        as embodied movement, 159–
            60, 166–67
        tempo, 47, 138, 139, 160–61, 168
    in speech, 2–3, 78–79, 91
        pace, 78, 90–91, 98, 99, 102
    in sport, 125–27
    in traditional Korean music, 47, 159–60
    and traumatic experience, 77
    of walking, 119–20, 168, 169

salpuri (dance), 41–42, 47
Sedgwick, Eve, 104, 152
sermons, 109–10
Shim Jintae, 21–41, 23f, 26f, 30f, 44, 45f,
        48–49, 51, 60–61, 117, 134, 148–49,
        165, 167, 174–76
Shin Yu, 163, 166–67

silence, x–xi, xiii–xiv, 2–3, 8, 14, 18, 49, 59,
        67, 80, 85–86, 88–89, 91–92, 104,
        105–6, 153–54, 175–76
    discourses of
        atomic silence, 11–12, 86, 88–
            89, 91–92
        breaking the silence, 12–14, 79, 86,
            88, 105–6
        as embodied movement, 19–
            20, 159–60
    moments of, 11–12, 44, 47–48, 49, 91–92
    opening and closing doors, 18
    as practice of selfhood and identity, 8–9,
        19, 164, 169
    of refusal, 14, 104
    of self-restraint, 12
singing, 5, 8–9, 10–11, 14–15, 19–20, 24–25,
        40–41, 42–43, 48, 53–54, 55–60,
        108–9, 112, 113–14, 134f, 136–40,
        143–44, 149, 150–51, 154–67, 168–
        69, 172, 174–75
    in speech, 67–68, 81, 82, 85–86, 91, 98
    thresholds of, 60, 83–84, 85, 153
    thresholds of song and speech, 15, 85,
        109, 171
    of traumatic experience, 11–12, 81
    visual, 88
songs and song genres
    "Aoi sora wa" ("The Blue Sky"), 156
    "Arirang," 136, 137
    "Changbu taryeong" ("Ballad of the
        Travelling Entertainer"), 156n.4
    "Cheongchun-eul dollyeodayo" ("Please
        Send Back [My] Youth"), 137
    "Cheonyeo nonggun" ("Girl
        Farmer"), 174–75
    children's songs, 55–60
    "Dangsini joa" ("I Like You"), 140
    "Dongbaek agassi" ("Camellia Girl"), 162
    folk (80s genre), 41
    folksong (minyo), 4, 24–25, 42–43,
        53–54, 136, 150, 156, 157–
        58, 159–61
        "new folksong," 55–56, 136, 137
    "Fujisan" ("Mount Fuji"), 57
    "Gochu" ("Hot Pepper"), 159–61, 160f,
        164–65, 166–67, 168–69, 174–75
    "Gohyang eui bom" ("Spring in my
        Hometown"), 57–58
    "Gojang nan byeoksigye" ("The Broken
        Wall-Clock"), 136, 138–40, 176

songs and song genres (*cont.*)
  "Haebangga" ("Song of Liberation"),
    53n.1, 156
  "Han obaengnyeon" ("About 500
    Years"), 157–58
  "Haru ga kita" ("Spring Has
    Come"), 58–59
  "Hwatu taryeong" ("Ballad of the Flower
    Cards"), 53–54
  hymns (Christian), 108
  "If You're Happy and You Know
    It," 125–26
  "Ito ano hoshi" ("Beloved Star"), 112–13
  "Jam janeun gongju" ("Sleeping
    Princess"), 163, 164–67, 168–69
  "Ju Yesunim nae mame deureowa" ("Since
    Jesus Came into My Heart"), 108
  "Kohan no shōjo" ("The Lakeside
    Maiden"), 59
  "Kohan no yado" ("The Lakeside Inn"), 58
  "Kwaejina chingchingnane," 42–43
  military songs (*gunka*), 24–25, 58–59
  "Miryang arirang" ("Arirang of Miryang"),
    4, 42–43
  "Naui galgil da gadorok" ("All the Way My
    Savior Leads Me"), 108
  "Niizuma kagami" ("A New Wife's
    Mirror"), 137–38
  "Nodeul gangbyeon" (Nodeul
    Riverside), 137
  "Sakura, Sakura," 55–57
  "Saneun dongan" ("The Time of
    Living"), 168–69
  "Sarangga" ("Song of Love"), 42–43
  "Tahyang Sali" ("Living in a Foreign
    Land"), 137
  "Te wo tatakimashō" ("Let's Clap Our
    Hands"), 125–26
  teuroteu, 136, 137, 138, 148–49, 150, 154,
    155, 157, 159–61, 162, 163
  "Uleora yeolpung-a" ("Cry, Storm
    Wind"), 162–63
  "Ulgin wae ureo" ("Crying? Why
    Cry"), 137
  "Uri eomeoni" ("Our Mother"), 143–44
  "Yeojaui ilsaeng" ("A Woman's Life"),
    162, 163
  "Yūyake koyake" ("Sunset and Its
    Afterglow"), 58
song books, 10, 60, 112, 136, 156, 156*f*, 176

Special Act for Support of Korean Victims of
    the Atomic Bombs, 48–49, 152–53
speech prosody, 18
  pitch contour, 83–84, 99, 150
  rhythm, 2–3, 78–79, 90–91, 98, 99, 102
  timbre, 24–25, 78, 79, 98, 99–100
  volume, 23–24, 26, 62–63, 79, 90–91
swimming, 121–23, 133

table tennis, 125–27
Taylor, Malik, 176
testimony, ix–x, xxi, 2–3, 7–9, 12, 19–20, 23,
    40–41, 52, 65, 66, 70, 76, 78, 79–81,
    89, 90–91, 90*f*, 96, 104, 146, 148–49
timbre, 24–25, 78, 79, 98, 99–100, 159
traumatic experience and memory, 8, 11–12,
    13–14, 16–17, 19–20, 42, 49–50, 60,
    66, 69–70, 77, 79–80, 81, 87–88, 89,
    104–7, 114, 116

victim (*piheja*) concept
  victim nationalism (*piheja minjokjuui*) and
    victim consciousness, x, 13
  versus *huisaengja* (sacrificial
    victim), 45–46
  versus "survivor," xiv–xv, xiv–xvn.7
visual art, 1–2, 2*f*, 3*f*, 34, 40–41, 88, 93–94,
    94*f*, 95*f*, 115–16, 137, 138*f*
voice
  An Wolseon's, 59
  archetypal, 88
  Bae Ilmyeong's, 97, 98, 102, 105, 109, 112
  beyond language, 85
  bicultural and bilingual, 55, 62–63
  children's, 40–41
  cultivation, 19–20, 155, 172
  of the dead, 91–92
  envoicing
    the dead, 13n.8
    silence, 13–14
  Han Jeongsun's, 148–49, 150–55,
    171, 172
  Jeong Hoyeon's, 53–54
  Jeong Ilbun's, 53–54
  Kim Hyeongryul's, ix–x, 175–76
  Kim Iljo's, 54, 59
  Kim Imseon's, 66
  making, 19–20
  of modernity, 9–10, 65–66
  as practice of selfhood, 62–63

quiet voices, 1, 8–9, 63, 65–66, 78–79,
105, 153–54
rural, 9–10, 97
Shim Jintae's, 23–24, 25, 26
and silence, 11–12, 48, 88–89, 105–
6, 153–54
in testimony, ix–x, 2–3, 8–9, 79, 91
and thyroid, 9, 112
Yi Suyong's, 78–79, 81, 83, 84, 85, 86,
88–89, 175–76

walking, 67, 116–17, 118–21,
145f, 164–71
as activism, 169–71
continuum of song, walking, and
discourse, 164–65, 166–67, 168–
71, 170f
and dance, 19–20, 163–64
everyday practices, 167–68
and institutional life, 116–17, 118–
21, 125–26

as metaphor in song and speech, 159–61,
162, 163, 165–66, 170f
in movement discourse, 169–71, 170f
rhythm in, 132, 168
and speech, 169
struggle to walk, 146, 151, 154–55

Yi Hyojeong, 143
Yi Mihwa, 47
Yi Mija, 162, 163
Yi Namjae, 47
Yi Suyong, 1–3, 2f, 3f, 14, 19–20, 61, 63, 63f,
69–92, 70f, 72f, 83f, 87f, 90f, 93, 98,
102–3, 104, 105, 120, 121, 136, 141–
42, 153–54, 155, 175–76
Yi Tae-ho, 168–69
Yi Yongsu, 48
Yu Ji-na, 157, 159–60, 174–75
Yun Sugi, 9, 10, 52, 53, 63–66, 65f, 78–79,
117, 121–27, 122f, 126f, 128–29,
133, 140, 141–42, 175–76

Printed in the USA/Agawam, MA
November 11, 2022

801102.031